10th Web as Corpus Workshop (WAC-X 2016) and the EmpiriST Shared Task

Held at ACL 2016

Berlin, Germany
12 August 2016

ISBN: 978-1-5108-2769-1

ACL 2016

**The 54th Annual Meeting of the
Association for Computational Linguistics**

**Proceedings of the 10th Web as Corpus Workshop (WAC-X)
and the EmpiriST Shared Task**

August 12, 2016
Berlin, Germany

Introduction

These proceedings contain the papers presented at the 10th Web as Corpus Workshop (WAC-X 2016) organized by the ACL Special Interest Group on Web as Corpus (SIGWAC), co-located with the ACL conference 2016. It took place on August 12, 2016.

With WAC-X, the series of WAC workshops continues its successful tradition going back to 2005. Thematically, the WAC workshops have always been positioned between computational linguistics and theoretically oriented empirical linguistics, and this year is no exception. A majority of the accepted papers relates in some way to the **construction of web corpora** (Barbaresi, Salway et al., Krause, Würschinger et al., Mendels et al., Ljubešić and Fišer, Schäfer) with a clear tendency towards specialized corpora collected for individual research questions and towards data sources similar to but not identical to the web (such as Twitter). The extraction and generation of **meta data** for web-derived (or similar) corpora has also been a recurring theme in Web as Corpus workshops (Schäfer and Bildhauer, Barbaresi, Dalan and Sharoff). A lot of the accepted papers also deal with **research based on web data** (Krause, Würschinger et al., Mendels et al., Ljubešić and Fišer), demonstrating that web corpora are a unique source of data in (computational) linguistics and related fields.

We received a total of 15 full paper submissions for the main workshop (5 short, 10 long) of which 9 were accepted (2 short, 7 long), resulting in an overall acceptance rate of 60% as the result of a double-blind peer review process (three independent reviews per paper).

Adding to the success of the WAC-X event was the inclusion of the final presentations for the shared task on **Automatic Linguistic Annotation of Computer-Mediated Communication/Social Media (EmpiriST)**. The papers by the five competing teams and the introductory paper by the organizers are also included in these proceedings. System descriptions were reviewed non-anonymously by the task organizers and participants. Each submitted paper received two reviews. All papers meeting our formal requirements and quality standards after revisions were accepted for publication, regardless of whether they make a novel research contribution.

In these proceedings, the WAC-X papers are printed before the EmpiriST papers. In both groups, the papers are printed in the order of the corresponding presentations.

We would like to thank all authors for submitting their research to WAC-X and the members of the program committee for their hard work reviewing the papers and making valuable suggestions.

Paul C. Cook
Stefan Evert
Roland Schäfer
Egon Stemle

SIGWAC web page: `https://www.sigwac.org.uk`

Organizers:

Paul Cook, University of New Brunswick
Stefan Evert, Friedrich-Alexander Universität Erlangen-Nürnberg
Roland Schäfer, Freie Universität Berlin
Egon Stemle, European Academy of Bozen/Bolzano

Program Committee:

Adrien Barbaresi, Österreichische Akademie der Wissenschaften, Wien
Silvia Bernardini, Università di Bologna
Douglas Biber, Northern Arizona University, Flagstaff
Felix Bildhauer, Institut für Deutsche Sprache Mannheim
Katrien Depuydt, Instituut voor Nederlandse Lexicologie, Leiden
Jesse de Does, Instituut voor Nederlandse Lexicologie, Leiden
Cédrick Fairon, Université catholique de Louvain
William H. Fletcher, U.S. Naval Academy, Annapolis
Iztok Kosem, Trojina Institute for Applied Slovene Studies, Ljubljana
Simon Krek, Jožef Stefan Institute, Ljubljana
Lothar Lemnitzer, Berlin-Brandenburgische Akademie der Wissenschaften
Nikola Ljubešić, Sveučilišta u Zagrebu
Siva Reddy, University of Edinburgh
Steffen Remus, Technische Universität Darmstadt
Pavel Rychly, Masaryk University, Brno
Kevin Scannell, Saint Louis University
Serge Sharoff, University of Leeds
Klaus Schulz, Ludwig-Maximilians-Universität München
Kay-Michael Würzner, Berlin-Brandenburgische Akademie der Wissenschaften
Torsten Zesch, Universität Duisburg-Essen
Pierre Zweigenbaum, Laboratoire d'Informatique pour la Mécanique et les Sciences de l'Ingénieur, Orsay

Table of Contents

Conference Program

9:30–10:30	**WAC-X morning session**
9:30–9:40	***Welcome and Introduction***
9:40–10:00	*Automatic Classification by Topic Domain for Meta Data Generation, Web Corpus Evaluation, and Corpus Comparison* Roland Schäfer and Felix Bildhauer
10:00–10:30	*Efficient construction of metadata-enhanced web corpora* Adrien Barbaresi
11:00–12:30	**WAC-X noon session**
11:00–11:30	*Topically-focused Blog Corpora for Multiple Languages* Andrew Salway, Dag Elgesem, Knut Hofland, Øystein Reigem and Lubos Steskal
11:30–12:00	*The Challenges and Joys of Analysing Ongoing Language Change in Web-based Corpora: a Case Study* Anne Krause
12:00–12:30	*Using the Web and Social Media as Corpora for Monitoring the Spread of Neologisms. The case of 'rapefugee', 'rapeugee', and 'rapugee'.* Quirin Würschinger, Mohammad Fazleh Elahi, Desislava Zhekova and Hans-Jörg Schmid
13:30–14:30	**EmpiriST session**
13:30–13:50	*EmpiriST 2015: A Shared Task on the Automatic Linguistic Annotation of Computer-Mediated Communication and Web Corpora* Michael Beißwenger, Sabine Bartsch, Stefan Evert and Kay-Michael Würzner
13:50–14:10	*SoMaJo: State-of-the-art tokenization for German web and social media texts* Thomas Proisl and Peter Uhrig
14:10–14:30	*UdS-(retrain\distributional\surface): Improving POS Tagging for OOV Words in German CMC and Web Data* Jakob Prange, Andrea Horbach and Stefan Thater

14:30–15:10   WAC-X and EmpiriST Teaser Talks

14:30–14:35   *Babler - Data Collection from the Web to Support Speech Recognition and Keyword Search*
Gideon Mendels, Erica Cooper and Julia Hirschberg

14:35–14:40   *A Global Analysis of Emoji Usage*
Nikola Ljubešić and Darja Fišer

14:40–14:45   *Genre classification for a corpus of academic webpages*
Erika Dalan and Serge Sharoff

14:45–14:50   *On Bias-free Crawling and Representative Web Corpora*
Roland Schäfer

14:55–15:00   *EmpiriST: AIPHES - Robust Tokenization and POS-Tagging for Different Genres*
Steffen Remus, Gerold Hintz, Chris Biemann, Christian M. Meyer, Darina Benikova, Judith Eckle-Kohler, Margot Mieskes and Thomas Arnold

15:00–15:05   *bot.zen @ EmpiriST 2015 - A minimally-deep learning PoS-tagger (trained for German CMC and Web data)*
Egon Stemle

15:05–15:10   *LTL-UDE @ EmpiriST 2015: Tokenization and PoS Tagging of Social Media Text*
Tobias Horsmann and Torsten Zesch

15:10–16:30   WAC-X and EmpiriST Poster Session

Automatic Classification by Topic Domain for Meta Data Generation, Web Corpus Evaluation, and Corpus Comparison

Roland Schäfer
Freie Universität Berlin
Habelschwerdter Allee 45
14196 Berlin, Germany
roland.schaefer@fu-berlin.de

Felix Bildhauer
Institut für Deutsche Sprache
R5, 6–13
68161 Mannheim, Germany
bildhauer@ids-mannheim.de

Abstract

In this paper, we describe preliminary results from an ongoing experiment wherein we classify two large unstructured text corpora—a web corpus and a newspaper corpus—by topic domain (or subject area). Our primary goal is to develop a method that allows for the reliable annotation of large crawled web corpora with meta data required by many corpus linguists. We are especially interested in designing an annotation scheme whose categories are both intuitively interpretable by linguists and firmly rooted in the distribution of lexical material in the documents. Since we use data from a web corpus and a more traditional corpus, we also contribute to the important field of corpus comparison and corpus evaluation. Technically, we use (unsupervised) topic modeling to automatically induce topic distributions over gold standard corpora that were manually annotated for 13 coarse-grained topic domains. In a second step, we apply supervised machine learning to learn the manually annotated topic domains using the previously induced topics as features. We achieve around 70% accuracy in 10-fold cross validations. An analysis of the errors clearly indicates, however, that a revised classification scheme and larger gold standard corpora will likely lead to a substantial increase in accuracy.

1 Introduction

In the experiment reported here, we classified large unstructured text corpora by *topic domain*. The *topic domain* of a document—along with other high-level classifications such as *genre* or *register*—is among the types of meta data most essential to many corpus linguists. Therefore, the lack of reliable meta data in general is often mentioned as a major drawback of large, crawled web corpora, and the automatic generation of such meta data is an active field of research.[1] It must be noted, however, that such high-level annotations are not reliably available for many very large traditional corpora (such as newspaper corpora), either. When it comes to the automatic identification of high-level categories like register (such as *Opinion, Narrative, Informational Persuasion*; Biber and Egbert 2016), even very recent approaches based on very large amounts of training data cannot deliver satisfying (arguably not even encouraging) results. For instance, Biber and Egbert (2016, 23) report *accuracy*=0.421, *precision*=0.268, *recall*=0.3. It is not even clear whether categories such as register and genre can be operationalized such that a reliable annotation is possible for humans.

By contrast, automatic text categorization by *content* yielded much more promising results years ago already (Sebastiani, 2002). Furthermore, data-driven induction of topics (*topic modeling*) has proven quite successful, and it is in many respects a very objective way of organizing a collection of documents by content. Deriving topic classifications from text-internal criteria is also advocated in the EAGLES (1996) guidelines, among others. However, topic modeling usually does not come with category labels that are useful for linguistic corpus users. In our project, we explore the possibility of inferring a small, more traditional set of *topic domains* (or *subject areas*) from the topics induced in an unsupervised manner by Latent Semantic Indexing (Landauer and Dumais, 1994; Landauer and Dumais, 1997).

---

[1] See, for example, many of the contributions in Mehler et al. (2010).

Proceedings of the 10th Web as Corpus Workshop (WAC-X) and the EmpiriST Shared Task, pages 1–6,
Berlin, Germany, August 7-12, 2016. ©2016 Association for Computational Linguistics

Since we classify and compare one large German web corpus and one large German newspaper corpus with respect to their distribution of topic domains, our paper also contributes to the area of corpus comparison, another important issue in corpus linguistics (Kilgarriff, 2001; Biemann et al., 2013). For the construction of crawled web corpora, such comparisons are vital because next to nothing is known about their composition.

The computational tools used in our method (unsupervised topic induction and supervised classifiers) are by now well-established and highly developed. This paper contributes to the field of applying such methods and making them usable for real-life problems of data processing and the development of suitable annotation schemes rather than to the development of the underlying mathematics and algorithms.

2 Gold Standard Data

Our gold standard corpora were prepared by manual annotation of documents from two large German corpora. The first data set consists of 870 randomly selected documents from DECOW14A, a crawled web corpus (Schäfer and Bildhauer, 2012; Schäfer, 2015), henceforth *Web*. The second data set contains 886 documents randomly selected from DeReKo, a corpus composed predominantly of newspaper texts (Kupietz et al., 2010), henceforth *News*. Our choice of corpora was motivated by fact that we expected some overlap w. r. t. to topics covered in them, but also some major differences. The documents in these gold standard corpora were classified according to a custom annotation scheme for topic domain which builds on previous work by Sharoff (2006). The design goal was to a have moderate number (about 10–20) of topic domains that can be thought of as subsuming more fine-grained topic distinctions. We developed the annotation scheme in a cyclic fashion, taking into account annotator feedback after repeated annotation processes. For the experiment reported here, we used a version that distinguishes 13 topic domains, namely *Science, Technology, Medical, Public Life and Infrastructure, Politics and Society, History, Business, Law, Fine Arts, Philosophy, Beliefs, Life and Leisure, Individuals*.

3 Experiment Setup

Our general approach was to infer a topic distribution over a corpus using *unsupervised* topic modeling algorithms as a first step. In the second step, rather than examining and interpreting the inferred topical structure, we used the resulting document–topic matrix to learn topic domain distinctions for the documents from their assignment to the topics in a *supervised* manner. To achieve this, supervised classifiers were used. Through permutation of virtually all available classifiers (with the appropriate capabilities) available in the Weka toolkit (Hall and Witten, 2011), LM Trees (Landwehr et al., 2005) and SVMs with a Pearson VII kernel (Üstün et al., 2006) were found to be most accurate. Due to minimally higher accuracy, SVMs were used in all subsequent experiments. Some topic domains occurred only rarely in the gold standard, and we did not expect the classifier to be able to generalize well from just a few instances. Therefore, we evaluated the results on the *full* data set and a *reduced* data set with rare categories removed.

For the first step (unsupervised topic induction), we used LSI and LDA (Latent Dirichlet Allocation, Blei et al. 2003) as implemented in the Gensim toolkit (Řehůřek and Sojka, 2010). In our first experiments, the LDA topic distribution was unstable, and results were generally unusable, possibly due to the comparatively small gold standard corpora used. We consequently only report LSI results here and will return to LDA in further experiments (cf. Section 5). However, for any topic modeling algorithm, our corpora can be considered small. Therefore, we inferred topics not just based on the annotated gold standard data sets, but also on larger datasets which consisted of the gold standard mixed with additional documents from the source corpora. For the training of the SVM classifiers, the documents that had been mixed in were removed again because no gold standard annotation was available for them. We systematically increased the number of mixed-in document in increments of roughly half as many documents as contained in the gold standard corpora.

We pre-processed both corpora in exactly the same way (tokenization, lemmatization, POS-tagging, named entity recognition). Using the lemma and the simplified POS tags (such as *kindergarten_nn*) as terms in combination with some filters (use only lower-cased purely alphabetic common and proper noun lemmas between 4 and 30 characters long) usually gave the best results.

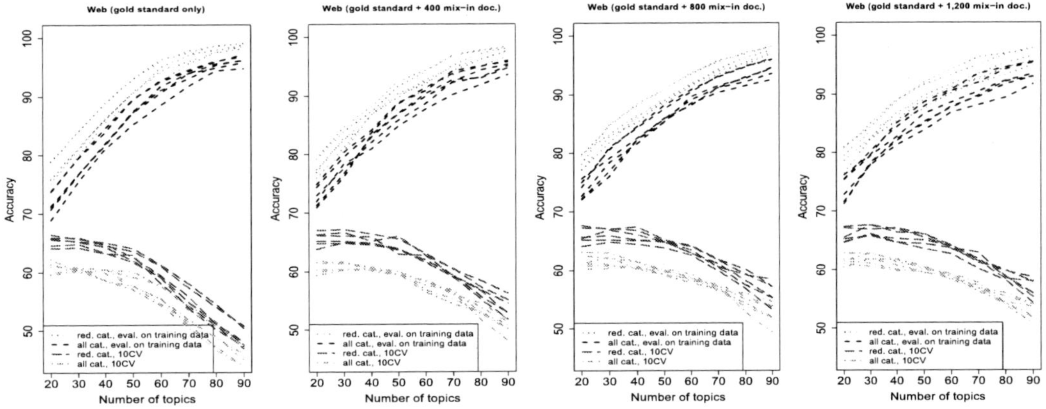

Figure 1: Accuracy with different numbers of topics for the Web dataset

4 Results

Figure 1 shows the classification accuracy using 20 to 90 LSI topics. Each line corresponds to one sub-experiment (with slightly different pre-processing options for lines of the same color and style), and the lines form well distinguishable bands. The highest accuracy is achieved with the reduced set of topic domains (minor categories removed) when the evaluation is performed on the training data. The full set of topic domains leads to a drop in accuracy of about 5%. The two lower bands show the classification accuracy in a 10-fold cross-validation (10CV), again with the reduced set of topic domains performing roughly 5% better. While a higher number of topics improves results on the training data, the accuracy in the cross-validation drops. Too large numbers of topics obviously allow the method to pick up idiosyncratic features of single documents or very small clusters of documents, leading to extreme overfitting.

The four panels show results based on different topic models. Panel (a) uses a topic model inferred only from the (more than 800) gold standard documents. Results in panel (b) through (d) are based on topic models inferred on larger data sets as described in Section 3. In the experiment reported in panel (d), for example, 1,200 documents were added to the 870 gold standard documents. While the results of the 10CV are slightly improved by mixing in more documents, the maximum achieved accuracy does not change significantly. We mixed in up to 8,000 additional documents (not all results shown here) with no significant change compared to panel (d) in Figure 1.

We consider the maximum 10CV accuracy with the reduced set of topic domains most informative w. r. t. the potential quality of our method, and we report it in Table 1.

A very similar plot for the News data is shown in Figure 3. The best results are also given in Table 1. The added accuracy (4.23% according to Table 1) is a side effect of the more skewed distribution of topic domains in the News gold standard data.

The κ statistic for the Web and Newspaper results from Table 1 is $\kappa_{\text{Web}} = 0.575$ and $\kappa_{\text{News}} = 0.582$, indicating that achieving a higher accuracy for the web data is actually slightly harder than for the newspaper data (see also the analysis of the confusion matrices below).

When the Web and News data are pooled, however, quality drops below any acceptable level, cf. Figure 3 and Table 1. Mixing in more documents (panels b–d) improves the evaluation results on the training data, but the 10CV results remains steady at around 50%. This is remarkable because larger training data sets should lead to increased, not degraded accuracy. While a deeper analysis of the LSI topic distributions remains to be undertaken, it is evident what most likely causes these below average results on the side of the SVM classifier when looking at the confusion matrices, cf. Table 2. In the Web gold standard (panel a), the dominant modal category is *Life and Leisure*. The distribution of topic domains is reasonably skewed, and the confusion is distributed roughly uniformly across categories. The News gold standard (panel b) consists mainly of two clusters of documents in the domains *Politics and Society* and *Life and Leisure*. For the pooled data set (panel c), this

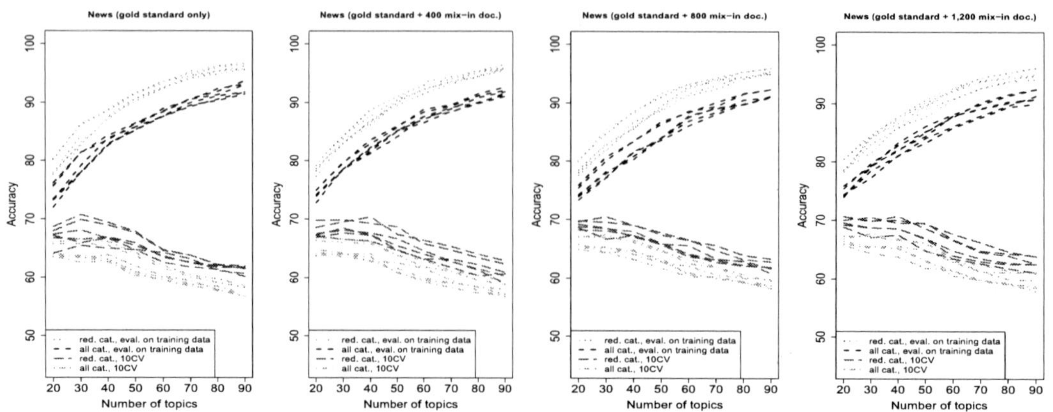

Figure 2: Accuracy with different numbers of topics for the News dataset

Corpus	Mixed-in	Attribute	Topics	Accuracy	Precision*	Recall*	F-Measure*
Web	3,200	token	20	68.765%	0.688	0.688	0.674
News	3,600	lemma + POS	40	72.999%	0.725	0.730	0.696
Web + News	0	lemma + POS	30	51.872%	0.431	0.519	0.417

Table 1: Evaluation at best achievable accuracy with the reduced set of topic domains in 10-fold cross-validation (*weighted average across all categories)

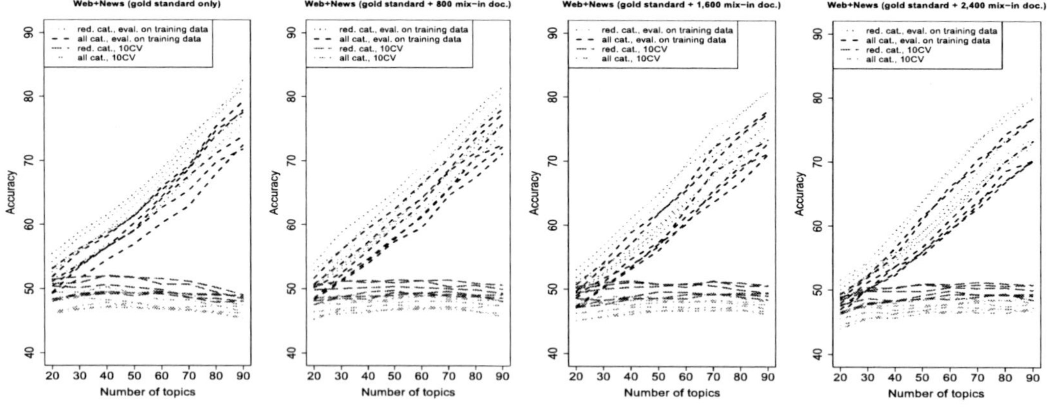

Figure 3: Accuracy with different numbers of topics for the pooled Web + News datasets

leads to a situation in which the classifier simply assigns most documents to *Life and Leisure* and the rest mostly to *Politics and Society*. This indicates that for such skewed distributions of topic domains, larger gold standard data sets are required. It is not indicative of a general failure of the method or a general incompatibility of newspaper and web data in the context of our method. The confusion matrices in Table 2 clearly indicate, however, that topic domains are represented quite differently in newspaper and web corpora.

5 Conclusions and Outlook

The results presented here are highly encouraging, and they clearly indicate the route to be taken in further experiments. First of all, there appears to be a connection between induced topic distributions and more general topic domains. The decreased performance in cross-validation experiments indicates that larger gold standard data sets are required. Such data sets are currently being annotated under our supervision.

Web (a)

Web (Annotated)	Classified							
	PolSoc	Busi	Life	Arts	Public	Law	Beliefs	Hist
PolSoc	**26**	12	10	1	1	0	1	0
Busi	5	**105**	40	7	1	2	1	1
Life	3	14	**286**	6	4	1	1	1
Arts	3	2	36	**78**	1	0	2	6
Public	0	3	11	0	**9**	1	0	0
Law	3	9	8	0	1	**8**	0	0
Beliefs	4	3	11	6	1	0	**30**	1
Hist	9	0	9	7	1	1	2	**15**

News (b)

News (Annotated)	Classified					
	PolSoc	Busi	Life	Indiv	Arts	Public
PolSoc	223	6	39	0	0	8
Busi	20	24	9	0	0	0
Life	24	1	324	0	0	1
Indiv	5	0	17	0	0	1
Arts	2	0	28	0	6	0
Public	35	0	30	0	0	34

Pooled (c)

Pooled (Annotated)	Classified								
	PolSoc	Busi	Medical	Life	Arts	Public	Law	Beliefs	Hist
PolSoc	**199**	7	0	109	0	12	0	0	0
Busi	18	**23**	0	172	0	2	0	0	0
Medical	6	0	**0**	29	0	1	0	0	0
Life	25	4	0	**632**	0	5	0	0	0
Arts	2	2	0	160	**0**	0	0	0	0
Public	46	2	0	56	0	**19**	0	0	0
Law	8	0	0	31	0	0	**0**	0	0
Beliefs	0	0	0	59	0	0	0	**0**	0
Hist	4	0	0	50	0	0	0	0	**0**

Table 2: Confusion matrices for the best achievable results on the Web (a), News (b), and pooled (c) data sets as reported in Table 1; different sets of categories are the result of excluding low-frequency topic domains (below 20 for Web and News, below 30 for pooled data)

Secondly, there appears to be a significant difference in the topic distribution and the topic/domain mapping in newspaper and web corpora. This might be one of the reasons behind the collapse of the classifier when newspaper and web data are pooled. In future experiments, it remains to be discovered whether larger gold standard corpora can alleviate such problems. This will eventually enable us to decide whether separate models or pooled models for the two kinds of corpora are more appropriate.

Thirdly, the highly skewed topic distributions in both newspaper and web corpora indicate that splitting up some topic domains might lead to a better fit. In fact, annotators have independently asked whether *Politics and Society* and *Life and Leisure*—the critical categories which make the classifier collapse (cf. Section 4)—could not be split up into at least two categories each.

Additionally, we will investigate whether alternative topic modeling algorithms lead to a better fit.[2] Moreover, as suggested by an anonymous reviewer, our results could be compared with a baseline classification that does not make use of topic modeling algorithms. Finally, we are currently experimenting with an extended annotation scheme that allows for multiple weighted assignments of documents to topic domains.

The ultimate goal of our project is to automatically annotate existing web corpora that are several billion tokens large with meta data such as their topic domain and to release the data freely (under a maximally permissive Creative Commons Attribution license).[3] The experiments reported here indicate that with some tweaking, it will be possible to create such free resources and achieve very high levels of quality.

Acknowledgments

Roland Schäfer's research on the project presented here was funded by the German Research Council (Deutsche Forschungsgemeinschaft, DFG) through grant SHA/1916-1 *Linguistic Web Characterization*.

References

Douglas Biber and Jesse Egbert. 2016. Using grammatical features for automatic register identification in an unrestricted corpus of documents from the open web. *Journal of Research Design and Statistics in Linguistics and Communication Science*, 2:3–36.

Chris Biemann, Felix Bildhauer, Stefan Evert, Dirk Goldhahn, Uwe Quasthoff, Roland Schäfer, Johannes Simon, Leonard Swiezinski, and Torsten Zesch. 2013. Scalable construction of high-quality web corpora. *Journal for Language Technology and Computational Linguistics*, 28(2):23–60.

David M. Blei, Andrew Y. Ng, and Michael I. Jordan. 2003. Latent dirichlet allocation. *Journal of Machine Learning Research*, 3:993–1022.

EAGLES. 1996. Preliminary recommendations on text typology. Technical report EAG-TCWG-TTYP/P, EAGLES.

Mark Hall and Ian H. Witten. 2011. *Data mining: practical machine learning tools and techniques*. Kaufmann, Burlington, 3rd edition.

Adam Kilgarriff. 2001. Comparing corpora. *International Journal of Corpus Linguistics*, 6(1):97–133.

Marc Kupietz, Cyril Belica, Holger Keibel, and Andreas Witt. 2010. The German reference corpus DeReKo: A primordial sample for linguistic research. In Nicoletta Calzolari, Khalid Choukri, Bente Maegaard, Joseph Mariani, Jan Odijk, Stelios

---

[2]The Gensim toolkit offers a wide array of algorithms, including *doc2vec* and an alternative LDA implementation *ldamallet*.

[3]The software and the classifiers will be made available under permissive open source licenses allowing even their use in commercial applications.

Piperidis, Mike Rosner, and Daniel Tapias, editors, *Proceedings of the Seventh International Conference on Language Resources and Evaluation (LREC '10)*, pages 1848–1854, Valletta, Malta. European Language Resources Association (ELRA).

Thomas K. Landauer and Susan T. Dumais. 1994. Latent semantic analysis and the measurement of knowledge. In R. M. Kaplan and J. C. Burstein, editors, *Educational testing service conference on natural language processing techniques and technology in assessment and education*. Educational Testing Service, Princeton, NJ.

Thomas K. Landauer and Susan T. Dumais. 1997. A solution to plato's problem: the latent semantic analysis theory of acquisition, induction and representation of knowledge. *Psychological Review*, 104(2):211–240.

Niels Landwehr, Mark Hall, and Eibe Frank. 2005. Logistic model trees. *Machine Learning*, 95(1–2):161–205.

Alexander Mehler, Serge Sharoff, and Marina Santini, editors. 2010. *Genres on the Web. Computational Models and Empirical Studies*, volume 42 of *Text, Speech and Language Technology*. Springer, Dordrecht.

Radim Řehůřek and Petr Sojka. 2010. Software Framework for Topic Modelling with Large Corpora. In *Proceedings of the LREC 2010 Workshop on New Challenges for NLP Frameworks*, pages 45–50, Valletta, Malta. ELRA.

Roland Schäfer and Felix Bildhauer. 2012. Building large corpora from the web using a new efficient tool chain. In Nicoletta Calzolari, Khalid Choukri, Thierry Declerck, Mehmet Uğur Doğan, Bente Maegaard, Joseph Mariani, Jan Odijk, and Stelios Piperidis, editors, *Proceedings of the Eight International Conference on Language Resources and Evaluation (LREC'12)*, pages 486–493, Istanbul. ELRA.

Roland Schäfer. 2015. Processing and querying large web corpora with the COW14 architecture. In Piotr Bański, Hanno Biber, Evelyn Breiteneder, Marc Kupietz, Harald Lüngen, and Andreas Witt, editors, *Proceedings of Challenges in the Management of Large Corpora 3 (CMLC-3)*, Lancaster. UCREL.

Fabrizio Sebastiani. 2002. Machine learning in automated text categorization. *ACM Computing Surveys*, 34(1):1–47.

Serge Sharoff. 2006. Creating general-purpose corpora using automated search engine queries. In Marco Baroni and Silvia Bernardini, editors, *Wacky! Working papers on the Web as Corpus*. GEDIT, Bologna.

Bülent Üstün, Willem J. Melssen, and Lutgarde M.C. Buydens. 2006. Facilitating the application of Support Vector Regression by using a universal Pearson VII function based kernel. *Chemometrics and Intelligent Laboratory Systems*, 81:29–40.

Efficient construction of metadata-enhanced web corpora

Adrien Barbaresi
Austrian Academy of Sciences – Berlin-Brandenburg Academy of Sciences
`adrien.barbaresi@oeaw.ac.at`

Abstract

Metadata extraction is known to be a problem in general-purpose Web corpora, and so is extensive crawling with little yield. The contributions of this paper are threefold: a method to find and download large numbers of WordPress pages; a targeted extraction of content featuring much needed metadata; and an analysis of the documents in the corpus with insights of actual blog uses.

The study focuses on a publishing software (WordPress), which allows for reliable extraction of structural elements such as metadata, posts, and comments. The download of about 9 million documents in the course of two experiments leads after processing to 2.7 billion tokens with usable metadata. This comparatively high yield is a step towards more efficiency with respect to machine power and "Hi-Fi" web corpora.

The resulting corpus complies with formal requirements on metadata-enhanced corpora and on weblogs considered as a series of dated entries. However, existing typologies on Web texts have to be revised in the light of this hybrid genre.

1 Introduction

1.1 Context

This article introduces work on focused web corpus construction with linguistic research in mind. The purpose of focused web corpora is to complement existing collections, as they allow for better coverage of specific written text types and genres, user-generated content, as well as latest language evolutions. However, it is quite rare to find ready-made resources. Specific issues include first the discovery of relevant web documents, and second the extraction of text and metadata, e.g. because of exotic markup and text genres (Schäfer et al., 2013). Nonetheless, proper extraction is necessary for the corpora to be established as scientific objects, as science needs an agreed scheme for identifying and registering research data (Sampson, 2000). Web corpus yield is another recurrent problem (Suchomel and Pomikálek, 2012; Schäfer et al., 2014). The shift from web *as* corpus to web *for* corpus – mostly due to an expanding Web universe and the need for better text quality (Versley and Panchenko, 2012) – as well as the limited resources of research institutions make extensive downloads costly and prompt for handy solutions (Barbaresi, 2015).

The DWDS lexicography project[1] at the Berlin-Brandenburg Academy of Sciences already features a good coverage of specific written text genres (Geyken, 2007). Further experiments including internet-based text genres are currently conducted in joint work with the Austrian Academy of Sciences (Academy Corpora). The common absence of metadata known to the philological tradition such as authorship and publication date accounts for a certain defiance regarding Web resources, as linguistic evidence cannot be cited or identified properly in the sense of the tradition. Thus, missing or erroneous metadata in "one size fits all" web corpora may undermine the relevance of web texts for linguistic purposes and in the humanities in general. Additionally, nearly all existing text extraction and classification techniques have been developed in the field of information retrieval, that is not with linguistic objectives in mind.

---

[1] Digital Dictionary of German, http://zwei.dwds.de

Proceedings of the 10th Web as Corpus Workshop (WAC-X) and the EmpiriST Shared Task, pages 7–16,
Berlin, Germany, August 7-12, 2016. ©2016 Association for Computational Linguistics

The contributions of this paper are threefold:
(**1**) a method to find and download large amounts of WordPress pages;
(**2**) a targeted extraction of content featuring much needed metadata;
(**3**) an analysis of the documents in the corpus with insights of actual uses of the blog genre.
My study focuses on a publishing software with two experiments, first on the official platform wordpress.com and second on the .at-domain. WordPress is used by about a quarter of the web-sites worldwide[2], the software has become so broadly used that its current deployments can be expected to differ from the original ones. A number of 158,719 blogs in German have previously been found on wordpress.com (Barbaresi and Würzner, 2014). The .at-domain (Austria) is in quantitative terms the 32th top-level domain with about 3,7 million hosts reported.[3]

1.2 Definitional and typological criteria

From the beginning of research on blogs/weblogs, the main definitional criterion has always been their form, a "reverse chronological sequences of dated entries" (Kumar et al., 2003). Another formal criterion is the use of dedicated software to articulate and publish the entries, a "weblog publishing software tool" (Glance et al., 2004), "public-domain blog software" (Kumar et al., 2003), or Content Management System (CMS). These tools largely impact the way blogs are created and run. 1996 seems to be the acknowledged beginning of the blog/weblog genre, with an exponential increase of their use starting in 1999 with the emergence of several user-friendly publishing tools (Kumar et al., 2003; Herring et al., 2004).

Whether a blog is to be considered to be a web page in its whole (Glance et al., 2004) or a website containing a series of dated entries, or posts, (Kehoe and Gee, 2012) being each a web page, there are invariant elements, such as "a persistent side-bar containing profile information" as well as links to other blogs (Kumar et al., 2003), or blogroll. For that matter, blogs are intricately intertwined in what has been called the blogosphere: "The cross-linking that takes place between blogs, through blogrolls, explicit linking, trackbacks, and referrals has helped create a strong sense of community in the weblogging world." (Glance et al., 2004).

This means that a comprehensive crawl could lead to better yields.

Regarding the classification of blogs, Blood (2002) distinguishes three basic types: filters, personal journals, and notebooks, while Krishnamurthy (2002) builds a typology based on function and intention of the blogs: online diaries, support group, enhanced column, collaborative content creation. More comprehensive typologies established on one hand several genres: online journal, self-declared expert, news filter, writer/artist, spam/advertisement; and on the other hand distinctive "variations": collaborative writing, comments from readers, means of publishing (Glance et al., 2004).

2 Related work

2.1 (Meta-)Data Extraction

Data extraction has first been based on "wrappers" (nowadays: "scrapers") which were mostly relying on manual design and tended to be brittle and hard to maintain (Crescenzi et al., 2001). These extraction procedures have also been used early on by blogs search engines (Glance et al., 2004). Since the genre of "web diaries" was established before the blogs in Japan, there have been attempts to target not only blog software but also regular pages (Nanno et al., 2004), in which the extraction of metadata also allows for a distinction based on heuristics.

Efforts were made to generate wrappers automatically, with emphasis on three different approaches (Guo et al., 2010): wrapper induction (e.g. by building a grammar to parse a web page), sequence labeling (e.g. labeled examples or a schema of data in the page), and statistical analysis and series of resulting heuristics. This analysis combined to the inspection of DOM tree characteristics (Wang et al., 2009; Guo et al., 2010) is a common ground to the information retrieval and web corpus linguistics communities, with the categorization of HTML elements and linguistic features (Ziegler and Skubacz, 2007) for the former, and markup and boilerplate removal operations known to the latter community (Schäfer and Bildhauer, 2013).

Regarding content-based wrappers for blogs in particular, targets include the title of the entry, the date, the author, the content, the number of comments, the archived link, and the trackback link (Glance et al., 2004); they can also aim at com-

---

[2] http://w3techs.com/technologies/details/cm-wordpress/all/all

[3] http://ftp.isc.org/www/survey/reports/2016/01/bynum.txt

ments specifically (Mishne and Glance, 2006).

2.2 Blog corpus construction

The first and foremost issue in blog corpus construction still holds true today: "there is no comprehensive directory of weblogs, although several small directories exist" (Glance et al., 2004). Previous work established several modes of construction, from broad, opportunistic approaches, to the focus on a particular method or platform due to the convenience of retrieval processes. Corpus size and length of downloads are frequently mentioned as potential obstacles. Glance et al. (2004) performed URL harvesting through specialized directories, and found a practical upper bound at about 100,000 active weblogs, which were used as a corpus in their study.

The first comprehensive studies used feeds to collect blog texts (Gruhl et al., 2004), since they are a convenient way to bypass extensive crawling and to harvest blog posts (and more rarely comments) without needing any boilerplate removal.

An approach based on RSS and Atom feeds is featured in the TREC-Blog collection[4] (Macdonald and Ounis, 2006), a reference in Information Extraction which has been used in a number of evaluation tasks. 100,649 blogs were predetermined, they are top blogs in terms of popularity, but no further information is given. Spam blogs, and hand-picked relevant blogs (no information on the criteria either) are used to complement and to balance the corpus to make it more versatile. The corpus is built by fetching feeds describing recent postings, whose permalinks are used as a reference. From initial figures totaling 3,215,171 permalinks and 324,880 homepages, most recent ones from 2008 mention 1,303,520 feeds and 28,488,766 permalink documents.[5]

Another way to enhance the quality of data and the ease of retrieval is the focus on a particular platform. To study authorship attribution, Schler et al. (2006) gathered a total of 71,000 blogs on the Google-owned Blogger platform, which allowed for easier extraction of content, although no comments are included in the corpus.

The Birmingham Blog Corpus (Kehoe and Gee, 2012) is a more recent approach to comprehensive corpus construction. Two platforms are taken into consideration: Blogger and wordpress.com,

with the "freshly pressed" page on WordPress as well as a series of trending blogs used as seed for the crawls, leading to 222,245 blog posts and 2,253,855 comments from Blogger and WordPress combined, totaling about 95 million tokens (for the posts) and 86 million tokens (for the comments).

The YACIS Corpus (Ptaszynski et al., 2012) is a Japanese corpus consisting of blogs collected from a single blog platform, which features mostly users in the target language as well as a clear HTML structure. Its creators were able to gather about 13 million webpages from 60,000 bloggers for a total of 5.6 billion tokens.

Last, focused crawl on the German version of the platform wordpress.com led to the construction of a corpus of 100 million tokens under Creative Commons licenses (Barbaresi and Würzner, 2014), albeit with a much lower proportion of comments (present on 12.7% of the posts). In fact, comments have been shown to be strongly related to the popularity of a blog (Mishne and Glance, 2006), so that the number of comments is much lower when blogs are taken at random.

The sharp decrease in publication of work documenting blog corpus construction after 2008 signalizes a shift of focus, not only because web corpus construction does not often get the attention it deserves, but also because of the growing popularity of short message services like Twitter, which allow for comprehensive studies on social networks and internet-based communication, with a larger number of users and messages as well as clear data on network range (e.g. followers).

3 Method

3.1 Discovery

A detection phase is needed to be able to observe bloggers "in the wild" without needing to resort to large-scale crawling. In fact, guessing if a website uses WordPress by analyzing HTML code is straightforward if nothing was been done to hide it, which is almost always the case. However, downloading even a reasonable number of web pages may take a lot of time. That is why I chose to perform massive scans in order to find websites using WordPress, which to my best knowledge has not yet been tried in the literature. The detection process is twofold, the first filter is URL-based whereas the final selection uses shallow HTTP requests.

---

[4] http://ir.dcs.gla.ac.uk/wiki/TREC-BLOG

[5] https://web.archive.org/web/20160313020503/
http://ir.dcs.gla.ac.uk/test_collections/blogs08info.html

The permalinks settings[6] in WordPress define five common URL structures: *default* (?p= or ?page_id= or ?paged=), *date* (/year/ and/or /month/ and/or /day/ and so on), *post number* (/keyword/number – where keyword is for example "archives"), *tag or category* (/tag/, /category/, or cross-language equivalents), and finally *post name* (long URLs containing a lot of hyphens). Patterns derived from those structures can serve as a first filter, although the patterns are not always reliable: news websites tend to use dates very frequently in URLs, in that case the accuracy of the prediction is poor.

The most accurate method would be a scan of fully-rendered HTML documents with clear heuristics such as the "generator" meta tag in the header, which by default points to WordPress. In this study, HTTP HEAD[7] requests are used to spare bandwidth and get cleaner, faster results. HEAD requests are part of the HTTP protocol. Like the most frequent request, GET, which fetches the content, they are supposed to be implemented by every web server. A HEAD request fetches the meta-information written in response headers without downloading the actual content, which makes it much faster, but also more resource-friendly, as according to my method less than three requests per domain name are sufficient.

The following rules come from from the official documentation and have been field-tested:
(1) A request sent to the homepage is bound to yield pingback information to use via the XML-RPC protocol in the *X-Pingback* header. Note that if there is a redirect, this header usually points to the "real" domain name and/or path, ending in *xmlrpc.php*. What is more, frequently used WordPress modules may leave a trace in the header as well, e.g. *WP-Super-Cache*, which identifies a WordPress-run website with certainty.
(2) A request sent to */login* or */wp-login.php* should yield a HTTP status corresponding to an existing page (2XX, 3XX, more rarely 401).
(3) A request sent to */feed* or */wp-feed.php* should yield the header *Location*.

The criteria can be used separately or in combination. I chose to use a simple decision tree. The information provided is rarely tampered on or misleading, since almost all WordPress installations stick to the defaults. Sending more than one request makes the guess more precise, it also acts like a redirection check which provides the effectively used domain name behind a URL. Thus, since the requests help deduplicating a URL list, they are doubly valuable.

3.2 Sources and crawls

This study falls doubly into the category of focused or scoped crawling (Olston and Najork, 2010): the emphasis lies on German or on the .at-domain, and a certain type of websites are examined based on structural characteristics.

I have previously shown that the diversity of sources has a positive impact on yield and quality (Barbaresi, 2014). Aside from URL lists from this and other previous experiments (Barbaresi, 2013) and URLs extracted from each batch of downloaded web documents (proper crawls), several sources were queried, not in the orthodox BootCat way with randomized tuples (Baroni and Bernardini, 2004) but based on formal URL characteristics as described above:
(1) URLs from the CommonCrawl[8], a repository already used in web corpus construction (Habernal et al., 2016; Schäfer, 2016);
(2) the CDX index query frontend of the internet Archive;[9]
(3) public instances of the metasearch engine Searx.[10]

A further restriction resides in the downloads of sitemaps for document retrieval. A majority of websites are optimized in this respect, and experiments showed that crawls otherwise depend on unclear directory structures such as posts classified by categories or month, as well as on variables (e.g. *page*) in URL structures, which leads to numerous duplicates and an inefficient crawl. Another advantage is that websites offering sitemaps are almost systematically robot-friendly, which solves ethical robots.txt-related issues such as the crawl delay, which is frequently mentioned as an obstacle in the literature.

3.3 Extraction

I designed a text extraction targeting specifically WordPress pages, which is transferable to a whole range of self-hosted websites using WordPress, allowing to reach various blogger profiles thanks

---

[6] http://codex.wordpress.org/Using_Permalinks
[7] http://www.w3.org/Protocols/rfc2616/rfc2616
[8] http://commoncrawl.org
[9] https://github.com/internetarchive/wayback/tree/master/wayback-cdx-server
[10] https://github.com/asciimoo/searx/wiki/Searx-instances

to a comparable if not identical content structure. The extractor acts like a state-of-the-art wrapper: after parsing the HTML page, XPATH-expressions select subtrees and operate on them through pruning and tag conversion to (1) write the data with the desired amount of markup and (2) convert the desired HTML tags into the output XML format in strict compliance to the guidelines of the Text Encoding Initiative[11], in order to allow for a greater interoperability within the research community.

The extraction of metadata targets the following fields, if available: title of post, title of blog, date of publication, canonical URL, author, categories, and tags. The multiple plugins cause strong divergences in the rendered HTML code, additionally not all websites use all the fields at their disposal. Thus, titles and canonical URL are the most often extracted data, followed by date, categories, tags, and author.

Content extraction allows for a distinction between post and comments, the latter being listed as a series of paragraphs with text formatting. The main difference with extractors used in information retrieval is that structural boundaries are kept (titles, paragraphs), whereas links are discarded for corpus use. A special attention is given to dates. Documents with non-existent or missed date or entry content are discarded during processing and are not part of the corpus, which through the dated entries is a corpus of "blogs" in a formal sense. Removal of duplicates is performed on entry basis.

3.4 Content analysis

In the first experiment, language detection is performed with langid.py (Lui and Baldwin, 2012) and sources are evaluated using the Filtering and Language identification for URL Crawling Seeds[12] toolchain (Barbaresi, 2014), which includes obvious spam and non-text documents filtering, redirection checks, collection of host- and markup-based data, HTML code stripping, document validity check, and language identification. No language detection is undertaken is the second experiment since no such filtering is intended. That being said, a large majority of webpages are expected to be in German, as has been shown for another German-speaking country in the .de-TLD

<hr>

[11]http://www.tei-c.org/
[12]https://github.com/adbar/flux-toolchain

(Schäfer et al., 2013).

The token counts below are produced by the WASTE tokenizer (Jurish and Würzner, 2013).

4 Experiment 1: Retrieving German blogs

4.1 General figures on harvested content

In a previous experiment, the largest platform for WordPress-hosted websites, wordpress.com, blogs under CC license were targeted (Barbaresi and Würzner, 2014). In the summer of 2015, sitemaps were retrieved for all known home pages, which lead to the integral download of 145,507 different websites for a total number of 6,605,078 documents (390 Gb), leaving 6,095,630 files after processing (36 Gb). There are 6,024,187 "valid" files (with usable date and content) from 141,648 websites, whose text amounts to about 2.11 billion tokens.

The distribution of harvested documents in the course of years is documented in table 6, there are 6,095,206 documents with at least a reliable indication of publication year, i.e. 92.3% of all documents. Contrarily to dates in the literature, these results are not from reported permalinks dates from feeds, but directly from page metadata; nonetheless, there is also a fair share of implausible dates, comparable to the 3% of the TREC blog corpus (Macdonald and Ounis, 2006). This indicates that these dates are not an extraction problem but rather a creative license on the side of the authors.

Year	Docs.
2003	1,746
2004	4,993
2005	13,916
2006	62,901
2007	191,898
2008	377,271
2009	575,923
2010	733,397
2011	871,108
2012	1,066,996
2013	1,108,495
2014	717,861
2015	362,633
rest	6,068

Table 1: Distribution of documents among plausible years in the first experiment

4.2 Typology

An analysis of the top domain names in canonical URLs extracted from the documents, by total number of documents in the corpus (see table 2) yields a typology clearly oriented towards community blogging mostly centered on creative activities or hobbies.

Domain name	URLs
mariusebertsblog.com	2,954
allesnaehbar.de	1,730
zuckerzimtundliebe.de	1,194
lyrikzeitung.com	1,104
der-retrosalon.com	1,092
rhein-main-startups.com	1,046
sciencefiles.org	1,042
des-belles-choses.com	1,014
twinklinstar.com	1,013
wirsindeins.org	1,007

Table 2: Most frequent domains names in URL queue in the first experiment

There are 4,777,546 pages with categories, 10,288,861 uses and 312,055 different categories in total, the top-15 results are displayed in table 3.

	Name	Freq.	Translation
1	Uncategorized	588,638	*(defaut category)*
2	Allgemein	239,796	*general*
3	Politik	71,534	*politics*
4	Allgemeines	60,178	*general*
5	News	58,281	*(also German)*
6	Musik	46,238	*music*
7	Gesellschaft	35,675	*society*
8	Fotografie	35,042	*photography*
9	Deutschland	33,841	*Germany*
10	Aktuelles	33,117	*current topics*
11	Medien	30,914	*media*
12	Alltag	29,839	*everyday life*
13	Leben	27,897	*life*
14	Fotos	26,107	*pictures*
15	Sonstiges	24,431	*misc.*

Table 3: Most frequent categories in the first experiment

There are 2,312,843 pages with tags, 15,856,481 uses in total, and 2,431,920 different tags, the top-15 results are displayed in table 4. They are as general as the top categories but slightly more informative.

All in all, the observed metadata are in line with the expectations, even if the high proportion of photoblogs is not ideal for text collection. Comments were extracted for 1,454,752 files (24%), this proportion confirms the hypothesis that the wordpress.com-platform leads primarily to the publication of blogs in a traditional fashion. On the contrary, the typology has to be more detailed in the second experiment due to the absence of previous knowledge about the collection.

	Name	Freq.	Translation
1	Fotografie	35,910	*photography*
2	Berlin	34,553	
3	Deutschland	30,351	*Germany*
4	Leben	29,597	*life*
5	Politik	26,315	*politics*
6	Musik	26,221	*music*
7	Foto	26,202	
8	Liebe	24,865	*love*
9	Kunst	24,382	*art*
10	USA	21,059	
11	Fotos	20,829	*pictures*
12	Natur	17,490	*nature*
13	Gedanken	16,542	*thoughts*
14	Weihnachten	16,344	*christmas*
15	Video	16,329	

Table 4: Most frequent tags in the first experiment

5 Experiment 2: Targeting the .at-domain

5.1 General figures on harvested content

The iterations summed up in table 5 took place during the 2nd half of 2015. Each time, all links in the .at top level domain were extracted, and analyzed as to their potential to be using WordPress. If so, potential sitemaps were retrieved and the URLs added to the queue if they were new. When necessary (e.g. after stages 5 and 6), the crawls have been refreshed with new material described in sources. After 11 iterations, seed exhaustion was nearing as new WordPress websites with sitemaps were hard to come by, and the experiment was stopped.

batch	domains	no. files	Gb
1	2,020	571,888	31
2	525	103,211	5.5
3	1,269	695,827	34
4	109	49,488	3.3
5	84	433	0.02
6	206	37,632	1.7
7	1,405	483,566	21
8	1,603	175,456	11
9	458	62,103	4.1
10	1,887	456,419	27
11	2,988	417,951	20

Table 5: Iterations and yields in the second experiment

A total of 3,053,974 different URLs have been downloaded (159 Gb), which left after processing and canonicalization 2,589,674 files (14 Gb). There are about 2 million "valid" files (with usable date and content), whose text amounts to about 550 million tokens. There are 5,664 different domain names before processing, and 7,275 after (due to the resolution of canonical URLs).

5.2 Typology

Of all canonical domain names, only 240 contain the word *blog*. Comments were extracted for 181,246 files (7%), which is explained mainly by the actual absence of comments and partly by difficulty of extraction in the case of third-party comment systems.

The distribution of harvested documents in the course of years is documented in table 6. There are 2,083,535 documents with at least a reliable indication of publication year, i.e. 80.5% of all documents. The relative amount of "creative" dates is slightly higher than in experiment 1, which hints at a larger diversity of form and content.

The increase in the number of documents exceeds by far the increase of domains registered in the .at-TLD[13], which seems to hint at the growing popularity of WordPress and maybe also at the ephemeral character of blogs.

Year	Docs.
2003	17,263
2004	30,009
2005	28,177
2006	35,853
2007	47,934
2008	78,895
2009	104,604
2010	152,422
2011	176,231
2012	197,819
2013	297,143
2014	371,605
2015	517,073
rest	28,507

Table 6: Distribution of documents among plausible years in the second experiment

An analysis of the top-50 domains names in canonical URLs extracted from the documents, by total number of documents in the corpus (see table 7) gives the following typology: informational for general news websites (9), promotional/commercial for websites which list ads, deals, jobs or products (12), specialized for focused news and community websites (16), entertainment (3), political (3), personal for websites dedicated to a person or an organization (3), adult (2), forum (1).

There are 260,468 pages with categories, 834,284 uses and 11,813 different categories in total, the top-15 results are displayed in table 8. The

[13]1,594,059 in January 2005; 3,112,683 in January 2010; 3,630,078 in January 2015
Source: http://ftp.isc.org/www/survey/reports/

Domain name	URLs	Genre
vol.at	333,690	informational
triple-s.at	312,714	informational
salzburg24.at	134,230	informational
vienna.at	96,654	informational
vorarlbergernachrichten.at	49,816	informational
dealdoktor.de	25,445	promotional
sportreport.biz	24,796	informational
cba.fro.at	21,895	informational
juve-verlag.at	21,548	promotional
eventfotos24.at	17,805	entertainment
unibrennt.at	16,497	political
dolomitenstadt.at	16,484	informational
sparhamster.at	13,997	promotional
freizeitalpin.com	12,440	specialized
webdeals.at	11,472	promotional
hans-wurst.net	10,717	entertainment
autorevue.at	9,840	specialized
katja.at	9,833	political
spielweb.at	9,541	promotional
medmedia.at	9,125	specialized
adiweiss.at	8,741	personal
sciam-online.at	8,058	specialized
electronicbeats.net	7,255	specialized
antiquariat-getau.at	7,205	promotional
greenpeace.org	7,031	political
photoboerse.at	6,945	promotional
salzburgresearch.at	6,802	professional
mittelstand-nachrichten.at	6,694	informational
sturm12.at	6,672	specialized
raketa.at	6,170	entertainment
platzpirsch.at	6,127	promotional
sexyinsider.at	6,024	adult
rebell.at	5,782	specialized
jusportal.at	5,739	specialized
aktuelle-veranstaltungen.at	5,733	specialized
ffmoedling.at	5,633	personal
zddk.eu	5,386	forum
kosmetik-transparent.at	5,381	specialized
sportwetteninfo.at	5,366	specialized
autoguru.at	5,142	specialized
ps4news.at	5,102	specialized
gastronomiejobs.wien	5,035	promotional
psychohelp.at	4,836	promotional
porno-austria.at	4,822	adult
christianmari.at	4,709	promotional
blog.sprachreisen.at	4,493	personal
w6-tabletop.at	4,488	specialized
ellert.at	4,381	promotional
demonic-nights.at	4,353	specialized
todesanzeigen.vol.at	4,296	specialized

Table 7: Most frequent domains names in URL queue in the second experiment

fact that "blog" is used as a category shows that it is not taken for granted.

There are 279,083 pages with tags, 5,093,088 uses in total, and 192,352 different tags, the top-15 results are displayed in table 9. The tags reflect a number of different preoccupations, including family, holidays, sex, job and labor legislation. "Homemade" and "amateur" can be used in German, albeit rarely, these words give more insights on the genre (most probably adult entertainment)

	Name	Freq.	Translation
1	Allgemein	28,005	*general*
2	Blu-ray	10,445	*(laser disc standard)*
3	MedienFamilie	9,662	*media-family*
4	Blog	9,652	
5	Familienleben	9,278	*family life*
6	News	8,857	*(also German)*
7	Film	8,222	*movies*
8	Absolut-Reisen	6,964	*absolute travels*
9	Buch	6,146	*book*
10	Schule	6,108	*school*
11	Spiele	5,939	*games*
12	Familienpolitik	5,781	*family policies*
13	Gewinnspiel	5,607	*competition*
14	In eigener Sache	5,463	*in our own cause*
15	Uncategorized	5,150	*(defaut category)*

Table 8: Most frequent categories in the second experiment

	Name	Freq.	Translation
1	Wien	18,973	*Vienna*
2	Deutschland	18,895	*Germany*
3	Usermeldungen	14,409	*user reports*
4	sterreich	10,886	*Austria*
5	Angebot aus DE	10,155	*offer from Germany*
6	sex	10,112	
7	Frauen	9,541	*women*
8	Kinder	8,968	*children*
9	USA	8,013	
10	Urlaub	7,767	*holiday*
11	homemade	7,666	
12	amateur	7,660	
13	mydirtyhobby	7,635	
14	Recht	7,611	*law*
15	Arbeitsrecht	7,294	*labor legislation*

Table 9: Most frequent tags in the second experiment

than on content language.

All in all, the distribution of categories and tags indicates that the majority of texts target as expected German-speaking users.

6 Discussion

Although the definition of blogs as a hybrid genre neither fundamentally new nor unique (Herring et al., 2004) holds true, several assumptions about weblogs cannot be considered to be accurate anymore in the light of frequencies in the corpus. Blogs are not always "authored by a single individual" (Kumar et al., 2003), nor does the frequency criterion given by the Oxford English Dictionary (Kehoe and Gee, 2012) – "frequently updated web site" – necessarily correspond to the reality. Even if both experiments gathered blogs in a formal sense, there are differences between the websites on the platform wordpress.com and freely hosted websites. The former are cleaner in form and content, they are in line with a certain tradition. The "local community interactions between a small number of bloggers" (Kumar et al., 2003) of the beginnings have been relegated by websites corresponding to the original criteria of a blog but whose finality is to sell information, entertainment, or concrete products and services.

Consequently, the expectation that "blog software makes Web pages truly interactive, even if that interactive potential has yet to be fully exploited" (Herring et al., 2004) is either outdated or yet to come. Beside these transformations and the emergence of other social networks, the whole range from top to barely known websites shows that the number of comments per post and per website is largely inferior to the "bursting" phase of webblogging, where comments were "a substantial part of the blogosphere" (Mishne and Glance, 2006). The evolution of the Web as well as the scope of this study cast the typical profile of a passive internet consumer, a "prosumer" at best, which should be taken in consideration in web corpus construction and computer-mediated communication studies. If blogs still bridge a technological gap between HTML-enhanced CMC and CMC-enhanced Web pages (Herring et al., 2004), a typological gap exists between original and current studies as well as between users of a platform and users of a content management system.

7 Conclusion

The trade-off to gain metadata using focused downloads following strict rules seems to get enough traction to build larger web corpora, since a total of 550 Gb of actually downloaded material allows after processing for the construction of a corpus of about 2.7 billion tokens with rich metadata. This comparatively high yield is a step towards more efficiency with respect to machine power and "Hi-Fi" web corpora, which could help promoting the cause of web sources and modernization of research methodology.

The resulting corpus complies with formal requirements on metadata-enhanced corpora and on weblogs considered as a series of dated entries. The interlinking of blogs and their rising popularity certainly don't stay in the way. However, addressing the tricky question of web genres seems inevitable in order to be able to properly qualify my findings and subsequent linguistic inquiries. More than ever, blogs are a hybrid genre, and their ecology tends to mimic existing text types, audiences, and motivations, with a focus on information (general, specialized, or community-based) as well as on promotional goals.

References

Adrien Barbaresi and Kay-Michael Würzner. 2014. For a fistful of blogs: Discovery and comparative benchmarking of republishable German content. In *KONVENS 2014, NLP4CMC workshop proceedings*, pages 2–10. Hildesheim University Press.

Adrien Barbaresi. 2013. Crawling microblogging services to gather language-classified URLs. Workflow and case study. In *Proceedings of the 51th Annual Meeting of the ACL, Student Research Workshop*, pages 9–15.

Adrien Barbaresi. 2014. Finding Viable Seed URLs for Web Corpora: A Scouting Approach and Comparative Study of Available Sources. In *Proceedings of the 9th Web as Corpus Workshop*, pages 1–8.

Adrien Barbaresi. 2015. *Ad hoc and general-purpose web corpus construction*. Ph.D. thesis, École Normale Supérieure de Lyon.

Marco Baroni and Silvia Bernardini. 2004. BootCaT: Bootstrapping Corpora and Terms from the Web. In *Proceedings of LREC*.

Rebecca Blood. 2002. *The Weblog Handbook: Practical Advice on Creating and Maintaining your Blog*. Basic Books.

Valter Crescenzi, Giansalvatore Mecca, and Paolo Merialdo. 2001. Roadrunner: Towards Automatic Data Extraction From Large Web Sites. In *Proceedings of the 27th VLDB Conference*, pages 109–118.

Alexander Geyken. 2007. The DWDS corpus: A reference corpus for the German language of the 20th century. In Christiane Fellbaum, editor, *Collocations and Idioms: Linguistic, lexicographic, and computational aspects*, pages 23–41. Continuum Press.

Natalie Glance, Matthew Hurst, and Takashi Tomokiyo. 2004. Blogpulse: Automated Trend Discovery for Weblogs. In *WWW 2004 Workshop on the Weblogging Ecosystem: Aggregation, Analysis and Dynamics*.

Daniel Gruhl, Ramanathan Guha, David Liben-Nowell, and Andrew Tomkins. 2004. Information Diffusion through Blogspace. In *Proceedings of the 13th international conference on World Wide Web*, pages 491–501. ACM.

Yan Guo, Huifeng Tang, Linhai Song, Yu Wang, and Guodong Ding. 2010. ECON: an Approach to Extract Content from Web News Page. In *Proceedings of 12th International Asia-Pacific Web Conference (APWEB)*, pages 314–320. IEEE.

Ivan Habernal, Omnia Zayed, and Iryna Gurevych. 2016. C4corpus: Multilingual web-size corpus with free license. In *Proceedings of LREC*, pages 914–922.

Susan C Herring, Lois Ann Scheidt, Sabrina Bonus, and Elijah Wright. 2004. Bridging the Gap: A Genre Analysis of Weblogs. In *Proceedings of the 37th Annual Hawaii International Conference on System Sciences*, pages 11–21. IEEE.

Bryan Jurish and Kay-Michael Würzner. 2013. Word and Sentence Tokenization with Hidden Markov Models. *JLCL*, 28(2):61–83.

Andrew Kehoe and Matt Gee. 2012. Reader comments as an aboutness indicator in online texts: introducing the Birmingham Blog Corpus. *Studies in Variation, Contacts and Change in English*, 12.

Sandeep Krishnamurthy. 2002. The Multidimensionality of Blog Conversations: The Virtual Enactment of September 11. *Internet Research*, 3.

Ravi Kumar, Jasmine Novak, Prabhakar Raghavan, and Andrew Tomkins. 2003. On the Bursty Evolution of Blogspace. In *Proceedings of WWW 2003*, pages 568–576.

Marco Lui and Timothy Baldwin. 2012. langid.py: An Off-the-shelf Language Identification Tool. In *Proceedings of the ACL 2012 system demonstrations*, pages 25–30.

Craig Macdonald and Iadh Ounis. 2006. The TREC Blogs06 Collection: Creating and Analysing a Blog Test Collection. Technical report, Department of Computer Science, University of Glasgow.

Gilad Mishne and Natalie Glance. 2006. Leave a Reply: An Analysis of Weblog Comments. In *Third Annual Workshop on the Weblogging Ecosystem, WWW 2006*.

Tomoyuki Nanno, Toshiaki Fujiki, Yasuhiro Suzuki, and Manabu Okumura. 2004. Automatically Collecting, Monitoring, and Mining Japanese Weblogs. In *Proceedings of the 13th international World Wide Web conference on Alternate track papers & posters*, pages 320–321. ACM.

Christopher Olston and Marc Najork. 2010. Web Crawling. *Foundations and Trends in Information Retrieval*, 4(3):175–246.

Michal Ptaszynski, Pawel Dybala, Rafal Rzepka, Kenji Araki, and Yoshio Momouchi. 2012. YACIS: A five-billion-word corpus of Japanese blogs fully annotated with syntactic and affective information. In *Proceedings of The AISB/IACAP World Congress*, pages 40–49.

Geoffrey Sampson. 2000. The role of taxonomy in language engineering. *Philosophical Transactions of the Royal Society of London. Series A: Mathematical, Physical and Engineering Sciences*, 358(1769):1339–1355.

Roland Schäfer and Felix Bildhauer. 2013. *Web Corpus Construction*. Synthesis Lectures on Human Language Technologies. Morgan & Claypool.

Roland Schäfer, Adrien Barbaresi, and Felix Bildhauer. 2013. The Good, the Bad, and the Hazy: Design Decisions in Web Corpus Construction. In *Proceedings of the 8th Web as Corpus Workshop*, pages 7–15.

Roland Schäfer, Adrien Barbaresi, and Felix Bildhauer. 2014. Focused Web Corpus Crawling. In *Proceedings of the 9th Web as Corpus workshop (WAC-9)*, pages 9–15.

Roland Schäfer. 2016. CommonCOW: massively huge web corpora from CommonCrawl data and a method to distribute them freely under restrictive EU copyright laws. In *Proceedings of LREC*, pages 4500–4504.

Jonathan Schler, Moshe Koppel, Shlomo Argamon, and James W Pennebaker. 2006. Effects of Age and Gender on Blogging. In *AAAI Spring Symposium: Computational Approaches to Analyzing Weblogs*, volume 6, pages 199–205.

Vít Suchomel and Jan Pomikálek. 2012. Efficient Webcrawling for large text corpora. In *Proceedings of the 7th Web as Corpus Workshop*, pages 40–44.

Yannick Versley and Yana Panchenko. 2012. Not just bigger: Towards better-quality Web corpora. In *Proceedings of the 7th Web as Corpus Workshop*, pages 44–52.

Junfeng Wang, Xiaofei He, Can Wang, Jian Pei, Jiajun Bu, Chun Chen, Ziyu Guan, and Gang Lu. 2009. News Article Extraction with Template-Independent Wrapper. In *Proceedings of the WWW 2009*, pages 1085–1086. ACM.

Cai-Nicolas Ziegler and Michal Skubacz. 2007. Content Extraction from News Pages using Particle Swarm Optimization on Linguistic and Structural Features. In *Proceedings of the IEEE/WIC/ACM International Conference on Web Intelligence*, pages 242–249. IEEE.

Topically-focused Blog Corpora for Multiple Languages

Andrew Salway[1], Dag Elgesem[2], Knut Hofland[1], Øystein Reigem[1], Lubos Steskal[2]
[1]Uni Research, Bergen, Norway   [2]University of Bergen, Norway
{andrew.salway, knut.hofland, oystein.reigem}@uni.no
{dag.elgesem, lubos.steskal}@uib.no

Abstract

This paper describes the construction of three corpora, intended for use in social science research, comprising English-language, French-language and Norwegian-language blogs related to the topic of climate change. The approach, techniques and lessons learnt should be applicable for creating other topically-focused blog corpora.

1 Introduction

Since the 1990s blogs have emerged as an important medium in which users can easily create and share content on the Internet. The emergence of the blogosphere has brought changes to the online public sphere, to the role of the mainstream media, to the production, contestation and dissemination of scientific knowledge, and to political deliberation. As a site for large-scale discourses about socially-relevant issues, the blogosphere has received considerable attention from social scientists during the last decade (Rettberg, 2013; Bruns and Jacobs, 2006).

Important questions relate to the democratic potential of blogs, i.e. whether they do indeed provide a new platform for open democratic participation (Benkler, 2007), or whether a minority of blogs get most of the attention (Hindman, 2008). Researchers have studied the roles of blogs in connection with political campaigns (Adamic and Glance, 2005; Bruns and Jacobs, 2006; Moe, 2011) and controversial political issues, like climate change, where the diffusion of information may influence the formation of opinions (Sharman, 2014; Elgesem et al., 2015). One aspect is whether the linking practices of bloggers contribute to the polarization of online political debate and the fragmentation of the online public sphere (Sunstein, 2008). Also, the relationship between mainstream media and blogs has been studied, e.g. to see whether blogs influ-

ence the audience's attention to news (Bruns, 2005; Leccese, 2009; Elgesem et al., 2016).

Despite the great interest in the content of the blogosphere, there is a lack of commonly available large-scale blog corpora to support empirical research. Most blog corpora created for social science research have been relatively small since they were concentrated on what were perceived to be the most important blogs for certain research questions (e.g. Adamic and Glance, 2005; Song et al., 2007; Sharman, 2014). Larger blog corpora have been created but these were not focused on particular topics or were not designed to support social science research (e.g. Glance et al., 2004; Bansal and Koudas, 2007; Kehoe and Gee, 2012; Meinel et al., 2015).

One exception is our previous development of a large climate change blog corpus (Salway et al., 2013; Elgesem et al., 2015). However, the method used in that work was somewhat ad hoc in its selection of blogs when crawling. The method's reliance on human judgment means that it is hard to replicate, i.e. in order to update the corpus, create corpora for other languages and topics, and critique it as part of social science methodology. Further, crawling-based methods may be problematic when a topically-defined area of the blogosphere is fragmented. It may be expected that there are few, if any, connections between some communities in the climate change blogosphere.

This paper describes the construction of large topically-focused blog corpora which are intended for use in social science research. The topic is climate change and the languages are English, French and Norwegian. It is hoped that the approach and techniques can be usefully replicated for other topics and languages. By topically-focused we mean a corpus that contains "all" blogs related to a socially-relevant issue, like climate change. By providing, as far as possible, an unbiased and comprehensive collection of relevant blogs, including core blogs and the

17

Proceedings of the 10th Web as Corpus Workshop (WAC-X) and the EmpiriST Shared Task, pages 17–26,
Berlin, Germany, August 7-12, 2016. ©2016 Association for Computational Linguistics

broader discourse around them, such a corpus supports a variety of social science research.

2   Task definition and approach

An important aspect of the blogosphere is the interaction between bloggers as evidenced by their linking patterns. Thus blog corpora should contain data about hyperlinks as well as the main text component of every blog post. The date of each blog post is needed for investigating the development of blog communities and information diffusion. A blog contains various pages, e.g. a homepage, archive pages, and posts. We seek to harvest all the posts for each chosen blog, but not other pages. So, in simple terms, the task at hand is to create a corpus containing all posts – with text, link and date data – from all blogs in a chosen language and that relate to a chosen topic. In this section we describe and discuss how the notions of blog, topic and language are defined and operationalized in our approach.

Blogs are commonly understood to be discussion or informational websites with posts presented in reverse chronological order. For practical reasons we define a blog to be a website that is produced using one of several blog authoring platforms, and, more specifically, a website that mentions the platform in its domain name. The platforms were chosen based on search engine results for queries in order to establish which platforms dominated searches for terms related to the topic. Searching for "climate change" and "global warming" in blogs showed that around 95% of all hits came from blogs on the Word-Press, Blogspot and TypePad platforms. No other platform had more than 1% of the hits. The same platforms dominated for Norwegian; for French, OverBlog swapped with TypePad.

This operational definition of blog – as a website that mentions a blog platform in its domain name – means it is trivial to identify blogs in a consistent way when searching and crawling. Selecting only a few blog platforms means that we can afford to optimize data extraction techniques in a platform-specific way. The obvious negatives are that we miss blogs on other platforms, and also blogs that are produced on the chosen platforms but that only use a domain name that does not contain the platform name. Results from the work reported in this paper suggest that some of the most important blogs are known by such domain names (see 4.4).

A topic like climate change is very broad and rather nebulous. People may blog about climate change from scientific, political and social perspectives, within which there are competing viewpoints. Blogs further vary in how they focus on the existence of climate change, its causes, its effects and ways in which to mitigate or adapt. The discussions may be in the context of local geographic areas, countries or the whole world. Some blogs will be specifically about climate change issues, but many other scientific, political and socially-concerned blogs mention it.

For blog corpora to be used in social science research it is important to minimize bias towards particular people, perspectives and viewpoints. As far as possible the method for selecting blogs should be transparent. Thus, we chose to define the topic of climate change with only a few generic terms, i.e. for English, "climate change", "global warming" and "greenhouse effect". These terms were chosen following the work of Schmidt et al. (2013) who conducted an extensive review of research into climate change communication: they considered the three terms to refer to the same phenomena and used them, and variant forms like 'climat* NEAR chang*', to select relevant newspaper stories. Whilst query expansion methods could be used to add many other search terms related to the topic, e.g. "sea level", "climate sceptic", "carbon tax", etc., we feel that this could introduce unaccountable bias into the selection of the material.

In our approach the search terms are used with search engine APIs in order to identify relevant blogs. In brief, the method retrieves blog posts containing the search terms and then selects blogs that have >1 posts containing >1 instances of a search term (see 3.1). This criterion is deliberately inclusive, i.e. it is intended to include blogs with only very few mentions of search terms because: (i) some blogs may focus on a specific aspect of the climate change debate without mentioning the generic terms very often; (ii) some blogs may be tangentially related to the climate change debate whilst still being of interest to some researchers. Researchers can later apply stricter criteria to select sub-corpora as necessary for specific research questions.

It is problematic to define and operationalize the concepts of nationality and national language varieties in the blogosphere. A blogger may write in their native language but be living and writing in the context of another country, or write in a lingua franca for an international audience. Some blogs have multiple contributors of different nationalities using different languages. Even if it was desirable to classify blogs according to nationality, practically it is not possible to reliably connect a blog to a country from its url, nor ascertain the nationality of a blogger.

Our approach is to create English-language, French-language and Norwegian-language corpora, without associating blogs with countries or language varieties. So, for example, an English-language corpus may include blogs written in US, Australian and British varieties, etc., and bloggers of any nationality, including some writing in English as a second language. Language identification is achieved with language codes when querying search engines (3.1), and subsequently an off-the-shelf tool (3.3.3).

3 Pipeline

3.1 Identification of relevant blogs

For each language a set of potentially relevant blog posts was gathered from repeated querying of three search engine APIs (Google, Bing and Yahoo). It seemed appropriate to use multiple APIs to reduce bias from any single one, although because Bing and Yahoo allowed more results to be returned it may be that they have a bigger influence than Google. That said, it must be noted that the search engine APIs are "black boxes" to us, i.e. we cannot know how they determine result sets and there is a risk of "filter bubble" effects (Pariser, 2011).

Queries specified a search term, a blog platform and a language code. For English the terms were "climate change", "global warming" and "greenhouse effect"; these were translated into French (three terms with five inflections) and Norwegian (four terms with 12 inflections). It could be that the search engine APIs would expand search terms into their inflected forms, but it seems safer to be explicit, and perhaps it helps to reach further down the list of potential results.

Querying was done daily for 12 weeks from early June 2014 and the rate of previously unseen posts and blogs in the results was monitored. New posts in the results were due both to bloggers writing new posts, and to search engines re-ranking older ones. Since search engines limit the number of results returned (100-1000 per query), after two weeks the set of query terms was expanded with n-grams containing the initial search terms and a function word, e.g. "of climate change". For each initial search term we took the 10 most frequent n-grams from the posts returned from the search engines at that point. This allowed us to reach much further down the search engines' results lists. Whilst this helped to

retrieve many more relevant posts, it also meant that for Norwegian, and to some extent French, some retrieved posts were rather tangential to the topic. It was also noted that about 20% of the posts returned for Norwegian were actually in Danish and had to be removed: this was done using a list of frequent Danish words that are rare in Norwegian. The total cost for using the APIs was approximately $2000. Table 1 shows for each language: the search terms, blog platforms and the number of blog posts that were retrieved.

English (WordPress, BlogSpot, TypePad) climate change, global warming, greenhouse effect → 95,662 posts
French (WordPress, BlogSpot, OverBlog) changement climatique, changements climatiques, réchauffement climatique, effet de serre, effets de serre → 68,853 posts
Norwegian (WordPress, BlogSpot, TypePad) drivhuseffekt, drivhuseffekten, global oppvarming, globale oppvarmingen, klimaendring, klimaendringen, klimaendringene, klimaendringer, klimaforandring, klimaforandringen, klimaforandringene, klimaforandringer → 8,973 posts (after Danish removed)

Table 1: The search terms and blog platforms for each language, and the number of posts returned from querying search engine APIs.

The sets of retrieved blog posts were used to determine which blogs should be harvested. Data was generated about the occurrence of the search terms in the retrieved posts, and hence in the blogs which they came from. The main text of each post was extracted with *jusText* (Pomikálek, 2011) and concordance lines of the search terms were inspected in order to identify and remove striking examples of duplicates due to boilerplate and spam posts. This gave us "good enough" text extraction for this stage of the process.

Table 2 shows how many blogs had >0, >1, >2 and >3 posts that contained >0, >1, and >2 instances of search terms. For example, for English there were 5563 different blogs for which we had >1 posts that contained >1 instances of search terms. Drawing on domain expertise, the sets of blogs relating to the different frequencies were inspected in order to decide appropriate thresholds. In order to favor broad inclusion it was decided to harvest all posts from blogs for which we had gathered >1 posts containing >1 instances of key terms, i.e. 5563 English, 2088 French and 128 Norwegian blogs.

The values for "total posts" in Table 2 are lower than in Table 1 because text was not extracted from all posts; either there was no text in the post, or text extraction failed. After text extraction not all posts contained a search term, e.g. only 67,979 out of 84,536 English posts did. From preliminary inspection it seems that this is because search terms only occurred in the boilerplate of some blog posts, and hence not in the extracted texts. It could also be a sign of query expansion by the search engines.

Search terms	Total posts	Blogs >0 post	Blogs >1 post	Blogs >2 posts	Blogs >3 posts
English					
Total	84536	27873	7205	3995	2762
>0	67979	25190	6515	3541	2391
>1	56806	21231	**5563**	2998	2042
>2	46584	18007	4633	2493	1730
French					
Total	52029	13838	4552	2716	1931
>0	35578	12732	3926	2217	1526
>1	17655	6470	**2088**	1213	845
>2	10839	4187	1318	754	512
Norwegian					
Total	7194	613	505	293	224
>0	2794	1393	337	172	119
>1	943	470	**128**	65	42
>2	477	268	67	26	18

Table 2: The data used to select blogs, i.e. the occurrence of search terms in posts, and the occurrence of these posts in different blogs.

3.2 Harvesting, pre-processing and filtering

The aim was to harvest all posts from the selected blogs that were posted up until the end of 2014. The harvesting script was customized for each blog platform but in general it started at each blog's homepage, followed links to archive pages and got the urls from all links in them. Each url was tested to make sure it had the recognized features for a blog post and that it was from 2014 or earlier (the year is given in the url). The harvesting script was improved iteratively, and rerun, as we learnt more about the idiosyncrasies of each blog platform. For each post the html was run through *ftfy* (Speer, 2016) to address encoding issues, and the time of harvesting was recorded.

The same blog post can be referred to with different urls which causes duplication in the corpus. It also causes problems for analyzing the network between blog posts, i.e. when hyperlinks point to the same post using different urls. Normalization of urls used manually created look-up tables to resolve alternative domain names. Rules were applied to standardize character encoding, the use of www and http, and platform-specific formatting variants. For blog posts with the same urls after normalization, we used the first html file and kept a record of the urls that had been normalized to it. In the English and French material 4.8% of posts had duplicates (nearly always just one); 3.3% for Norwegian.

3.3 Data extraction from html

3.3.1 Boilerplate removal (aka text extraction)

To support social science research it is important to extract the main text of each blog post as accurately as possible, i.e. so that it is then possible to analyze and compare what was written where and when. This contrasts with some web as corpus initiatives in which the corpus may be treated as a bag of sentences in order to remove duplicates (Biemann et al., 2013).

We evaluated two general text extraction solutions – *jusText* (Pomikálek, 2011) and *Alchemy* (www.alchemyapi.com) – on a sample of 1000 posts. For about 20% of posts there was either text missing or extraneous text included. Thus it was considered necessary to develop our own text extraction tool which could take advantage of the fact that the posts it processed came from specific blog authoring platforms.

We assume that the main text of the blog post is continuous and that each blog platform has a certain amount of regularity in how html sequences indicate the start and end of the main text; cf. the BTE algorithm and jusText algorithm reviewed and combined by Endrédy and Novák (2013). For each platform, a set of heuristics – based on html cues – was iteratively developed to identify the start and end points of the main text within an html file. This involved counting frequent <div> elements, manual inspection of html files, and trial and error application of heuristics in which the matching heuristics were recorded and counted, so that the most useful ones became apparent.

The main text is taken to be all lines of html from the first instance of a start cue until the first instance of an end cue. From the selected lines all html tags, and other html sequences, were stripped except link, paragraph and break markers, ensuring white space was maintained. Finally we removed multiple whitespace, converted html entities to characters, and substituted a uniform marker for paragraphs and breaks.

When run over all harvested posts in the three corpora the start and end cues succeeded in matching for 99.7% of all posts, i.e. something was extracted as main text for nearly all of the posts. The quality of the extraction was evaluated with a set of 1463 randomly selected English-language posts, all from different blogs. The evaluator determined that there were only 11 posts (< 1%) in which part of the main text was missing. There were 72 (5%) posts with inappropriate text included at the beginning, 1 in the middle and 48 (3%) at the end.

3.3.2 Further boilerplate mark-up by 5-grams

In the case of a blog corpus, unwanted boilerplate text can manifest as near-duplicate paragraphs in the extracted article text for many posts within a blog, e.g. a slogan for the blog, or a request for donations. However, it should not be assumed that this kind of boilerplate will appear consistently on all posts in a blog since it may change during the life of a blog, or between different batches of a harvest.

Even if we are confident of getting a high precision rate in identifying blog-specific boilerplate within the previously extracted text, it seems better that we mark it up, rather than delete it and risk destroying some relevant material. This means that researchers can decide later what to include for their investigations; for some researchers blog-specific boilerplate might even be an object of study.

Our approach to marking-up blog-specific boilerplate text is based on identifying a set of suspicious 5-grams for each blog, i.e. 5-grams that occur on more than a certain percentage of posts. Through analysis and trial and error we determined a threshold of 15%. Because we had harvested posts in different batches it was important to keep the threshold percentage quite low, i.e. $\geq$ 15% (and frequency $\geq$ 10), in case boilerplate text changed from batch to batch. However we noticed that some genuine 5-grams did occur on more than 15% of a blog's posts, due to the idiosyncratic writing style of some bloggers. We also note that some boilerplate paragraphs may consist of fewer than 5 words but we tolerate these because 4-grams, and less, are too common in normal text.

Thus any paragraph for which 50% or more of the words comprise suspicious 5-grams was marked as boilerplate. We say 50% to capture boilerplate lines in which some content may vary, like a date or a name: it seems unlikely that 50% of a real paragraph would be made up of common 5-grams. Manual evaluation (see 3.3.1) showed that in 23 (9%) of 258 posts with boilerplate marked-up, one or more paragraphs had

been incorrectly marked-up as boilerplate. Whilst 9% is quite high, it is likely that only a small part of each post was incorrectly marked as boilerplate. Further, boilerplate was only marked-up at all on about 20% of all blogs.

3.3.3. Posts in wrong language

For several reasons it is possible that a blog in a corpus for one language contains some posts that are in a different language. Firstly, as noted previously, blogs may contain posts from different contributors or be written by someone in more than one language. Another problem, especially relating to English, is that our search terms may occur on blogs that are all in another language, e.g. as part of a quote or a scientific citation. Due to our low threshold for selecting blogs (see 3.1) a non-English blog would be selected for the English corpus if it had two posts each with two mentions of any English search terms. Further issues may arise from the reliance on search engines' language codes.

We anticipate that different users of the corpora will have different ideas about what should count as an English/French/Norwegian-language blog; and for some researchers the multilingualism of blogs could be of interest. Thus it does not seem appropriate to delete material but rather to record measures of how many posts in each corpus, and in each blog, are in the target language.

Every blog post was run through *langid.py* (Lui and Baldwin, 2012) and a Boolean value was recorded according to whether the post was most likely to be in the target language of its corpus or not. The results of correct language posts by corpus were: English, 96%; French, 81%; Norwegian, 89%. It may be that some blogs are bilingual, e.g. Canadian blogs in French and English, but this remains to be explored.

For each blog the percentage of posts in the correct language was calculated. For analysis, a threshold of 85% posts was taken to mean that a blog was principally in the correct language; the threshold was based on manual inspection of blogs with high numbers of incorrect language posts. This gave the following estimate of blogs in the correct language: English, 96%; French, 86%; Norwegian, 87%.

3.3.4 Link extraction

For each post we stored a set of article links, i.e. the urls (normalized as per 3.2) pointed to from all links found in the main text (article). These links are also marked up in the main text because when analyzing linking patterns in social media it is important to consider the text around links.

Data was also stored to facilitate network analysis based on blogroll links. A blogroll typically appears in a sidebar on all posts of a blog and includes links to other blogs that the blogger is assumed to have some affinity with. We explored extracting these links based on html structure but did not see sufficient regularity. Instead, going blog-by-blog, for each link we store the percentage of the blog's posts that it appears on (instances of links appearing within article text are not counted). A high percentage value for a link that points to another blog may be assumed to indicate a blog roll link (see 4.3).

3.3.5 Date extraction

On the four chosen blog platforms the url for a post normally includes values for month and year; WordPress urls also contain a value for day. For now we simply record these values for a blog post's date. For 490 French OverBlog blogs date information was not available from urls. Work has been done to iteratively develop heuristics to extract date data, including day values, from html for all platforms; see the approach to text extraction, 3.3.1. Preliminary evaluation is encouraging based on comparing month and year values extracted from the html with those from urls. However, date data from html has not been incorporated into the corpora yet.

4 Analysis of the corpora

Table 3 records the content of the three corpora. It counts posts considered to be in the target language of each corpus (see 3.3.3), and words in the main texts of posts, excluding paragraphs marked-up as boilerplate (see 3.3.1 and 3.3.2). The total number of blogs is 123 (1.6%) less than stated in Table 2: this is due to a combination of harvesting and text extraction problems, including the fact that some blogs were no longer available for harvest.

	Blogs	Posts	Words
English	5497	10,539,575	4,837,481,377
French	2033	2,335,174	1,224,657,286
Norwegian	126	46,775	21,212,686

Table 3: The content of the three climate change blog corpora.

Figure 1 shows, for the English corpus, the cumulative total percentage of posts in the corpus against the rank of each blog by number of posts.

For example, it shows that the top 20 blogs account for 10% of the corpus by posts, and the top 200 blogs for 40%. The weighting towards top ranked blogs in the French and Norwegian corpora is even greater. From initial inspection it seems that most of these very large blogs are only loosely related to climate change, if at all. Users of the corpora may consider excluding some of them from their investigations.

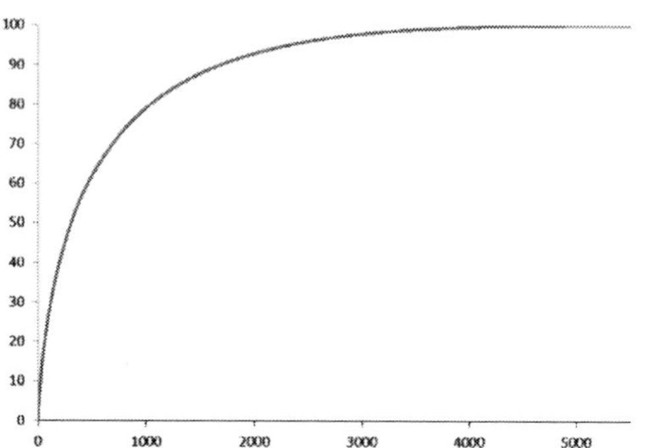

Figure 1: Cumulative total percentage of posts in the English corpus against rank of blog by number of posts.

4.1 Text analysis

As a first step to understand the extent to which the English corpus relates to the topic of climate change, Table 4 gives a view of the distribution of the three search terms used to select blogs. For each term it gives the percentage of blogs that have at least one post containing it, and the percentage of all posts containing it. The fact that 99.2% of blogs, and not 100%, contain any search term suggests minor problems with either harvesting or with text extraction.

The table also gives '% pwc' which sums the word count for all posts containing the term and shows this as a percentage of all words in the corpus. Thus about 14% of the corpus (by word count) comprises blog posts with at least one mention of a search term. Work is ongoing to determine how many further posts contain other terms related to climate change.

	freq.	% blogs	% posts	% pwc
Any term	2,415,596	99.2	6.4	13.9
climate change	1,486,549	96.5	4.8	11.6
global warming	900,918	96.1	3.3	8.7
g'house effect	28,129	47.6	0.1	0.6

Table 4: The distribution of search terms in the English-language corpus.

Another view of the distribution of the terms was obtained by considering, for each blog, the percentage of posts that contain at least one term. This showed that a large number of the blogs appear to be only tangentially related to the topic, although an expanded set of terms needs to be considered before conclusions are made. Some 1041 blogs out of 5497 have only 0-2% of posts containing a search term. A further 1907 blogs have 2-10% posts with search terms, and 742 blogs have 10-20%. The remaining 1807 blogs are evenly spread between 30-100%.

4.2 Distribution of dates

For a temporal view, Figure 2 shows the rate of posting increasing steadily year-by-year in each corpus. Of course it is possible that there is a recency effect since search engines were used to identify relevant blogs: perhaps some blogs that were only active several years ago were missed.

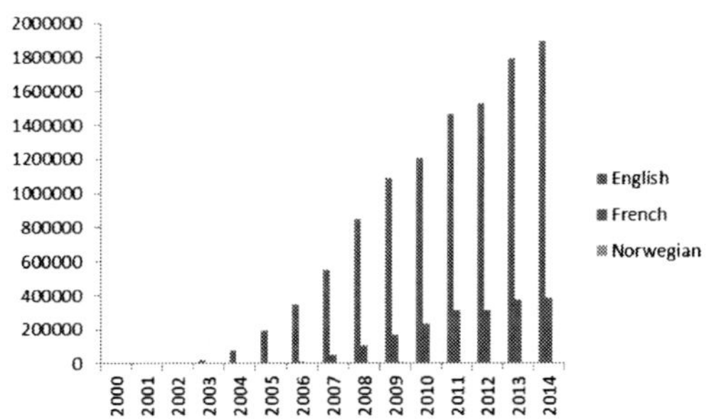

Figure 2: Number of blog posts per year.

By considering the date of the earliest post in each blog, Figure 3 shows a peak for blogs being started in 2009, with a fairly steady decline since then. When the date of the most recent post in each blog was examined it appeared that 56% of English blogs were still active at some point in 2014; French, 61%; Norwegian, 57%.

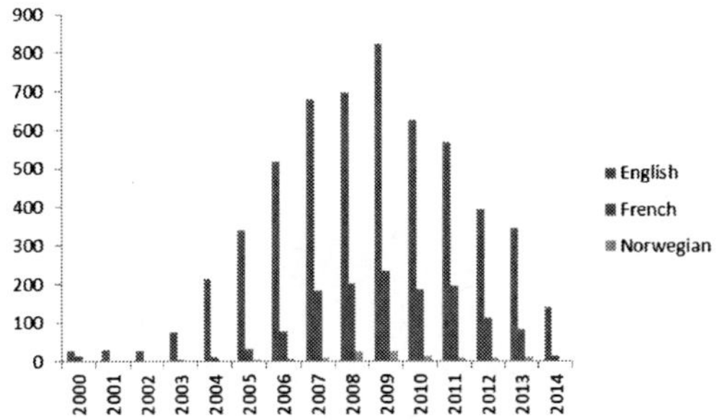

Figure 3: Number of blogs starting per year, i.e. the year of their earliest post.

4.3 Network analysis

As described in 3.3.4, for each non-article link found on a blog we calculated the percentage of posts in that blog that it appeared on. The assumption is that links pointing to the same url from most posts on a blog are blogroll links. Considering the distribution of these percentage values for the English-language corpus we see that non-article links tend to occur either on very few of a blog's posts, or on most of them: 70% of the 855,778 links occur on < 10% of the posts in the blogs they occur on; 24% occur on > 90% of the posts in the blogs they occur on. This leads us to take non-article links occurring on >90% of a blog's posts as blogroll links.

To analyze the network structure of the corpus this set of blogroll links was filtered to keep only those pointing to a blog that we had harvested. Then a directed blog network was created where there is a directed edge from blog A to blog B if there is a blogroll link from A to B. As is common in web networks, the degree distribution is power law like (Broder et al., 2000), ranging from 0 to 68. A few blogs have most of the in-links (links pointing to the blog), and most blogs have very few or none.

To visualize the network all nodes with an in-degree < 5 were removed. Figure 4 shows a network visualization made in Gephi (Bastian et al., 2009) with the ForceAtlas 2 layout algorithm (Jacomy et al., 2014): this tends to cluster highly interconnected nodes and repel weakly connected ones. On top of this, a modularity based community detection algorithm (Blondel et al., 2008) clustered the network into four densely connected groups distinguished by the shade of grey. Note, the size of a node reflects its in-degree. Manual inspection of core blogs in each of the four clusters suggested that one cluster comprised mostly skeptical blogs, one acceptor blogs, and one blogs concerned primarily with economic issues; the fourth cluster was less coherent.

4.4 How much of the climate change blogosphere was captured?

Generally it may be assumed that a blog's in-degree reflects its importance. Hence, one way to assess the coverage of the corpora, and to fill gaps, is to use blogroll links as a source of information about what are important blogs. Here we take some preliminary steps in this direction.

For the blogroll links, filtered by platform, from the English-language corpus (see 4.3) the in-degree for each linked-to blog was counted, including blogs not in the corpus. Table 5 shows the number of blogs with different in-degrees, and the percentage of these blogs that are present in the corpus. Assuming a minimum in-degree of 25 to mean that a blog is important, our method retrieved 22 (88%) of the important climate change blogs with the chosen platforms in their domain names. The missing blogs are about politics in general, rather than climate change specifically (dissectleft, nicedeb, gatewaypundit).

Minimum in-degree	Blogs in network	Blogs in corpus	"recall" %
1	19010	1255	6.6
2	3279	638	19.5
5	560	234	41.8
10	159	95	59.7
15	76	51	67.1
20	40	32	80.0
25	25	22	88.0

Table 5: Assessing coverage of the English-language corpus, where a high in-degree is assumed to indicate an important blog.

By taking blogroll links from the whole corpus the analysis is swamped by links from blogs that are mostly peripheral to the climate change blogosphere. To address this, we also examined all the blogroll links from six well known climate change blogs reflecting different perspectives and viewpoints (joannenova, realclimate, wattsupwiththat, tamino, climatechangeaction, climate-connections). In this case links to all blogs judged to be about climate change were included, i.e. not only blogs explicitly on the chosen platforms. This gave 71 blogs that are not present in the English-language corpus. Seven of these have 'wordpress' or 'blogspot' in their domain name, so could and should have been captured by our selection method.

Of the 64 missing blogs without any platform mentioned in their domain name, 17 had an in-degree (from the corpus) >25 and hence may be considered crucial omissions, although they vary in the extent to which they are about climate change or more general environmental and political topics. It is interesting that 17 out of 64 missing blogs not explicitly on any platform should be so important. This compares with 22 out of 5497 blogs explicitly on a chosen platform with an in-degree >25 (Table 5). This suggests a strong tendency for important blogs to use a domain name that does not include any blog platform. Hence it seems that, at least for some social science investigations, our blog selection method would have to be extended in order to capture more of the important blogs. This could be done by systematically using in-degree data to crawl from the initial corpus. However, human judgment would be required to determine what linked-to websites were blogs, and another test would be required for topic relevance.

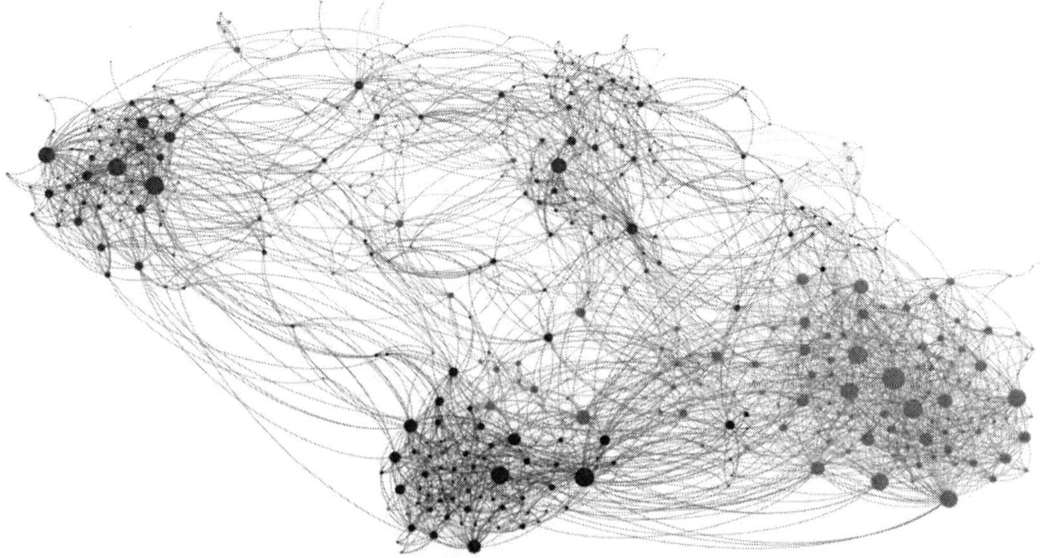

Figure 4: The directed blog network, based on blogroll links, from the English-language corpus. This shows most blogs are in one of four communities. The size of each node (blog) reflects its in-degree.

5   Closing remarks

It is not possible to make strong claims about how successful any method is in retrieving all blogs related to a topic. This is due to the fuzzy boundaries of topics and to the lack of a common definition of what constitutes a blog being related to a topic, rather than mentioning it in passing. However, the preliminary analyses in Section 4 allow us to say something about the efficacy of our approach and techniques. In brief, large-scale blog corpora were created with a reasonable amount of topical content, and intuitively correct temporal distribution and network structure.

To recap, the method relies on two main assumptions. Firstly, a blog is considered to be relevant if search engine APIs return >1 posts with >1 instances of the search terms which are chosen to be generic for the topic. This criterion could be considered to be too permissive, i.e. it includes blogs that are not really relevant to the topic. However, researchers have the option to apply stricter criteria and create sub-corpora that are better suited for specific research questions. The use of only a few generic search terms might mean that some niche sites that focus on a particular aspect of the topic are missed if they do not use the generic terms. We feel this is unlikely but it perhaps should be tested in future work.

Secondly, a website is considered to be a blog if it includes one of the selected blog platforms in its domain name. As discussed in 4.4 this leads to some important blogs being missed but this could remedied by selecting further blogs based on link data from the initial corpus and human judgement. Of course, a different approach would be to gather all blogs by crawling from an initial set of seed blogs, as we did in previous work (Salway et al., 2013; Elgesem et al., 2015). Two reasons seem to count against such an approach: (i) in fragmented blogospheres crawling may miss communities that are weakly connected to the rest; (ii) ensuring only topical blogs are included could entail downloading and analyzing a prohibitively large amount of most websites visited. Ideally, future work would make a systematic comparison of results from the two approaches and look to combine them.

Regarding the replicability and transparency of the method, a potential drawback is the reliance on search engine APIs whose ranking algorithms and query expansion techniques are unknown to us. Bias is mitigated to some extent by using multiple search engines, and by having a low threshold for what blogs are included (3.1). However, the ever changing nature of the algorithms counts against precise replicability.

We are currently preparing and documenting the corpora so that they can be made available for research purposes. In the first instance they will be released as they are currently, i.e. without removing 'further boilerplate' (3.3.2) and 'wrong language' material (3.3.3), and without adding further blogs (4.4). However, the corpora will include all the information needed to allow researchers to make their own decisions about how to customize the corpora to address specific research questions. Work is ongoing to integrate date data from html, and to extract data about comments. Also ongoing is work to further investigate the content of the corpora as part of social science investigations, e.g. to identify acceptor and sceptic communities and analyze the interactions between them, and to compare this between the different corpora.

Acknowledgements

This work was funded by the Research Council of Norway (VERDIKT program) and the Center for Big Data Analysis, Uni Research. We are very grateful for the technical support provided by Patcharee Thongtra and Eirik Thorsnes. Daniel Rognes and Samia Touileb helped with evaluation. Kjersti Fløttum and Anje Muller Gjesdal provided input regarding the content of the French corpus. Finally, many thanks to the three anonymous reviewers for their constructive feedback.

References

Lada A. Adamic and Natalie Glance. 2005. The political blogosphere and the 2004 US election: divided they blog. *LinkKDD '05: Proceedings of the 3rd International Workshop on Link Discovery*:36-43.

Nilesh Bansal and Nick Koudas. 2007. BlogScope: A System for Online Analysis of High Volume Text Streams. *Procs. VLDB '07*:1410-1413.

Mathieu Bastian, Sebastien Heymann, and Mathieu Jacomy. 2009. Gephi: an open source software for exploring and manipulating networks. Procs. Third International AAAI Conference on Weblogs and Social Media: 361-362.

Yochai Benkler. 2007. *The Wealth of Networks: How Social Production Transforms Markets and Freedom*. Yale University Press.

Chris Biemann, Felix Bildhauer, Stefan Evert, Dirk

Goldhahn, Uwe Quasthoff, Roland Schäfer, Johannes Simon, Leonard Swiezinski, and Torsten Zesch. 2013. Scalable Construction of High-Quality Web Corpora. *Journal for Language Technology and Computational Linguistics* 28(2):23-59.

Vincent D. Blondel, Jean-Loup Guillaume, Renaud Lambiotte, and Etienne Lefebvre. 2008. Fast unfolding of communities in large networks. *Journal of Statistical Mechanics: Theory and Experiment* 10, P10008.

Andrei Broder, Ravi Kumar, Farzin Maghoul, Prabhakar Raghavan, Sridhar Rajagopalan, Raymie Stata, Andrew Tomkins, and Janet Wiener. 2000. Graph structure in the web. *Computer Networks* 33:1, 309-320.

Axel Bruns. 2005. *Gatewatching: Collaborative Online News Production*. Peter Lang, New York.

Axel Bruns and Joanne Jacobs, eds. 2006. *Uses of Blogs*. Peter Lang, New York.

Dag Elgesem, Lubos Steskal, and Nick Diakopoulos. 2015. Structure and Content of the Discourse on Climate Change in the Blogosphere: The Big Picture. *Environmental Communication* 9(2):169-188.

Dag Elgesem, Ingo Feinerer, and Lubos Steskal. 2016. Bloggers' Responses to the Snowden Affair: Combining Automated and Manual Methods in the Analysis of News Blogging. *Computer Supported Cooperative Work (CSCW)* 25(2):167-191.

István Endrédy and Attila Novák. 2013. More Effective Boilerplate Removal – the GoldMiner Algorithm. *Polibits* (48):79-83.

Natalie S. Glance, Matthew Hurst, and Takashi Tomokiyo. 2004. BlogPulse: Automated Trend Discovery for Weblogs. *WWW 2004 Workshop on the Weblogging Ecosystem*.

Matthew Hindman. 2008. *The Myth of Digital Democracy*. Princeton University Press.

Mathieu Jacomy, Tommaso Venturini, Sebastien Heymann, and Mathieu Bastian. 2014. ForceAtlas2, a continuous graph layout algorithm for handy network visualization designed for the Gephi software. *PloS one* 9.6: e98679.

Andrew Kehoe and Matt Gee. 2012. Reader comments as an aboutness indicator in online texts: introducing the Birmingham Blog Corpus. *Studies in Variation, Contacts and Change in English* 12.

Mark Leccese. 2009. Online Information Sources of Political Blogs. *Journalism and Mass Communication Quarterly* 86(3):578-593.

Marco Lui and Timothy Baldwin. 2012. langid.py: An Off-the-shelf Language Identification Tool. *Procs. ACL 2012*: 25-30.

Christoph Meinel, Justus Broß, Philipp Berger, and

Patrick Hennig. 2015. *Blogosphere and its Exploration*. Springer-Verlag, Berlin.

Hallvard Moe. 2011. Mapping the Norwegian Blogosphere: Methodological Challenges in Internationalizing Internet Research. *Social Science Computer Review* 29(3):313-326.

Eli Pariser. 2011. *The filter bubble: What the Internet is hiding from you*. Penguin UK.

Jan Pomikálek. 2011. Removing boilerplate and duplicate content from web corpora. PhD thesis, Masaryk university, Faculty of Informatics, Brno, Czech Republic. Software: https://pypi.python.org/pypi/jusText

Jill Walker Rettberg. 2013. *Blogging*. Polity Press.

Andrew Salway, Samia Touileb, and Knut Hofland. 2013. Applying Corpus Techniques to Climate Change Blogs. In A. Hardie and R. Love (eds.) *Corpus Linguistics 2013 Abstract Book*.

Andreas Schmidt, Ana Ivanova, and Mike S. Schäfer. 2013. Media attention for climate change around the world: A comparative analysis of newspaper coverage in 27 countries. *Global Environmental Change* 23:1233-1248.

Amelia Sharman. 2014. Mapping the climate change blogosphere. *Global Environmental Change* 26:159-170.

Rob Speer. 2016. ftfy software: https://ftfy.readthedocs.io/en/latest/

Xiaodan Song, Yun Chi, Koji Hino, and Belle L. Tseng. 2007. Identifying Opinion Leaders in the Blogosphere. *Procs. ACM CIKM '07*: 971-974.

Cass R. Sunstein. 2008. *Republic.com 2.0*. Princeton University Press.

The Challenges and Joys of Analysing Ongoing Language Change in Web-based Corpora: a Case Study

Anne Krause

Leipzig University

Beethovenstraße 15

04107 Leipzig

anne.krause@uni-leipzig.de

Abstract

Researchers of language variation and change often need to go to great lengths to find sufficient data, particularly when they shall be used for a sound statistical analysis of the phenomenon in question. The recent analogical change in the formation of the imperative singular of German strong verbs with vowel gradation is a case in point, as it could not have been studied without the compilation of a web-based corpus. On the one hand, the investigation was faced with a number of challenges during the compilation of the corpus, the search for relevant hits and their annotation for a number of variables. On the other hand, results which would otherwise not have been obtained balance out this increased amount of manual labour. The present paper elaborates on some of these challenges and provides suggestions how they might be avoided in similar investigations in future. It concludes by presenting invaluable insights which would not have been gained without the present corpus study.

1 Introduction

It has been noted several times by different authors that the use of the web as corpus enriches investigations of linguistic variation and change by providing a higher number of authentic and more recent examples than traditional corpora can furnish. In contrast to such "opportunistic" uses of the web, researchers of recent language change may be forced to make "systematic" use of web-based corpora because they are "the only source for examples of very rare usages and constructions" (Mair, 2012, 245). In the present project, a web-based corpus has been compiled as the primary source of evidence, not only because the web yielded more examples than traditional corpora but because the only text type which yielded enough evidence is specific to the web.

Instead of consulting a large pre-existing web-based corpus, material from a very specific website was used in the current investigation; nevertheless, problems faced during corpus compilation and analysis and suggestions for avoiding them can be generalised to similar phenomena and languages to a great extent.

1.1 Change-in-progress in German verb inflection

There are a number of German strong verbs which exhibit a stem vowel change from the infinitive -e- to -i- in the imperative singular, for example the verb *geben* 'give' in Table 1:

		present	
number	person	indicative	imperative
	1st	*geb(e)*	
singular	2nd	*gibst*	***gib***
	3rd	*gibt*	
	1st	*geben*	
plural	2nd	*gebt*	*gebt*
	3rd	*geben*	

Table 1: Conjugation table for the German verb *geben* 'give'

The present project investigates the replacement of the established i-stem imperative singular of these strong verbs with vowel gradation by an e-stem variant formed in analogy to weak (regular) verb inflection, e.g. *sterben* 'to die': *stirb!* → *sterb(e)!*; *geben* 'to give': *gib!* → *geb(e)!*

Proceedings of the 10th Web as Corpus Workshop (WAC-X) and the EmpiriST Shared Task, pages 27–34,
Berlin, Germany, August 7-12, 2016. ©2016 Association for Computational Linguistics

1.2 The Conserving Effect

Along the lines of former usage-based analyses of analogical language change, it is hypothesised that the established i-stem imperative singular forms of lower frequency verbs are replaced by analogical variants earlier and faster than those of higher frequency verbs. For example, native speakers of German consistently stumble over the expression *Milk die Kuh!* 'Milk the cow!', employing the established i-stem imperative form of a low frequency verb, but they seem to accept both variants of verbs from a middle frequency region such as *bewirb dich!/ bewerb(e) dich!* 'apply (for sth.)!'. On the other end of the scale, the analogically formed variants of high frequency verbs in sentences like *Geb mir das Buch!* 'Give me the book!'/ *Seh es dir an!* 'Have a look at it!' are usually frowned at, whereas the i-stem variants of the same verbs are not.

The imperative singular forms of high frequency verbs are assumed to resist analogical change because they are highly entrenched in speakers' minds; this phenomenon is generally referred to as the "Conserving Effect" (Bybee and Thompson, 1997, 380). Although it has been explained from very early on that this frequency effect could be found in "modern leveling" as well (Hooper, 1976, 99), the majority of research in this area has been concerned with cases of completed language change. The present study thus fills two gaps by examining change-in-progress in German, a language in which the effects of type and token frequencies are still underresearched.

1.3 Imperative singular forms in corpora

It became apparent very soon that the change in the imperative singular of strong verbs with vowel gradation could not be examined with the help of "traditional" corpora (Mair, 2012) Although some of them are comparably large (e.g. DeReKo[1]) and contain spoken language (e.g. corpora in the DGD database[2]), where linguistic change usually starts out before it finds its way into written language, none of these corpora yielded enough tokens of the target imperative singular forms for a systematic (let alone statistical) analysis. Two reasons for the rarity of the imperative singular can be found in the Duden grammar (Dudenredaktion, 2009, 548-550): its use is tied to the condition that speakers

are on familiar terms (use of the informal second person singular pronoun *du*), and there are several other constructions used instead of the imperative to express requests or commands, such as indicative, modal and infinitive constructions.

Pre-existing large web-based corpora also have drawbacks. Most of them do not provide meta information about the authors of texts, a circumstance which has rather obvious reasons, given the wealth of data in the corpora, and which could be accepted. More serious for the study of a recent language change is the fact that no information is available about when the texts in these corpora were produced, as is the case, for example, in the deWaC (Baroni et al., 2008).

2 The Walkthrough Corpus

Instead of consulting traditional or existing web-based corpora, a corpus was specifically compiled for the present investigation. It consists of a web-specific text type, viz. walkthroughs, which contains a high number of instances of imperative singular forms. In addition, the website which was crawled contains very recent language material and the majority of texts on it have a timestamp, so that the development of imperative formation can be tracked.

2.1 Texts

Walkthroughs are guides for video games, i.e. computer, console and internet games, which help gamers complete a game successfully. They include step-by-step instructions, lists of achievements and items, cheats and other tips. Like in official strategy guides (usually in print), which are commissioned by the game publishers, their main focus is on a precise rendering of the game's content. In contrast to the former, these online guides are written by gamers and the texts are subject to a minimal amount of proofreading or revision. The conditions of their production are therefore very close to natural language.

Perhaps most importantly for the present investigation, the fact that members of the gaming community write walkthroughs for other members provides for an increased use of the imperative singular, e.g. *nimm den Gegenstand* 'take the item', *erstich den Feind* 'stab the enemy' etc., which is otherwise only rarely attested in corpora of German, spoken or written. A pilot search on the web revealed several candidate websites for the corpus

---

[1] http://www.ids-mannheim.de/cosmas2/
[2] http://dgd.ids-mannheim.de/

compilation, only one of which provided some of the required meta information (also see section 3 below):

The website *spieletipps.de*[3] exists since 2001 (in the present form). It was crawled in 2013; hence, the corpus covers a time span of 12 years. It is one of the main gaming websites in Germany, on which complete walkthroughs, individual cheats and tips and forums are available for the majority of existing platforms (including retro ones like Atari consoles). The final walkthrough corpus compiled from the website comprises approximately 7 m. tokens or word forms.

2.2 Crawler

A webcrawler (Java) was tailored to the website in order to download all walkthrough texts, cheats etc. Each text was stored in one line of a csv file. Available meta information about texts and authors were similarly stored in separate csv files. When queries were entered in the search interface (2.4), the data from these files were reunited through an inverted index.

2.3 Annotation

All texts contained in the corpus were then tagged for their part of speech using the Tree-Tagger (Schmid, 1995). This should enable the search for imperative forms of verbs (POS-tag VVIMP in STTS) and thereby reduce the number of word-level queries (however, see 3.1). The annotated versions of all texts were similarly stored in a csv file.

2.4 Interface

A simple search interface was created, comparable to those of popular web search engines. It allowed word-level, e.g. *gib*, and POS-level queries, e.g. *vvimp2geben* 'imperative forms of give'. It outputs csv files with one row for each query hit and columns for the query, sentence context and meta information.

3 Challenges

Challenges arose during the compilation of the corpus, the search for imperative singular forms in it and the annotation of the data for additional variables. One of these can be attributed to the researcher (3.1); others are specific to the website

(3.2 and 3.3), the corpus (3.4), the walkthrough genre (3.5 and 3.6) or the search interface (3.7).

3.1 Non-computational linguists

Linguists who want to investigate a potential language change-in-progress might find themselves in a situation when the phenomenon in question is not or only rarely attested in "traditional" corpora. Even though they might be able to perform a pilot search using one of the major web search engines, many (if not to say) most linguists do not possess the necessary programming skills for the compilation of a corpus of web data.

Since this was the case in the present paper, the compilation of the corpus itself was left in the hands of a computer scientist. However, the latter needs to be carefully instructed by the researcher in order that the final product yields the required results. Thus, the linguist should have a precise idea not only of which data and meta data are available during crawling (see 3.2 and 3.3) but also of how annotation for additional variables may be partly automatised by the use of an appropriate interface (see 3.7).

3.2 Meta information about corpus texts

Although the corpus compiler in the present case was instructed to retrieve each text on the website along with all available meta information, he can only include data in the corpus which is provided by the website (creators). A crucial piece of information for an investigation of language change in general, and perhaps ongoing change in particular, is the point in time when a linguistic utterance was produced.

Unfortunately, the original timestamp of posts on the website used for the present analysis was not given. However, in contrast to corpora such as the deWaC, which do not provide a date, either, two dates could be retrieved from the present website: i) when a member had registered, and ii) when the game to which the entry referred was released in Germany (or the earliest universal release, if no German version exists). The timestamp was extrapolated as the more recent of these two dates: a member cannot post a walkthrough or other tip for an existing game on the website before being registered, and even as a registered member, he/she cannot post a walkthrough or anything similar about a game which has not been released yet. The format of the timestamps was

---

[3]http://spieletipps.de

mixed; they were therefore reduced to only the posting year.

It turned out later that on the profiles of members, their last postings were listed with the original posting date. The comparison of the original and extrapolated timestamps for the instances in the final dataset revealed that 53.6% of the extrapolated posting years were correct and 22.0% could be replaced by the years listed on the member profiles. For the remaining 24.4% of observations, only the extrapolated dates were available (due to the author's active membership). Separate statistical analyses performed on the full dataset and a reduced dataset without these observations showed that extrapolation did not have an effect on the results of the investigation.

3.3 Meta information about authors

In times of heated discussion about data protection, it is easily understood that members of a website or forum wish to remain anonymous. On the website used for the present investigation, members can theoretically provide personal information such as their full name, age and residence on their profile page, and they can select which of these data to share with the public. The crawler could only include meta information about the authors of texts in the corpus which was visible on their public profile page. Therefore, in the final dataset, which was used for the statistical analysis, only 21.3% of the instances had an annotation for the author's age, 13.4% for gender (based on members' first names), and 6.8% for their residence. Analyses of the influence of sociolinguistic factors on the change in imperative singular formation of the strong verbs with vowel gradation were thus based on such small samples that they identified trends, but the results are not generalisable.

3.4 POS tagging

As mentioned before, the corpus search interface allowed word-level and POS-level queries. Unsurprisingly, the analogical e-stem imperative variants of verbs were incorrectly tagged as finite forms or as proper names; therefore, instead of using the POS-level query, these forms (e.g. *geb*, *gebe*) had to be searched on word-level for every individual verb. Perhaps more interestingly, even though the i-stem imperative is the established variant, only lower case instances of, for example, *gib* were recognised correctly, whereas

capitalised *Gib* was often incorrectly tagged as a noun or proper name and therefore not returned by the POS-level query.

The available options in the corpus search interface were thus sufficient to extract hits on the word (and POS) level, and the immediate sentence context in the output files provided enough information to distinguish finite forms of a verb from genuine imperative hits (1 vs. 2) and imperative forms of simplex verbs from those of particle verbs (2 vs. 3):

> (1) "<u>Ich</u> hab das Spiel bereits durchgespielt und **gebe** hier mal die Gegner bekannt"
> (nds/fluch-karibik-3/2620615)

> (2) "**Gebe** ihm das Glas und die Spirale"
> (pc/clever-smart/2742515)

> (3) "**Gebe** die ersten beiden Buchstaben <u>ein</u>"
> (snes/nba-jam/310511)

However, at least the distinction between examples (1) and (2) would have been largely performed by the TreeTagger if it had been trained accordingly, which would have reduced the amount of manual POS-tag correction. In similar investigations of variation or recent language change, it may be worth adapting the TreeTagger or supplying manually tagged training material with instances of the target construction or form before tagging the actual corpus texts.

3.5 Authorship confirmation

Although all imperative singular instances in the dataset were annotated for the member of the website who had contributed the text in which they occurred, it had to be ascertained that all of these instances were indeed produced by the specified author. For a number of reasons, the authors quote from inside the game whose walkthrough they are writing. Some of these quotes are readily recognisable as such from the use of quotation marks or their occurrence in tables of so-called "achievements", such as "Stiehl 30 Fahrzeuge" 'Steal 30 vehicles' (Gangstar Miami Vindication for iPhone). Other quoted imperative singular forms occurred in running text without any indication of being borrowed. The consultation of "Let's Play" videos[4] proved an efficient way of exposing the unmarked in-game imperative uses. In

---

[4]Youtube - http://youtube.com

these videos, gamers tape their computer or console screen while playing a particular game and comment on how (missions or chapters in) the game can be completed successfully. Thus, any in-game commands which were quoted in the walkthrough appear on the player's screen in the video and can be discarded from the dataset.

3.6 Skewed frequency data

While walkthroughs have the advantage of being practically the only text type to contain a very high number of instances of the imperative singular, their special topic presented another challenge. One of the aims of the present project was to test whether the Conserving Effect of high token frequency in analogical change is also found in the recent change in imperative singular formation of German strong verbs with vowel gradation. To this end, instances in the dataset should be annotated for the verb's token frequency in German.

Unfortunately, the plots of video games are very different from everyday life in the real world; therefore, token frequencies of words in walk-throughs are necessarily skewed. For example, avatars in first- and third-person shooters and a number of role-playing games do not eat, but *essen* 'to eat' is a strong verb with vowel grada-tion in German, hence one of the target verbs. If the token frequencies for this and other target verbs had been taken from the walkthrough cor-pus, the results of the analysis would have been skewed as well. In order to avoid this, verb to-ken frequencies needed to be extracted from refer-ence corpora (DeReWo[5]; Projekt Wortschatz Uni-versität Leipzig[6]), frequency dictionaries (Jones and Tschirner, 2006; Ruoff, 1990), and frequency counts provided in a dictionary of German (Duden online[7]).

3.7 Annotation for persistence

A close reading of some of the texts in the cor-pus revealed that the specific form of the imper-ative may in part depend on the preceding con-text. Benedikt Szmrecsanyi explained that lan-guage users are "creatures of habit" and tend to reuse words or patterns whenever possible (2005; 2006). This "persistence" strategy may be at work

[5]http://www1.ids-mannheim.de/kl/projekte/methoden/ derewo.html

[6]http://wortschatz.uni-leipzig.de/

[7]http://www.duden.de/woerterbuch/

in the formation of the imperative singular of the strong verbs with vowel gradation as well.

Imperative singular forms of German verbs can usually occur as a suffixed or unsuffixed variant: *red!/ rede!* 'talk!', *renn!/ renne!* 'run!', *steh!/ stehe!* 'stand!'. Similarly, the analogical e-stem variants of strong verbs with vowel gradation can occur with or without the suffix -e: *nehm!/ nehme!* 'take!'; however, the i-stem variant is never suf-fixed: *nimm!* It seemed that the authors of the walkthroughs developed a "routine", so that when they had used the suffixed variants of one or sev-eral consecutive verbs, e.g. *laufe ... gehe ... ver-lasse*, they wished to add a suffix to the following imperative singular form as well. If this next verb was a strong verb with vowel gradation, the author has no choice but to use the suffixed analogical e-stem variant because a suffixed i-stem imperative singular variant of these verbs does not exist. Ex-amples (4) and (5) illustrate this persistence effect of suffixed and unsuffixed previous imperatives.

> (4) -e → -e
> "2. Stell**e** deine Gäste einander vor und verkuppl**e** sie.
> 3. G**e**b**e** deinen Gästen genügend zu trinken, indem..."
> (ps2/playboy-mansion/2260012)

> (5) -ø → -ø
> "Nach der Cutszene, geh-**ø** zu Junes und geh-**ø** in die TV-Welt. Sobald du drin-nen bist spr**i**ch-**ø** mit Rise um den let-zten Boss zu suchen."
> (ps2/persona-4/3379622)

In order to test this hypothesis, all instances of im-perative singular forms of strong verbs with vowel gradation in the dataset need to be annotated for the form of imperative singular occurrences in their preceding context. As the interface which was created for the walkthrough corpus does not incorporate context queries, all imperative singu-lar forms preceding the target forms in the dataset were searched and annotated manually.

4 Joys

The compilation of the walkthrough corpus and the search for and annotation of relevant instances of the target construction presented many chal-lenges. Results which would otherwise not have been obtained, however, by far outweigh the costs of manual labour. Not only did the corpus study reveal frequency and persistence effects on imperative singular formation of the strong verbs with vowel gradation, but these results also served as input for a subsequent experimental study.

4.1 Results of the corpus study

After removing all false hits, the final dataset comprised 1939 observations of imperative singular forms of strong verbs with vowel gradation, i.e. instances of the established i-stem variant and the suffixed and unsuffixed analogical e-stem variants. Mixed-effects regression models were fitted on the dataset in order to determine which of the annotated predictor variables had an influence on stem vowel choice and suffixation of the imperative singular forms.

As expected, verb token frequency has a significant effect on stem vowel choice: imperative singular forms of lower frequency verbs show a high probability of occurring with the analogical e-stem, while higher frequency verbs retain the established i-stem. The Conserving Effect of high token frequency in analogical change is thus confirmed for morphological change-in-progress in German (see Figure 1).

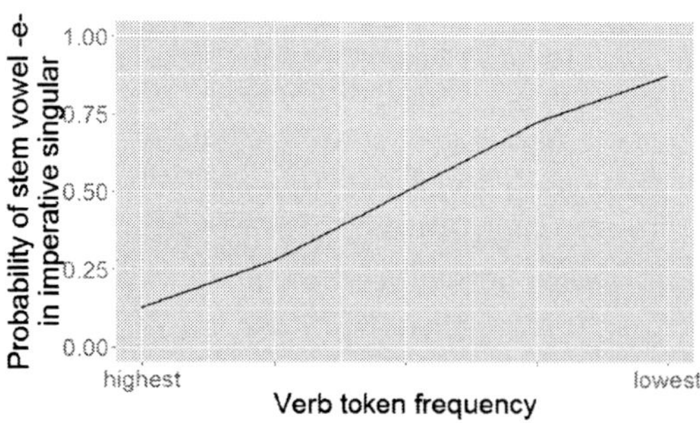

Figure 1: Conserving Effect of verb token frequency

The analysis also affirmed that the suffixation of the imperative forms (and thereby indirectly stem vowel choice) is significantly influenced by the occurrence of suffixed or unsuffixed imperative singular forms prior to the target imperatives: Imperative singular forms of strong verbs with vowel gradation show a high probability of being suffixed (e.g. *nehme*) when they are preceded by other suffixed imperative singular forms. Unsuffixed variants of the imperative singular of these verbs (e.g. *nimm, nehm*) occur more often after other unsuffixed imperative singular forms (see

examples 4 and 5). This effect is reinforced when the previously occurring verb itself is a strong verb with vowel gradation, e.g. *nehme* following *gebe* or *nimm* following *gib*.

4.2 Experimental Study

The Conserving Effect of high token frequency is generally explained on the basis of "entrenchment" (Langacker, 1987, 59): through repeated use, the imperative forms of higher frequency verbs have stronger mental representations than those of lower frequency verbs. Therefore, the forms of higher frequency verbs are more quickly retrieved from memory than the forms of lower frequency verbs. The longer they take to retrieve, the higher is the probability that the speaker forms the imperative in analogy to the weak verb paradigm. An instance of recent language change, such as the example of imperative singular formation examined in the present paper, is an excellent test case for the validity of this assumption.

In the experiment conducted as part of the current project, participants' reactions to the established i-stem and analogical e-stem imperative singular variants, presented in verbs of different token frequency, were measured. Once it was known from the corpus study that, in addition to the predictor verb token frequency, the presence of suffixed or unsuffixed imperative singular forms prior to the target imperative has a significant influence on the formation of the imperative singular of strong verbs with vowel gradation, this potentially disturbing persistence effect could be eliminated in the experiment and stimulus design. Furthermore, the corpus study showed up trends with regard to the influence of dialect on imperative formation (3.3) which inspired the inclusion of participant groups from different dialect areas in order to test this notion more systematically than was possible in the corpus study itself. Finally, sentences adapted from walkthrough texts can accommodate a large number of verbs from diverse semantic fields without appearing too absurd to the participants. Thus, the corpus texts served yet another purpose.

5 Suggestions for future research

The text type used in the present investigation was identified through the coincidence that the author relied on walkthroughs in order to complete several video games and was therefore aware of the high number of imperative singular forms contained in texts of this kind. In other studies, suitable web-specific genres/ text types may be identified by performing pilot searches on the web or in existing large web corpora and inspecting whether instances of a target construction predominate in a particular text type or web register. The situation might be further improved by attempts at recognising and classifying as many web registers as possible and identifying linguistic patterns associated with them (cf. Egbert and Biber, 2013; Biber et al., 2015).

As concerns the compilation of a corpus for a linguistic study, this task should preferably be delegated to a person who has experience with working with a linguistic corpus or is familiar with the kinds of questions linguists wish to answer with the help of corpora. In the current study, the presence of an "intermediary" or "translator", i.e. a linguist with extended IT knowledge, proved helpful while the research assistant was instructed on how to compile the walkthrough corpus (cf. 3.1). At the same time, the intermediary could answer the author's questions about how the corpus and its query interface are created.

However, even the best assistant (and intermediary) has to rely on the needs and demands which the employing researcher expresses, who in turn has to know the website(s) and features of the specific text type very well. If the website *spieletipps.de* would have been more thoroughly inspected before corpus compilation, the time stamps for walkthroughs could have been extracted primarily from the member profile pages; only if they were not available there, the programme would have to resort to the release date of the video game and the member registration date as a proxy (3.2). Similarly, as explained above, the persistence variables were manually annotated (3.7), i.e. the verb class and suffixation of imperative singular forms in the preceding context and the textual distance to the target imperative form were searched and counted by hand. Slight changes to the crawler could have reduced the amount of manual labour in both annotation steps. As the analysis of corpus data is at least as time-consuming as the compilation of a corpus, researchers might be tempted to push compilation forward before knowing the included sources well enough. The present investigation illustrates clearly that the manual effort which can be avoided

outweighs the costs of a thorough inspection of potential corpus texts, e.g. particular websites.

The analysis of sociolinguistic patterns of variation according to authors' age, gender and location only revealed trends in the present corpus study. In such cases, conducting additional studies, for example a psycholinguistic experiment (4.2) is an effective way of consolidating or falsifying these trends.

6 Conclusion

Even though the challenges of using web-based corpora for analysing recent language change seem to outweigh the joys in the present contribution, this is largely due to the fact that the former have been more elaborately discussed in order to serve as advice for researchers of similar phenomena in future. Some of the manual labour explained above might be increased in web-specific genres of the walkthrough kind and cannot be avoided completely, such as extracting frequency data from reference corpora or other sources. Other drawbacks of the present corpus have been avoided in the compilation of large existing web-based corpora: for example, the DE-COW (German web corpus by COW; Schäfer, 2015) is annotated for meta information like the "last modified" date. And yet others may be avoided by tailoring the corpus compilation process to the specific object of study, e.g. adjusting or training the TreeTagger on a target construction.

Nevertheless, it cannot be stressed too often that the walkthrough corpus offered data without which work on the present project would not have been possible. A bit of manual labour (after hours) was rewarded with many invaluable insights from the corpus analysis. Not only do these results explain the present stage of the change-in-progress in imperative formation of strong verbs with vowel gradation, but they also find their repercussions in the design of a subsequent experimental study.

Acknowledgements

Work on the present PhD project (including the compilation of the walkthrough corpus and payment for participants in the experiment) was funded by the *Deutsche Forschungsgemeinschaft* through the Research Training Group GRK DFG 1624 "Frequency Effects in Language".

I would like to thank three anonymous WAC-X reviewers for their helpful comments.

References

Marco Baroni, Silvia Bernardini, Adriano Ferraresi, and Eros Zanchetta. 2008. The WaCky Wide Web: A Collection of Very Large Linguistically Processed Web-Crawled Corpora. *Language Resources and Evaluation*, 43:209–226. [deWaC].

Douglas Biber, Jesse Egbert, and Mark Davies. 2015. Exploring the composition of the searchable web: a corpus-based taxonomy of web registers. *Corpora*, 10:11–45.

Joan Bybee and Sandra Thompson. 1997. Three frequency effects in syntax. In Matthew L. Juge and Jeri L. Moxley, editors, *Proceedings of the Twenty-Third Annual Meeting of the Berkeley Linguistics Society: General Session and Parasession on Pragmatics and Grammatical Structure*, pages 378–388.

Dudenredaktion, editor. 2009. *Duden - Die Grammatik: unentbehrlich für richtiges Deutsch*. Dudenverlag, Mannheim and Wien and Zürich.

Jesse Egbert and Douglas Biber. 2013. Developing a User-based Method of Web Register Classification. In *Proceedings of the 8th Web as Corpus Workshop*, pages 16–23.

Joan B. Hooper. 1976. Word frequency in lexical diffusion and the source of morphophonological change. In William Christie, editor, *Current progress in historical linguistics*, pages 95–105. North Holland, Amsterdam.

Randall L. Jones and Erwin Tschirner. 2006. *A Frequency Dictionary of German: Core Vocabulary for Learners*. Routledge, London.

Ronald W. Langacker. 1987. *Foundations of cognitive grammar: vol. 1: Theoretical Prerequisites*. Stanford University Press, Stanford.

Christian Mair. 2012. From opportunistic to systematic use of the web as corpus. In Terttu Nevalainen and Elisabeth Traugott, editors, *The Oxford Handbook of the History of English*, pages 245–255. Oxford University Press, New York.

Arno Ruoff. 1990. *Häufigkeitswörterbuch gesprochener Sprache*. Niemeyer, Tübingen.

Roland Schäfer. 2015. Processing and querying large web corpora with the COW14 architecture. In *Proceedings of Challenges in the Management of Large Corpora*, pages 28–34. [DECOW14].

Helmut Schmid. 1995. Improvements in Part-of-Speech Tagging with an Application to German. In *Proceedings of the ACL SIGDAT-Workshop*, pages 1–9. [TreeTagger].

Thomas Schmidt. 2014. Gesprächskorpora und Gesprächsdatenbanken am Beispiel von FOLK und DGD. *Gesprächsforschung*, 15:196–233. [DGD].

Benedikt Szmrecsanyi. 2005. Language users as creatures of habit: A corpus-based analysis of persistence in spoken English. *Corpus Linguistics and Linguistic Theory*, 1(1):113–150.

Benedikt Szmrecsanyi. 2006. *Morphosyntactic persistence in spoken English. A corpus study at the intersection of variationist sociolinguistics, psycholinguistics, and discourse analysis*. Trends in Linguistics. Studies and Monographs. De Gruyter, Berlin and New York.

Using the Web and Social Media as Corpora for Monitoring the Spread of Neologisms. The case of *rapefugee*, *rapeugee*, and *rapugee*.

Quirin Würschinger, Mohammad Fazleh Elahi, Desislava Zhekova and Hans-Jörg Schmid
LMU Munich
80539 Munich, Germany
`q.wuerschinger@lmu.de, fazleh.elahi@anglistik.uni-muenchen.de,`
`desi@cis.uni-muenchen.de, hans-joerg.schmid@anglistik.uni-muenchen.de`

Abstract

This paper employs both a web-as-corpus and a Twitter-as-corpus approach to present a longitudinal case study of the establishment of three recently coined, synonymous neologisms: *rapefugee, rapeugee* and *rapugee*. We describe the retrieval and processing of the web and Twitter data and discuss the dynamics of the competition between the three forms within and across both datasets based on quantitative summaries of the results. The results show that various language-external events boost the usage of the terms both on the web and on Twitter, with the latter typically ahead of the former by some days. Beside absolute frequencies, we distinguish between several special usages of the target words and their effects on the establishment process. For the web corpus, we examine target words appearing in the title of websites and metalinguistic usages; for the Twitter corpus, we examine hashtag uses and retweets. We find that the use of hashtags and retweets significantly affects the spread of the neologisms both on Twitter and on the web.

1 Introduction

Electronic mass communication offers unique opportunities for the study of new words and the early phases of their establishment. Using the web and social media like Twitter as corpora offers an economical way of investigating whether newly coined words are taken up by language users and begin to spread and diffuse into other domains of discourse. Such investigations require longitudinal studies which keep track of new occurrences of neologisms on the web and/or in posts on Twitter and other social media.

This paper presents a web-as-corpus and Twitter-as-corpus study of the spread of three recently coined words which emerged in 2015 and compete for encoding the same meaning: *rapefugee, rapeugee*, and *rapugee*. All three target words are formed by blending the source words *rape* and *refugee*, and all three are mainly used as derogatory propaganda terms by opponents of policies that welcome asylum-seekers. We would like to note that our work does not support, but only explores and analyses the use of these terms, equally applicable to any other neologism.

The approach chosen in this paper complements an earlier study by Kerremans et al. (2012), who investigated the competition between the meanings of one polysemous neologism, viz. the verb *to de-tweet*. Analyzing material collected by means of a tailor-made webcrawler, the so-called *Neo-Crawler*, the authors show how language users gradually begin to converge on one meaning, 'to sign off (from Twitter)', following a period where different users associate different meanings with the form and even explicitly promote them.

The current project addresses the mirror-image situation where several synonymous forms compete for encoding the same meaning. Investigations of this type are important for understanding how new words spread, because competition between forms is one of the factors that influence this process. Extending the methodology used in (Kerremans et al., 2012) in a second direction, we compare the data from the web with a second dataset collected for the same period from Twitter. We aim to provide a dense-data longitudinal analysis of the rivalry between these three recent neologisms, both separately within the web and the Twitter data and in comparison between these two

Proceedings of the 10th Web as Corpus Workshop (WAC-X) and the EmpiriST Shared Task, pages 35–43,
Berlin, Germany, August 7-12, 2016. ©2016 Association for Computational Linguistics

data sources. In the course of this, we discuss the specific advantages and challenges involved in retrieving, processing and analyzing data from the web and from Twitter respectively.

2 Related work

Efforts to investigate neologisms with the help of web-based data have been stepped up considerably over the past years. There are numerous websites, run by dictionary publishers or based on crowdsourced user-content, which list and define new words and provide selected quotations, often including the first known attestation. Prominent examples are *New Words* by Merriam-Webster[1], *About words* by Cambridge University Press[2], *UrbanDictionary*[3], and *WordSpy: Dictionary of New Words*[4]. A comparable project for German is *Wortwarte*[5], which documents German neologisms based on newspaper data (Lemnitzer, 2011).

As far as research projects on neologisms which apply the web-as-corpus method are concerned, Bauer and Renouf (2000) investigate the contexts of use for 5000 neologisms in a newspaper corpus. Combining data from a newspaper corpus and the web, Renouf (2007) analyzes the recent productivity of prefixes such as *techno-* and *cyber-* and traces the frequency development of four neologisms in newspaper articles. Hohenhaus (2006) investigates the word *bouncebackability* by means of the web-as-corpus method. Paryzek (2008) reviews different methods of retrieving neologisms and extracts neologisms from a 45-million-word corpus based on Nature. Veale and Butnariu (2010) harvest neologisms from a corpus which is derived from the English version of Wikipedia. Like the study by Kerremans et al. (2012) mentioned above, Grieve et al. (2016) aim to unveil the factors behind the emergence and success of neologisms. This is also the question that motivates the work presented in this paper.

3 Operationalizing the research question

As pointed out above, we aim at a comparative longitudinal analysis of attestations of three synonymous words on the web and on Twitter in or-
der to investigate the dynamics of the competition between them. To operationalize this research question, the following types of data and data analyses must be provided by computational means:

- Absolute frequency counts of occurrences of the three words on the web and on Twitter over a defined period of time in a high temporal solution (i.e. weekly/daily counts of newly added occurrences). These counts are required to obtain a measure of *usage intensity as such* (cf. Stefanowitsch and Flach (forthcoming)).

- Relative frequency counts of the three words per time interval (days of weeks), i.e. the frequency of each word relative to the frequencies of the other two for the same time interval. For example, we detected a total number of 233 tokens across all three formal variants in the web corpus in the third week of January 2016. The variant *rapefugee* amounts to 191 occurrences, which corresponds to a relative frequency of about 0.82. These relative frequency counts are required to measure the *current relative success* of the three forms to occupy the onomasiological target space.

- A longitudinal analysis of the changes in absolute and relative frequencies over time: this is required to measure *the dynamics of the temporal development of relative success*. Examples can be found in Figure 1 and Figure 3.

- Classificatory analyses of different usage types of the three words which are suspected to have *differential effects on their chances* of being taken up again and thus being spread. Specifically, what we are interested in are:

  - *single* object-linguistic uses as opposed to
  - *metalinguistic* uses of talking about the word rather than actually using it (e.g. *Whenever people hear "refugee" they need to think #rapefugee.* (Tweet from 7 January 2016))
  - *multiple* uses within one web page / tweet as well as repetitions via *retweets*
  - uses as *hashtags* on Twitter or as parts of *titles* of web pages.

4 Data acquisition

4.1 Web as a corpus

We used the NeoCrawler (Kerremans et al., 2012) to collect timestamped web pages containing

---

[1]http://nws.merriam-webster.com/opendictionary
[2]https://dictionaryblog.cambridge.org/category/new-words/
[3]www.urbandictionary.com
[4]http://www.wordspy.com/
[5]www.wortwarte.de

	single	multiple	title	metalinguistic	total # words
rapefugee	169	849	125	59	273,961
rapeugee	122	281	24	3	627,077
rapugee	21	41	6	1	51,590

Table 1: Descriptive summary of data from the web corpus

tokens of the three neologisms on the web. In order to have a comparable sample, we restricted the search to the timespan in which the Twitter data has been collected (see Section 4.2), namely from October 19th, 2015 until March 16th, 2016. The NeoCrawler uses Google searches for collecting web pages, as this has several benefits for neologism research (Lewandowski, 2008; Kerremans et al., 2012): Google provides the largest number of indexed pages, its index is updated fastest in comparison to other search engines, and it provides the web pages which are most relevant for a given search string.

The NeoCrawler searches by means of an automated version of the processes carried out in manual Google searches. The system builds a search string[6] defining values for a number of parameters (such as language, date, token etc.). There are several advantages of this approach over other Google search APIs[7], such as *Custom Search Engine* or *Google Site Search*. While the main functionality provided by *Custom Search Engine* is to search across a set of sites specified, it can also be configured to search the whole web. However, in that case, it provides a smaller number and less relevant search results than a manual Google search, which is not desirable if the project requires maximum recall. *Google Site Search* is an edition of *Google Custom Search* that provides additional functionality, but does not solve the problem either. Therefore, neither of these APIs is suitable for our goal, as we need to search the whole web in order to get as many relevant search results as possible. The automated version of the Google manual search implemented in the NeoCrawler is an optimal fit for our purpose. However, a large number of potential hits returned by Google searches turn out to be either false positives (i.e.

pages that do not contain the search token), duplicate copies or otherwise useless pages. Therefore, we extracted only the pages containing the search token excluding duplicates and empty pages.

Following the operationalization procedure outlined in Section 3 above, we distinguished between single (each page is counted as a single occurrence independently of how often a neologism has been used on it) and multiple occurrences per page (each token on the page is counted separately), and between special usage types (i.e. usage in the title of a document) and metalinguistic usage (operationalized as uses in inverted commas). Table 1 shows a summary of the web data.

A key requirement for the longitudinal analysis of the temporal dynamics is to identify the correct timestamp of the web content that contains a given token. However, due to the decentralized nature of timestamps and the lack of standard meta-data for time and date, reliable timestamps are frequently not available for web documents. In its previous version, the NeoCrawler extracted the remote timestamp of the retrieved document using the CURL module for PHP, which is a library for getting files from various Internet protocols including HTTP/HTTPS. However, since CURL relies on the *Last-Modified* header value of the HTML page to extract the timestamp, which is often missing, it was impossible to extract a timestamp from a large proportion of the documents. Therefore, we have extended the NeoCrawler to extract the timestamp from the Google search page directly, where Google provides the timestamp of the content containing the token instead of that of the last update of the web page. Moreover, the NeoCrawler extracts both the absolute (i.e. 12/01/2016) and the relative (i.e. *a week ago*) timestamp found on the web page. It must be conceded, however, that Google's timestamps are not always correct either, among other things because the location of the content and its respective timestamp on the page is ambiguous, or because there are several tokens added at different dates to

---

[6]`https://encrypted.google.com/search?`
`num=100&hl=en&lr=lang_en&start=0&tbs=`
`lr%3Alang_1en%2Ccdr%3A1%2Ccd_min%3A10%`
`2F01%2F2015%2Ccd_max%3A03%2F16%2F2016&q=`
`%22rapefugee%22`
[7]`https://developers.google.com/`
`custom-search/json-api/v1/overview`

	single	multiple	hashtag	direct	tweet	retweet	total # words
rapefugee	3,777	3,786	3,303	451	1,024	2,753	77,369
rapeugee	272	277	220	52	87	185	5,909
rapugee	92	92	88	4	22	70	1,740

Table 2: Descriptive summary of data from the Twitter corpus

the same page. In the latter case, only a single timestamp is provided by Google. Results related to the temporal development will be given in Section 5 below.

4.2 Twitter as a corpus

Unlike the web, Twitter cannot be queried for past events in an unlimited manner. Only the Firehose Twitter API[8], which is of highly limited access, can be used to collect all public statuses. An open access equivalent for part of this functionality is the Twitter Streaming API[9] which provides low latency access to Twitter's current global stream of data (i.e. a sample of the current stream fulfilling the query). However, the current Twitter stream cannot aid us in our attempt to observe how the three neologisms *rapefugee*, *rapeugee* and *rapugee* have been used since the time of their coining. The Twitter Search API, searches only against a sampling of recent Tweets published in the past seven days. Yet, the tokens have been in use a lot longer than seven days.

The only way to query Twitter for older posts is via using previously collected Twitter corpora. Based on the fact that the neologisms of interest are different blends of *rape* and *refugee*, we made use of an extended version of the REFUGEE corpus (Zhekova, 2016), which consists of tweets that were collected from October 19th, 2015 until March 16th, 2016 via the Twitter Streaming API by tracking the token *refugee*. We assume that the linguistic relation between the three neologisms and *refugee* will result in a representative sample of Twitter data containing these new words.

Another difference between Twitter and web data is that the meta-information is readily available in Twitter. Unlike in the web data, all relevant tweets are precisely timestamped. With respect to token identification and classification (single, multiple, metalinguistic use), we followed

---

[8]https://dev.twitter.com/streaming/
firehose

[9]https://dev.twitter.com/streaming/
overview

the same approach as for the web data. Additionally, for the Twitter corpus, we observed the difference between direct vs. hashtag usage (i.e. *No rapefugees!* vs. *No #rapefugees!*) and normal tweets vs. retweets (i.e. *No #rapefugees!* vs. *RT No #rapefugees!*). Table 2 provides a basic summary of the occurrences of the three neologisms in the Twitter data.

5 Results

5.1 Web corpus

Usage intensity. In order to measure usage intensity (Stefanowitsch and Flach, forthcoming), we conduct absolute frequency counts of tokens for all three types (*rapefugee*, *rapeugee* and *rapugee*) in both datasets. We count multiple tokens per type within one website or one tweet separately. The counts are accumulated in weekly intervals corresponding to each calendar week in the timespan between October 19th, 2015 (i.e. 15_CW_43 – to be read as the 43rd calendar week of 2015) and March 16th, 2016. Figure 1 presents the absolute usage frequencies in the web corpus.

The graph shows a very small number of uses of the three types before 16_CW_02, with a maximum of 9 tokens of the form *rapeugee* in 15_CW_50. The period after New Year marks a turning point, after which numbers rapidly increase, with a maximum of 233 tokens in 16_CW_03.

The first attestation of any of the three target forms on the web is a single occurrence of *rapefugee* on January 19, 2015 (15_CW_43 in Figure 1).

Only a few days later, however, the type *rapeugee* appears and initially supersedes the other two types in popularity, representing an accumulated 79 % of all tokens of all three types in the period before the New Year turn. In 16_CW_02, the numbers for all three types rise significantly, indicating an increasing communicative need for expressing the underlying concept 'rape / refugee'. The use of *rapeugee* rises considerably and re-

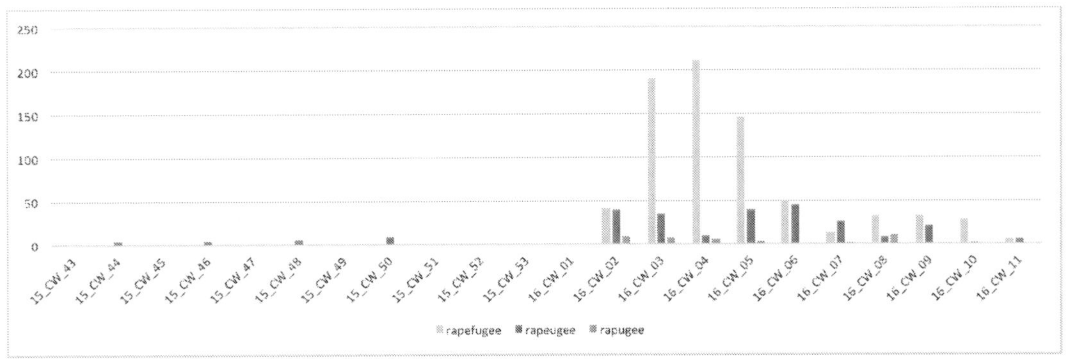

Figure 1: Absolute frequencies in the web corpus

mains fairly stable over the next few weeks. The form *rapugee*, which had up to this point been used only once, is used with moderate frequency until it vanishes again in 16_CW_09. Lastly, the form *rapefugee* shows the most radical increase by far. It reaches a maximum of 211 new tokens on 30 different websites in 16_CW_04. After New Year's Eve it represents an accumulated 73 % of tokens across all three types, making it the most dominant form in this period.

Figure 1 indicates that the spread of words expressing the concept 'rape / refugee' seems to happen in several spurts which do not follow a linear trend. Manual sample checks of the corpus data reveal that these spikes are closely related to real-life events in which refugees play an important role. Most often these events were various sexual harrassments, as we will exemplify further.

The first attestation of *rapeugee* we found is from a forum of an extremist propaganda website called *Shitskin Plantation*. On 29 October 2015, the user *canuckfmj* used the title *Denmark has a rapeugee problem* to publish the following post: *They want to give the new 'migrants' classes so they don't rape the locals and the livestock. Sorry but classes aren't going to help with these savages.* The post contains a hyperlink to another extremist website which strongly criticises the introduction of sexual education in courses for refugees in Denmark. The use of the word *rapeugee* is clearly related to this particular recent political decision which serves as a trigger for coining the new term. The author expresses their critical attitude by questioning the adequacy of the neutral term *migrants* by using it in metalinguistic quotes. Instead, the author chooses the new term *rapeugee* to emphasize the propagated association between

'refugees' and 'rape'. In the following week, the new word seems to have already vanished again with the decreasing relevance of the real-life context, however, as we have not been able to find a single attestion of *rapeugee*. Similar patterns and connections to real-life events can be observed for the other spikes of *rapeugee* before New Year's Eve.

The turning point in the web corpus data is marked by the steep increase in the use of all three tokens after New Year's Eve and can be explained in the same manner. However this time, the variant *rapefugee* is preferred by most speakers. Its first attestation in 2016 is another blog post on a right-wing extremist blog named *Neoreactive*. A reader of the blog named Matt Bracken created a post entitled: *A Reader Says That The Cologne #Rapefugee Attacks Are Just A Pep Rally For The Coming Intifada In Europe*. Again, the author explicitly refers to the events in Cologne on New Year's Eve, when German media reported sexual assaults by refugees, and also instrumentalizes the blend of *rape* and *refugee* for anti-refugee propaganda.

The scale of the Cologne events and their presence in public media and in the Internet explain the explosive increase and the longer-lasting effect displayed in Figure 1. The numbers of new occurrences remain very high for a period of three weeks before the popularity of the three terms seems to run out of steam again after 16_CW_05.

The combination between such real-life triggers and the specific, quite uniform propaganda motivation of associating refugees with rape can be seen as the driving force behind the characteristic spurts in the usage intensity of the terms illustrated in Figure 1. These patterns are in line with previous research by Kerremans (2015) who classified comparable cases as 'recurrent semi-conventionalization'.

Usage types. As pointed out in Section 3, besides measuring usage intensity as such, we examined different usage types of these words and their effects on the establishment process more closely.

Firstly, we investigated the tokens' position on the websites by counting tokens contained in titles separately. Across all three types, a high proportion of about 16 % of the tokens were used in the titles of websites. This fits the presumed motivation behind using the tokens as provocative propaganda terms in order to attract the readers' attention. We did not detect significant differences in usage frequencies regarding token position between the three types.

Secondly, we examined whether tokens were used in metalinguistic contexts. In these cases, speakers reflect/talk *about* the terms rather than just regularly using them. To identify these uses, we extracted quoted instances of all formal variants (i.e. *"rapefugee"*, *'rapugee'*). In total, about 7 % of the tokens were metalinguistic usages. On the one hand, we found that in most cases authors used inverted commas to distance themselves from the right-wing ideology behind the terms. For example, the website of the New York Post, an established conservative newspaper, published an article entitled *German clash over 'rapefugees' who carried out mass sex attack* (10 January 2016) in which they used the term *rapefugee* several times with a metalinguistic function. The article does not attack refugees, but the alarming growth of right-wing German extremists using the term for propaganda purposes. On the other hand, albeit in a much smaller number of cases, the terms are also sometimes used metalinguistically by anti-refugee activists who consciously try to spread them as propaganda terms. The results concerning metalinguistic uses indicate that they strongly differ from objectlinguistic uses and that they provide valuable information about the coinage and spread of neologisms.

5.2 Twitter corpus

Usage intensity. Figure 2 provides an overview of the Twitter data. In terms of usage intensity, the overall pattern is similar to that of the web corpus. The frequency of all three types remains relatively low before New Year, shows a steep increase in the first weeks of the new year and then declines to a lower level after that. However, there are also some differences.

First of all, there are no instances of *rapefugee* or *rapugee* before the New Year turn. This means that the dominance of *rapeugee* before New Year is even stronger in the Twitter data. There are only three weeks (15_CW_46 until 15_CW_48) that contain any tokens at all, and they only amount to a total of 15 tokens. Compared with the much higher usage intensity after the turn to 2016, this means an even steeper increase of use at the start of January than in the web corpus.

Secondly, the NY increase starts off earlier than in the web corpus. As a comparison of Figure 1 and Figure 2 shows, the turning point of usage intensity for all types on Twitter precedes that on the web by one week. This offset indicates that Twitter is the medium in which this change can be first observed. Being more flexible, social media are apparently faster in reacting to noteworthy events than web domains like blogs and forums.

The first tweet for *rapefugee* in 16_CW_01 in our dataset is *Refugee = rapist. Flüchtling = Vergewaltiger. #Cologne #rapefugees*, posted on Wednesday, 6 January 2016, and directly followed by its retweet. This tweet connects the neologism to the 2016 New Year's Eve sexual assaults in Cologne. Supposedly, these events were the trigger for the highly rapid boost in usage intensity for all three neologisms on Twitter. This is supported by the analysis of further tweets: The most frequent tweet for *rapefugee* in 16_CW_01 is *RT @DavidJo52951945: RT pictures from protest in Germany against immigrant/refugee abuse gangs #rapefugees https://t.co/USHsiXOtKZ*, which occurs 190 times during this week and also connects it to the sexual assaults in Germany.

The tweet *Where were the police water cannons when the Muslim rapeugees were terrorizing Cologne on NYE?!? https://t.co/dRcTMY9UJm*, retweeted twice, is the most frequent tweet for *rapeugee* during 16_CW_01 – also connected to the events in Cologne.

For *rapugee*, the two tweets during 16_CW_01: *@BBCBreaking @BBCWorld gangs of men??? Refugee men – say it: #rapugee https://t.co/AZK4fYLZLo* and a modified version of it, also relate it to these events.

The connection of the neologisms with the New

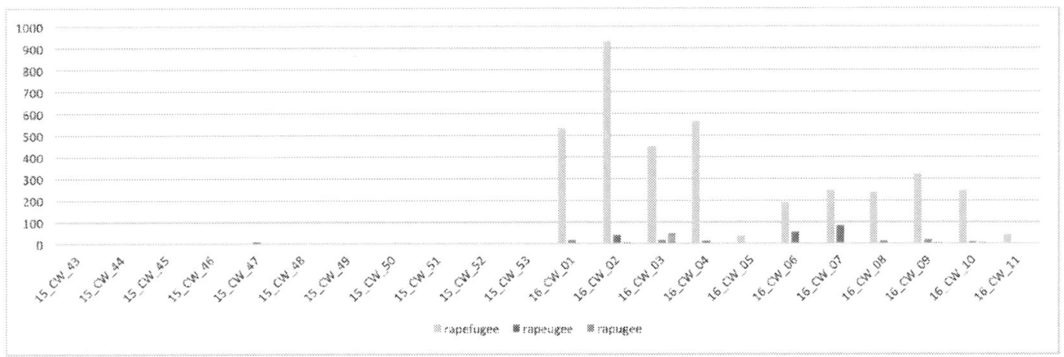

Figure 2: Absolute frequencies in the Twitter corpus

Year events and their respective usage intensity and relative success indicate that important real-life events play a significant role for the coining, rivalry and establishment of neologisms competing for occupying the same onomasiological space.

Usage types. With respect to usage types, a first distinction can be drawn between tweets and retweets. Retweets provide users with a very economical and efficient way of sharing tweets by other users with their own followers. As the original content is preserved and retweets are marked with the prefix *RT*, this can essentially be considered a quoting mechanism. The average number of retweets per tweets for all three forms is 2.7. This affects the establishment of words in at least two ways. On the one hand, it significantly increases the number of people reading the target words, which raises the chances that they will retweet or actively use it too. On the other hand, retweets are exact copies. So if the original author chooses the variant *rapefugee*, this choice is being replicated for all retweets. It is quite likely that these factors have contributed to the success of the form *rapefugee* on Twitter in the wake of New Year's Eve.

A second distinction can be drawn between hashtags and direct, i.e. normal uses of words. Hashtags are a second key feature of Twitter which has the potential to cause new effects on the pathways of the establishment of new words. Users can prefix words with # in order to turn them into labels. These labels build a fluctuating system tweeters use to refer to certain events or entities. Across all three types, we observed that 87 % of the tokens were used as hashtags. The very high proportion of tokens used as hashtags can be explained by their presumed communicative purpose. As was pointed out above, these terms mainly serve propaganda functions as they are used to label refugees as (potential) rapists. The establishment of a label like *#rapefugee* contributes to fixing the choice of the dominant variant.

5.3 Competition across both corpora

The composition and the sizes of the web corpus (about 950,000 words) and the Twitter corpus (about 85,000 words) differ greatly, which makes it hard to compare competition effects across both corpora. In order to measure the relative success of the three forms, we therefore normalized each type's frequency measures by the total frequency of all types within that dataset. The rationale behind this procedure is that the three forms lend themselves to encoding the same portion of semantic space and are thus in onomasiological competition. Even though the choice of individual language users may be determined by various factors such as whether they are familiar with all three terms, what they have heard or read just before (a priming effect possibly leading to the large numbers of retweets), or what they have become accustomed to (an entrenchment effect), this proportional measure is a good indicator of the relative success and spread of the three forms.

Figure 3 shows the relative counts for the web data where *rapeugee* appears to be the predominant type of choice between 15_CW_43 and 16_CW_02. 16_CW_02 marks the turning-point of the success of *rapefugee*. While *rapugee* still occurs following this period, there is a clear preference for the other two forms in the timespan from

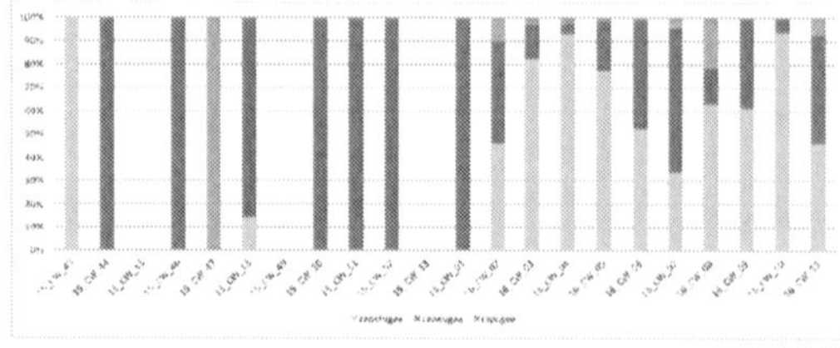

Figure 3: Relative frequencies in the web corpus

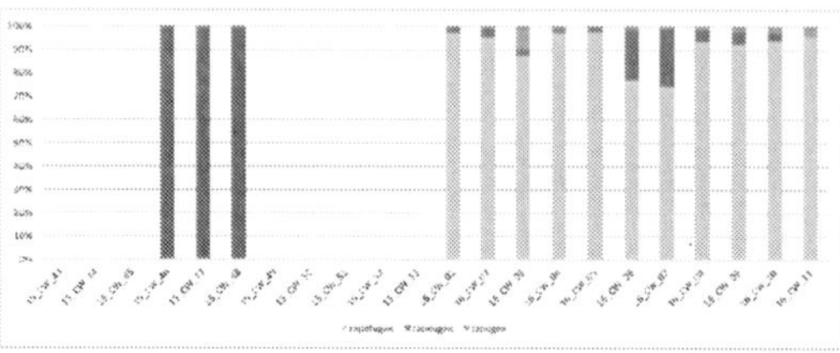

Figure 4: Relative frequencies in the Twitter corpus

16_CW_02 onwards, with an ongoing competition between them whose outcome does not seem to be determined at present.

In the Twitter data, which is visualized in Figure 4, the situation is considerably different. As mentioned above, the turning point in the relative success of the three types is one week before the one on the web, namely 16_CW_01. From this point onwards *rapefugee* is clearly the predominant choice although the other two types are also occasionally made use of.

Comparing the development in the web corpus to the Twitter data suggests that Twitter might have influenced the competition between the three competing forms in both domains decisively. Firstly, tweeters react to the events in Cologne on New Year's Eve more quickly than authors on the web. Secondly, the early establishment of the hashtag *#rapefugee* might have fuelled the increasing dominance of this formal variant. This is also supported by the fact that the type *rapefugee* often appears with the Twitter prefix # on the web in the early weeks of 2016, even though the hashtag does not serve any technical labelling function on the corresponding web pages. Thirdly, the high number of retweets seems to have supported the increasing dominance of the variant *rapefugee*. This is a particularly interesting finding, because it indicates that social media provide new ways of promoting the spread of new words.

What should be taken into consideration, however, is that all three of our target words are propaganda terms, whose users aim to spread their ideas and concepts. The people using these terms seem to belong to a like-minded community sharing the same communicative goals. This promotes the uniform use of the terms and the high number of retweets. Further research into less 'loaded' words will have to show whether the establishment process we observed is a special mechanism in the present case.

6 Conclusion

We have investigated the competition between three synonymous neologisms – *rapefugee*, *rapeugee* and *rapugee* – in a web and a Twitter corpus over a period of 22 weeks and found that the spread of the terms is closely related to preceding real-life events. Most importantly, the sexual assaults on New Year's Eve in Cologne lead to a steep increase in the use of these terms, mainly by right-wing extremists. Overall, the form *rapefugee* turned out to be the most likely candidate for establishment, although the final outcome remains uncertain at the present stage.

Analyzing data from the Twitter corpus allowed us to evaluate the web corpus' results more closely. We observed the same general development of the three neologisms in both datasets. Together with the language-external evidence of real-life events, this can be regarded as a cross-validation of both approaches. However, we also found that certain communicative practices within the Twitter domain, such as retweeting and hashtags, significantly influence the establishment of new words. Firstly, these mechanisms affected the competition between the three formal variants within the Twitter domain. It was presumably due to its high prominence in retweets and as a hashtag, that the variant *rapefugee* took the lead after New Year. Secondly, the Twitter domain seems to have influenced the use of the terms on the web. While the observed one-week offset could simply be due to the speed of social media, the use of hashtags on the web clearly suggests a causal explanation.

The results show that social media can be an important driving force in the coining of new words, and that social media corpora are thus an important data source for their detection and observation. Yet, the comparison of results between both datasets also shows that particular rules or conventions on social media platforms like Twitter significantly shape the linguistic behaviour of users on that platform. Therefore, platform-specific features and mechanisms like retweeting and hashtags need to be taken into account to arrive at an adequate interpretation of results. A big advantage of using the web as a data source is its heterogeneity. It provides a much broader set of linguistic varieties, text types, authors and readers which makes it a much more representative sample. Platforms like Twitter might certainly often spark or react more quickly to the establishment of new words, yet their use on the heterogeneous and pervasive World Wide Web provides a more balanced indication for their eventual conventionalization.

7   Future work

As we have shown, differences between the linguistic behaviour of speakers on Twitter and on the web significantly influence the spread of neologisms in both domains. Given the heterogeneity of the Word Wide Web, it would be desirable to further classify different domains-of-discourse within the web corpus in order to observe how these sub-domains differ regarding the use of neologisms. For example, our case study indicates that the use of terms like *rapefugee* differs strongly between private domains like personal blogs and professional domains like newspaper websites. While the former seem to function as a driving force in the early spread of the term, the latter tend to use the term less frequently and more critically, which is also reflected in the increased proportion of metalinguistic uses.

For future work, automatic classifications of domains-of-discourse for the web should thus be implemented. When investigating a large set of neologisms, this would allow to monitor in which domains they first appear and whether and how their use extends to other domains-of-discourse. This promises very valuable information, as the diffusion of neologisms across several domains plays an important role in their conventionalization process.

References

Laurie Bauer and Antoinette Renouf. 2000. Contextual clues to word-meaning. *International Journal of Corpus Linguistics*, 5:231–258.

Jack Grieve, Andrea Nini, and Diansheng Guo. 2016. Analyzing lexical emergence in Modern American English online. *English Language and Linguistics*.

Peter Hohenhaus. 2006. Bouncebackability. A web-as-corpus-based study of a new formation, its interpretation, generalization/spread and subsequent decline. *SKASE Journal of Theoretical Linguistics*, 3:17–27.

Daphné Kerremans, Susanne Stegmayr, and Hans-Jörg Schmid. 2012. The Neocrawler: identifying and retrieving neologisms from the internet and monitoring ongoing change. In Kathryn Allan and Justyna A. Robinson, editors, *Current Methods in Historical Semantics*, pages 59–96. Berlin: de Gruyter Mouton.

Daphné Kerremans. 2015. *A Web of New Words: A Corpus-based Study of the Conventionalization Process of English Neologisms*. Frankfurt am Main: Peter Lang.

Lothar Lemnitzer. 2011. Making sense of nonce words. In Margrethe Heidemann Andersen and Jörgen Nörby Jensen, editors, *Sprognaevets Konferenceserie 1*, pages 7–18. Nye Ord. Kopenhagen.

Dirk Lewandowski. 2008. A three-year study on the freshness of Web search engine databases. *Journal of Information Science*, 34(6):817–831.

Piotr Paryzek. 2008. Comparison of selected methods for the retrieval of neologisms. *Investigationes Linguisicae*, 16:163–181.

Antoinette Renouf. 2007. Tracing lexical productivity and creativity in the British Media: 'The Chavs and the Chav-Nots'. *Lexical Creativity, Texts and Contexts*, pages 61–92.

Anatol Stefanowitsch and Susanne Flach. (forthcoming). The corpus-based perspective on entrenchment. In Hans-Jörg Schmid, editor, *Entrenchment and the Psychology of Language Learning: How We Reorganize and Adapt Linguistic Knowledge*. American Psychology Association and de Gruyter Mouton, Boston, USA.

Tony Veale and Cristina Butnariu. 2010. Harvesting and understanding on-line neologisms. *Cognitive perspectives on word formation*, pages 399–418.

Desislava Zhekova. 2016. Using Contemporary Media for the Humanities: The REFUGEE Twitter Corpus. *Digital Scholarship in the Humanities*. (submitted).

EmpiriST 2015: A Shared Task on the Automatic Linguistic Annotation of Computer-Mediated Communication and Web Corpora

Michael Beißwenger
Universität Duisburg-Essen
45127 Essen, Germany
`michael.beisswenger`
`@uni-due.de`

Sabine Bartsch
Technische Universität Darmstadt
64293 Darmstadt
`bartsch`
`@linglit.tu-darmstadt.de`

Stefan Evert
FAU Erlangen-Nürnberg
91054 Erlangen, Germany
`stefan.evert@fau.de`

Kay-Michael Würzner
Berlin-Brandenburgische
Akademie der Wissenschaften
10405 Berlin, Germany
`wuerzner@bbaw.de`

Abstract

This paper describes the goals, design and results of a shared task on the automatic linguistic annotation of German language data from genres of computer-mediated communication (CMC), social media interactions and Web corpora. The two subtasks of tokenization and part-of-speech tagging were performed on two data sets: (i) a genuine *CMC data set* with samples from several CMC genres, and (ii) a *Web corpora data set* of CC-licensed Web pages which represents the type of data found in large corpora crawled from the Web. The teams participating in the shared task achieved a substantial improvement over current off-the-shelf tools for German. The best tokenizer reached an F_1-score of 99.57% (vs. 98.95% off-the-shelf baseline), while the best tagger reached an accuracy of 90.44% (vs. 84.86% baseline). The gold standard (more than 20,000 tokens of training and test data) is freely available online together with detailed annotation guidelines.

1 Motivation, premises and goals

Over the past decade, there has been a growing interest in collecting, processing and analyzing data from genres of computer-mediated communication and social media interactions (henceforth referred to as CMC) such as chats, blogs, forums, tweets, newsgroups, messaging applications (SMS, WhatsApp), interactions on "social network" sites and on wiki talk pages. The development of resources, tools and best practices for automatic linguistic processing and annotation of CMC discourse has turned out to be a desideratum for several fields of research in the humanities:

1. Large corpora crawled from the Web often contain substantial amounts of CMC (blogs, forums, etc.) and similar forms of non-canonical language. Such data are often regarded as "bycatch" that proves difficult for linguistic annotation by means of standard natural language processing (NLP) tools that are optimized for edited text (Giesbrecht and Evert, 2009).

2. For corpus-based variational linguistics, corpora of CMC discourse are an important resource that closes the "CMC gap" in corpora of contemporary written language and language-in-interaction. With a considerable part of contemporary everyday communication being mediated through CMC technologies, up-to-date investigations of language change and linguistic variation need to be able to include CMC discourse in their empirical analyses.

In order to harness the full potential of corpus-based research, the preparation of any type of linguistic corpus which includes CMC discourse—whether a genuine CMC corpus or a broad-coverage Web corpus—faces the challenge of handling and annotating the linguistic peculiarities characteristic for the types of written discourse found in CMC genres. Two fundamental (but non-trivial) tasks are (i) accurate tokenization and (ii) sufficiently reliable part-of-speech (PoS) annotation. Together, they provide a layer of basic linguistic information on the token level that is a pre-

Proceedings of the 10th Web as Corpus Workshop (WAC-X) and the EmpiriST Shared Task, pages 44–56,
Berlin, Germany, August 7-12, 2016. ©2016 Association for Computational Linguistics

requisite for any form of advanced linguistic analysis on the word, sentence and interaction level.

The linguistic peculiarities of discourse in CMC and social media genres have been extensively described in the literature (for an overview of features with a focus on German CMC see e.g. Haase et al., 1997; Runkehl et al., 1998; Beißwenger, 2000; Storrer, 2001; Dürscheid, 2005; Androutsopoulos, 2007; Bartz et al., 2013; for English CMC see e.g. Crystal, 2001, 2003; Herring, 1996, 2010, 2011). Due to its dialogic nature and depending on the degree to which the interlocutors consider their interaction as an informal, private exchange, CMC discourse typically includes a range of deviations from the syntactic and orthographic norms of the written standard (often referred to as non-canonical phenomena) such as colloquial spellings (e.g., clitics and schwa elisions) and lexical items which typically occur in spoken interactions rather than monologic texts (interjections, intensifiers, focus and gradation particles, modal particles and downtoners, etc.). The word order and syntax of CMC posts exhibit features that are characteristic of spoken or "conceptually oral" language use in colloquial registers (e.g., ellipses, German *weil* or *obwohl* with V2 clause). High speed typing causes speedwriting phenomena such as typos, the omission of upper case or the use of acronyms; other deviations from the orthographic standard have to be considered as intended, creative spellings (*nice2CU*, *good n8*). The need for emotion markers leads to the use of emoticons and emoji; upper case and letter iterations serve as suprasegmental forms of emphasis in the written medium (*LASS DAS!*, *suuuuuper!!!!*). Addressing terms and hashtags indicate reference between user posts and link individual posts to discourse topics.

Tackling the linguistic peculiarities of CMC data with NLP tools is an open issue in corpus and computational linguistics, which has been addressed by an increasing number of papers and approaches over the past years (as a desideratum e.g. Beißwenger and Storrer, 2008; King, 2009; for the development of NLP tools e.g. Ritter et al., 2011; Gimpel et al., 2011; Owoputi et al., 2015; Avontuur et al., 2012; Bartz et al., 2013; Neunerdt et al., 2013; Rehbein, 2013; Rehbein et al., 2013; Horbach et al., 2015; Zinsmeister et al., 2014; Ljubešić et al., 2015). Issues of processing and annotating CMC data have also been a central topic

of the DFG-funded scientific network *Empirical Research of Internet-Based Communication (Empirikom)*, which brought together researchers interested in building and analyzing CMC, social media and Web corpora for research questions in linguistics, computational linguistics and language technology during the years 2010–2014.[1] As a result from discussions in the network, it was decided to set up a community shared task to foster the development of approaches for automatic linguistic annotation of CMC data for German in a competitive setting. The task was named *Empirikom* Shared Task on Automatic Linguistic Annotation of Computer-Mediated Communication and Social Media (EmpiriST 2015).

The design of EmpiriST 2015 was based on the following two premises:

1. It should take into consideration not only the compilation of CMC corpora for research and teaching purposes in linguistics but also the handling of portions of CMC data as part of large Web corpora.
2. It should be based on a freely available gold standard created with a well-defined PoS tagset and precise guidelines for tokenization and PoS annotation (see Sec. 2).

The main goals and research questions are:

1. To what extent can the performance of automatic tools for tokenization and PoS tagging of German CMC discourse be improved, using our gold standard for training or domain adaptation?
2. Can both genuine CMC corpora and Web corpora (where CMC phenomena typically occur much less frequently) be processed by the same approaches and models, or do we need different tools for the two types of corpora?

2 The EmpiriST gold standard

The gold standard developed for the shared task comprises roughly 10,000 tokens of training data provided to participants as well as roughly 10,000 tokens of unseen test data used in the evaluation phase. It was compiled from data samples considered representative for the two types of corpora: (i) a CMC subset covering discourse from a range of CMC/social media genres, and (ii) a Web corpora subset containing CC-licensed Web pages from different genres.

---

[1] http://www.empirikom.net/

2.1 Data sets

The **CMC subset** includes samples from several CMC genres and different sources:

- a selection of donated tweets from (i) the Twitter channel of an academy project used for (monologic) project-related announcements, (ii) the Twitter channel of a lecturer used for discussions with the students accompanying a university class (= dialogic use of tweets);
- a selection of data taken from the *Dortmund Chat Corpus* (Beißwenger, 2013) representing discourse from different types of chat: (i) *social chat* recorded in multiparty chatrooms where people met mainly for recreational purposes, (ii) *professional chat* comprising professional uses of chatrooms, e.g. advisory chats and chats in the context of learning and teaching;
- a selection of threads retrieved from Wikipedia talk pages;
- a selection of WhatsApp interactions taken from the data collected in the project *Whats up, Deutschland?*;[2]
- a selection of blog comments from CC-licensed weblogs collected by Adrien Barbaresi.

For the **Web corpora subset**, roughly 50,000 running words of text were collected by Web crawling. In order to ensure a broad coverage of Web genres and topics, the crawl was based on a set of manually pre-selected seed words. The following list gives an impression of the distribution of genres in the data:

- Web sites on topics such as hobbies, travel and IT;
- blogs on topics such as hobbies, travel and legal issues;
- Wikipedia articles on topics such as biology, botany and cities;
- Wikinews on topics such as IT security and ecology.

The largest portion of these data is comprised of Web pages, blog entries and commentaries, a smaller portion consists of genres such as Wikipedia articles, Wikinews etc. An important requirement was that all texts must be published

under a suitable Creative Commons licence so that the resulting corpus can be made freely available to the community without any legal issues.

From the available data, we selected roughly 5,000 tokens of training data for each subset, which were provided to task participants with manual tokenization and PoS tagging. Another 5,000 tokens per subset were used as unseen test data, with a similar distribution of genres and sources as in the training data. The precise data sizes of the training and test sets are listed in Tab. 1.

	CMC subset	Web subset
training data	5,109 (8 samples)	4,944 (11 samples)
test data	5,234 (6 samples)	7,568 (12 samples)

Table 1: Sizes of the training and test data sets, specified in number of tokens (above) and number of text samples (below).

2.2 Annotation guidelines

For **tokenization**, we developed a guideline with detailed rules for handling CMC-specific tokenization issues (Beißwenger et al., 2015a). It was tested and refined for a range of CMC and Web genres with the help of several student annotators in Berlin, Darmstadt, Dortmund and Erlangen.

For **PoS tagging**, we used the 'STTS_IBK' tag set which had been defined as a result from discussions in the *Empirikom* network and at three workshops dedicated to the adaptation and extension of the canonical version of the *Stuttgart-Tübingen-Tagset* ('STTS 1.0'; Schiller et al., 1999) to the peculiarities of "non-standard" genres (Zinsmeister et al., 2013, 2014). STTS_IBK introduces two types of new tags: (i) tags for phenomena that are specific to CMC and social media discourse, (ii) tags for phenomena that are typical for spontaneous (spoken or "conceptually oral") language in colloquial registers (cf. Tab. 2). These extensions are useful for corpus-based research on CMC as well as spoken conversation. STTS_IBK is downward compatible to STTS 1.0 and therefore allows for interoperability with existing corpora and tools. In addition, the tag set extensions in STTS_IBK are compatible with the STTS extensions defined at IDS Mannheim for the PoS

---

[2]http://www.whatsup-deutschland.de/

PoS tag	Category	Examples
I. Tags for phenomena specific for CMC / social media discourse:		
EMOASC	ASCII emoticon	`:-) :-( ^^ O.O`
EMOIMG	Graphic emoticon (emoji)	☺ ☺ ●
AKW	Interaction word	`*lach*, freu, grübel, *lol*`
HST	Hash tag	`Kreta war super! #Urlaub`
ADR	Addressing term	`@lothar: Wie isset so?`
URL	Uniform resource locator	`http://tu-dortmund.de`
EML	E-mail address	`peterklein@web.de`
II. Tags for phenomena typical for spontaneous spoken ('conceptually oral') language in colloquial registers:		
VVPPER		`schreibste, machste`
APPRART		`vorm, überm, fürn`
VMPPER	Tags for different types of colloquial contractions	`willste, darfste, musste`
VAPPER	thate are frequent in CMC (APPRART already	`haste, biste, isses`
KOUSPPER	exists in STTS 1.0)	`wenns, weils, obse`
PPERPPER		`ichs, dus, ers`
ADVART		`son, sone`
PTKIFG	Intensifier, focus and gradation particles	sehr schön, höchst eigenartig, nur sie, voll geil
PTKMA	Modal particles and downtoners	Das ist ja / vielleicht doof. Ist das denn richtig so? Das war halt echt nicht einfach.
PTKMWL	Particle as part of a multi-word lexeme	keine mehr, noch mal, schon wieder
DM	Discourse markers	weil, obwohl, nur, also, ...*with V2 clauses*
ONO	Onomatopoeia	`boing, miau, zisch`

Table 2: Tagset extensions for CMC phenomena in STTS_IBK. More examples with context can be found in the detailed annotation guidelines on the EmpiriST Web site (available in German and English).

annotation of FOLK[3], the Mannheim "Research and Teaching Corpus of Spoken German" (Westpfahl and Schmidt, 2013; Westpfahl, 2013). The tag set is described in an annotation guideline (Beißwenger et al., 2015b) and has been tested with data from several CMC genres in advance.

The complete annotation guidelines (in German) as well as supplementary documentation are available online from the shared task Web site.[4] For international participants, an English translation of the tagging guideline is also provided.

2.3 Annotation procedure

All data sets were manually tokenized and PoS tagged by multiple annotators, based on the official tokenization (Beißwenger et al., 2015a) and tagging guidelines (Schiller et al., 1999; Beißwenger et al., 2015b), see Sec. 2.2. Cases of disagreement were then adjudicated by the task or-

ganizers to produce the final gold standard. During the annotation of the training data, minor changes to the annotation guidelines were made based on experience from the adjudication procedure. In addition, various problematic cases were collected in a supplementary document available to the annotators.

The manual tokenization was carried out in a plain text editor, starting from whitespace-tokenized files in one-token-per-line format. Annotators were instructed to make no other changes to the files than inserting additional line breaks as token boundaries (except for a few special cases), but were allowed to mark unclear cases with comments. The tokenizations were compared and adjudicated using the `kdiff3` utility.[5]

In the next step, manual tagging was partly carried out with the Web-based annotation platform *CorA*[6] (Bollmann et al., 2014), partly with

<hr>

[3] `http://agd.ids-mannheim.de/folk.shtml`
[4] `https://sites.google.com/site/empirist2015/home/annotation-guidelines`

[5] `http://kdiff3.sourceforge.net/`
[6] `https://www.linguistics.rub.de/comphist/resources/cora/`

	BT	FW
gold	96.04	94.05
BT		91.05

Table 3: Agreement between annotators and gold standard for PoS tagging of the CMC data subset (training and test sets). Values are accuracy (acc) percentages.

our own Web-based tool *MiniMarker*. In both cases annotators worked independently with separate password-protected accounts and were encouraged to document interesting or difficult phenomena in free-form comments. CorA has the advantage that tokenization errors can be corrected at the tagging stage, while MiniMarker enables annotators to look up how specific word forms are tagged in the TIGER treebank corpus in order to ensure consistent annotation. For adjudication of the PoS tagging, we pre-annotated unanmimous annotator decisions and filled in the remaining disputed tags with MiniMarker.

Agreement between annotators as well as the agreement of each annotator with the final gold standard was determined using the same evaluation metrics as for systems participating in the shared task (see Sec. 3.2).

2.3.1 CMC subset

In a preliminary study on the manual tokenization of CMC (cf. Beißwenger et al., 2013), we observed very high inter-annotator agreement with F_1 scores ranging from 98.6% to 99.7%, showing that manual tokenization of such data provides a valid and reliable gold standard. For training and test data of the CMC subset, we therefore decided to pursue a "sequential double keying" approach. The initial tokenization was done at a very early stage of the task preparation; it was later double-checked and revised according to the final tokenization guidelines by a second expert annotator.

PoS tags were added by two independent annotators. Tab. 3 shows the observed agreement between the annotators and the adjudicated gold standard in terms of accuracy (acc).

Frequent errors involved the new particle classes in STTS_IBK (PTKIFG, PTKMA, PTKMWL), punctuation ($ (vs. $.), the distinction between common (NN) and proper nouns (NE) and the correct classification of non-inflected adjectives (ADJD).

It is interesting to note that for both annotators the agreement between each annotator and the gold standard is much higher than the agreement between the two annotators. One possible explanation is that each annotator had difficulties with specific types of phenomena. Looking at the error classes, this assumption turns out to be true: For example, annotator FW tended to misclassify adverbs as intensifier particles (PTKIFG, $n = 66$) whereas annotator BT made this mistake only six times. On the other hand, BT misjudged more than twice as many adjectives (ADJA vs. ADJD) than FW.

2.3.2 Web corpora subset

The test data of the Web corpora subset were manually tokenized by five primary annotators, and then adjudicated in two phases by one of the task organizers. Tab. 4 shows pairwise agreement between annotators and the agreement of each annotator with the gold standard in terms of F_1 scores for token boundaries. Agreement is very high between all pairs of annotators, indicating that the manual tokenization is reliable.

	AM	AS	DP	JM	LS
gold	99.56	99.74	99.70	99.78	99.93
AM		99.75	99.67	99.66	99.62
AS			99.88	99.89	99.80
DP				99.87	99.71
JM					99.73

Table 4: Agreement between annotators and gold standard for tokenization of the Web corpora test data. Values are F_1 scores given as percentages.

	AM	AS	JM	LS
gold	92.64	96.15	95.49	91.77
AM		91.54	90.80	88.42
AS			93.04	89.51
JM				90.27

Table 5: Agreement between annotators and gold standard for PoS tagging of the Web corpora test data. Values are accuracy (acc) percentages.

PoS tags were manually added by 4 independent annotators, based on the adjudicated tokenization. No further corrections of the tokenization were found to be necessary in this phase. Tab. 5 shows agreement between the annotators and the gold standard in terms of observed accuracy (acc). Due to the low probability of chance agreement (approx. 7.5%), there is no need to compute κ values or other adjusted scores. Agreement for the manual tagging is less satisfactory than for the tokenization. Major sources of disagreement were the newly introduced particle classes—in particular PTKIFG and PTKMA—as well as unintuitive or poorly defined category boundaries in the original STTS 1.0 tag set—in particular common nouns (NN) vs. proper nouns (NE) vs. foreign text (FM), and adverbs (ADV) vs. adverbial adjectives (ADJD). It is also noticeable that the training and experience of individual annotators played an important role: two annotators (AS and JM) agree fairly well with each other and with the adjudicated gold standard, while the other two annotators performed considerably worse.

Despite these issues, most errors and misinterpretations were caught by our adjudication of the four-fold annotation. A fifth independent tagging carried out by annotator SM at a later stage showed an agreement of acc $= 95.90\%$ with the final gold standard.

The training data of the Web corpora subset were manually tokenized by three independent annotators and tagged by five independent annotators, with adjudication by one of the task organizers after each stage. Agreement between annotators and the gold standard is similar to the test data.

2.4 Availability

All gold standard data sets, the specification of the extended STTS tag set and the guidelines for tokenization and PoS tagging have been published on the EmpiriST Web site[7] and will remain available for use in future research. We used simple UTF-8 encoded text formats for both raw and annotated versions of the data. Annotated files are provided in one-token-per-line format with empty lines serving as posting or paragraph boundary markers. Corresponding PoS tags are given in an additional column separated from the token text by a single tab stop. Metadata for each posting or Web page are inserted as empty XML elements on separate lines. A small excerpt from one of the files is shown in Fig. 1.

Apart from the actual contents, the EmpiriST 2015 data package comes with a description of the tag set, evaluation scripts and licensing informa-

```
<posting info="User 15:08, 26.09.10" />
Das        ART
ständige           ADJA
Revertieren        NN
von        APPR
Phi        NE
damit      PAV
auch       ADV
...        $.
```

Figure 1: Excerpt from the CMC subset of the EmpiriST 2015 shared task training data.

tion. All files are released under the *Creative Commons* CC BY-SA 3.0 licence.[8]

3 The shared task

3.1 Layout of the task

The EmpiriST 2015 shared task was divided into three major stages: (i) preparation, (ii) training and (iii) evaluation.

The preparation stage started with the release of the annotation guidelines together with roughly 2,000 tokens of trial data from each subset in October 2015. The trial data were intended to illustrate the required input and output file formats and to give an impression of the specific characteristics of the CMC and Web texts to be processed. They were based on preliminary versions of the guidelines and were produced without multiple annotation. Participants were instructed that they should not be relied on for training the final systems. During the preparation stage, there was also a fruitful dialogue between interested parties and the shared task organizers, leading to clarifications and corrections of the guidelines.

The second stage was dedicated to the training and adaptation of the competing systems. It started with the release of the complete training data on the shared task Web site in December 2015. The registration deadline fell within this stage, enabling participants to make an initial assessment of their performance before registering.

The evaluation stage was divided into two consecutive phases so that (i) tokenization and tagging quality could be evaluated separately and (ii) the same test data could be used for both subtasks. In each phase, unannotated test data were released via the shared task Web site; participants then had to submit their system output within five days by e-mail. For the tokenization phase, raw texts were

---

[7]https://sites.google.com/site/
empirist2015/home/gold

[8]https://creativecommons.org/licenses/
by-sa/3.0/

released, padded with additional filler data in order to prevent tuning of systems to the test data before the second phase. For the tagging phase, manually tokenized versions of the texts were released. The two phases took place in two consecutive weeks in February 2016.

3.2 Evaluation metrics

Evaluation of the submissions to EmpiriST 2015 was carried out by the task organizers. Following Jurish and Würzner (2013), results for the tokenization task were evaluated based on the unweighted harmonic average (F_1) between precision (pr) and recall (rc) of the token boundaries in the participants' submissions. Formally, let $B_{\mathrm{retrieved}}$ be the set of token boundaries predicted by the tokenization procedure to be evaluated and B_{relevant} those present in the gold standard; then:

$$\mathrm{pr} = \frac{|B_{\mathrm{relevant}} \cap B_{\mathrm{retrieved}}|}{|B_{\mathrm{retrieved}}|} \tag{1}$$

$$\mathrm{rc} = \frac{|B_{\mathrm{relevant}} \cap B_{\mathrm{retrieved}}|}{|B_{\mathrm{relevant}}|} \tag{2}$$

$$F_1 = \frac{2 \cdot \mathrm{pr} \cdot \mathrm{rc}}{\mathrm{pr} + \mathrm{rc}} \tag{3}$$

For technical reasons, the trivial token boundary at the beginning of each text file is included in the evaluation, but not the boundary at its end.[9]

Following Giesbrecht and Evert (2009), the PoS tagging task was evaluated in terms of the accuracy (acc) of the PoS tag assignments in the participants' submissions. Formally, let n_{correct} be the number of tokens whose tags agree with the gold standard, and n_{total} the total number of tokens in the data set; then:

$$\mathrm{acc} = \frac{n_{\mathrm{correct}}}{n_{\mathrm{total}}} \tag{4}$$

In order to support participants in development and self-evaluation of their submissions, both evaluation metrics were implemented as Perl scripts by the organizers and published together with the training and test data sets.

4 Participating systems

Tab. 6 gives an overview of the participating teams and systems. Team UdS submitted three related systems (UdS-distributional, UDS-retrain, UDS-surface). In addition, each system was permitted

Team	Reference
	Tokenization
AIPHES	Remus et al. (2016)
COW	Schäfer and Bildhauer (2012)[1]
LTL-UDE	Horsmann and Zesch (2016)
SoMaJo	Proisl and Uhrig (2016)
$WAGMOB[†]	—
	PoS tagging
AIPHES	Remus et al. (2016)
bot.zen*	Stemle (2016)
COW[†]	Schäfer and Bildhauer (2012)[1]
LTL-UDE	Horsmann and Zesch (2016)
$WAGMOB[†]	—
UdS	Prange et al. (2016)

* late submission

[†] non-competitive submission

[1] see also Schäfer (2015)

Table 6: Overview of the participants with reference to the corresponding system description.

to submit up to 3 different runs, with only the best run being included in the task results.

4.1 Summary of competing approaches

As shown in Tab. 6, we had five submissions for the **tokenization** subtask, one of them non-competitive.[10] All five systems employed rule-based tokenization approaches. Two of them (AIPHES and LTL-UDE) used a "split and merge" strategy that splits tokens into atomic units in the first pass. In subsequent passes, higher-order rules implement merging strategies for dealing with complex phenomena such as URLs, abbreviations or emoticons. In contrast, COW used an "under segmentation" strategy protecting certain token sequences in the first pass and further segmenting them in a second. SoMaJo used complex, cascaded regular expressions successively dealing with the aforementioned classes of phenomena.

All approaches made use of additional lists of abbreviations, proper names, emoticons, etc. in order to improve correct tokenization of special characters and punctuation.

We had six submissions for the **PoS tagging** subtask, two of them non-competitive.[11] From the

---

[9]This trick simplified the implementation of the evaluation script considerably. It was deemed to be acceptable with a typical effect of less than 0.01% on the evaluation metrics.

[10]$WAGMOB was a student team from a Bachelor seminar taught by one of the task organizers

[11]COW is an existing annotation pipeline for large Web corpora, which was entered into the task with minimal adap-

four regular submissions, one (bot.zen) was sent in after the submission deadline and is thus not included in the official ranking. In contrast to tokenization, all systems competing in the PoS tagging subtask made use of statistical models specially trained or re-trained for the purpose of EmpiriST 2015. The types of models employed reflect all state-of-the-art approaches to the task of PoS tagging. All approaches have in common that they extend the EmpiriST training data with additional corpora and linguistic resources.

The three UdS systems built on a classical *hidden Markov model* (HMM; Rabiner, 1989). In addition, they focused on improvements in the analysis of out-of-vocabulary (OOV) words by adding domain-specific training material and a list of likely PoS tags for OOV items. LTL-UDE and AIPHES used *conditional random fields* (CRF; Lafferty et al., 2001). Both systems differed in the selection of features and the additional resources used in the training process. Team bot.zen employed a long short-term memory (LSTM; Hochreiter and Schmidhuber, 1997) recurrent neural network in combination with neural word embeddings as input representations (Mikolov et al., 2013).

5   Results

In order to put the performance of the shared task submissions into perspective, we also evaluated several widely-used off-the-shelf tools as baselines:

- the WASTE tokenizer (Jurish and Würzner, 2013);[12]
- TreeTagger v3.2 (Schmid, 1995);[13]
- Stanford tagger v3.6.0 (Toutanova et al., 2003);[14]

---

tations to account for the tokenization principles and extended tag set of EmpiriST. It may therefore be more appropriate to compare COW with the baseline systems than with the other task participants.

[12]We used WASTE as shipped with the moot package (v2.0.13, `http://kaskade.dwds.de/waste/`) and trained a model solely using the EmpiriST training data.

[13]We used the German UTF-8 parameter file downloaded from `http://www.cis.uni-muenchen.de/~schmid/tools/TreeTagger/` on 21 June 2016.

[14]We used the `german-dewac` parameter file from the distribution released on 9 Dec 2015. Substantial automatic and manual post-editing was required to undo character transformations made by the tokenizer, replace non-STTS tags (e.g. `$[` instead of `$(`), and account for the systematic mistagging of parentheses and brackets as TRUNC.

- the COW pipeline (Schäfer and Bildhauer, 2012; Schäfer, 2015).[15]

Tab. 7 (tokenization) and Tab. 8 (PoS tagging) show the results obtained by all task participants and baseline systems on the CMC and Web corpora subsets. Within each subset, results are micro-averaged across the text samples. The overall score is the macro-average over both subsets, ensuring that CMC and Web corpora carry the same weight. For systems that submitted multiple runs, only the best run is shown in the table (indicated by a subscript appended to the team name). The official ranking ("podium") includes only competitive and timely submissions. Since team UdS entered three closely related systems into the competition, only one of them was selected for the official podium. Detailed results for individual runs and text samples are available on the EmpiriST Web page.[16]

Since the existing off-the-shelf taggers used as a baseline are not aware of the new PoS tags in STTS_IBK, the evaluation was carried out both at the level of STTS_IBK and at the level of the established STTS 1.0 tag set (Schiller et al., 1999). For this purpose, one or more alternative STTS 1.0 tags were also accepted for each extended tag in the gold standard. The precise mapping rules are specified in Tab. 9. The official ranking is always based on the full STTS_IBK tag set.

6   Conclusion

The systems submitted to the EmpiriST2015 shared task have improved the state-of-the-art for tokenization and PoS tagging of CMC and Web corpora. The best submitted tokenizer achieved an F_1-score of 99.54% (vs. 98.47% baseline) for the CMC data set and an F_1-score of 99.77% (vs. 99.42% baseline) for the Web corpora data set. For PoS tagging, the results are still far from optimal. Nevertheless, the improvement against baseline systems is striking especially for the CMC subset: The best submitted tagger achieved an accuracy of 87.33% evaluated against STTS_IBK (vs. 77.89% baseline), and an accuracy of 90.28% against STTS 1.0 (vs. 81.51% baseline). For the Web corpora subset, where the baseline systems already peform much better than on gen-

---

[15]COW results were submitted by the developers as a baseline participation in the PoS tagging subtask.

[16]`https://sites.google.com/site/empirist2015/home/results`

Team	CMC				Web				Overall		
	pr	rc	F_1	Rk	pr	rc	F_1	Rk	F_1	Rk	Pdm
SoMaJo	99.52	99.56	99.54	1	99.57	99.64	99.60	3	99.57	1	**1**
AIPHES	99.30	98.62	98.96	2	99.63	99.89	99.76	2	99.36	2	**2**
COW	98.31	98.07	98.18	5	99.84	99.71	99.77	1	98.98	3	**3**
WASTE[†]	99.41	97.57	98.47	4	99.59	99.26	99.42	4	98.95	4	-
LTL-UDE	99.01	98.18	98.58	3	98.92	99.54	99.22	8	98.90	5	**4**
$WAGMOB*	98.97	96.79	97.83	6	99.41	99.38	99.39	5	98.61	6	-
Stanford[†]	97.19	97.69	97.41	7	98.97	99.71	99.34	7	98.38	7	-
TreeTagger[†]	94.95	95.01	94.96	8	99.58	99.14	99.36	6	97.16	8	-

Table 7: Results of the tokenization subtask including non-competitive submissions (marked with *) and baseline systems (marked with [†]). The last column gives the official EmpiriST 2015 "podium" ranking. pr, rc, and F_1 are given as percentages for better readability.

Team	CMC				Web				Overall		
	STTS_IBK		STTS 1.0		STTS_IBK		STTS 1.0		STTS_IBK		
	acc	Rk	acc	Rk	acc	Rk	acc	Rk	acc	Rk	Pdm
UdS-distributional$_2$	87.33	1	90.28	1	93.55	1	94.62	1	90.44	1	**1**
UdS-retrain$_2$	86.40	3	89.07	3	92.79	3	93.86	3	89.60	2	-
UdS-surface$_2$	86.45	2	89.28	2	92.43	4	93.50	4	89.44	3	-
LTL-UDE$_2$	86.07	4	88.84	4	92.10	5	93.12	5	89.09	4	**2**
AIPHES	84.22	7	87.10	6	93.27	2	94.30	2	88.75	5	**3**
bot.zen$_3^*$	85.42	5	87.47	5	90.63	8	91.74	9	88.03	6	-
COW[†]	77.89	8	81.51	8	91.82	6	92.96	6	84.86	7	-
$WAGMOB*	84.77	6	87.03	7	84.51	10	85.57	10	84.64	8	-
TreeTagger[†]	73.21	9	76.81	9	91.75	7	92.89	7	82.48	9	-
Stanford[†]	70.60	10	75.83	10	89.42	9	92.52	8	80.01	10	-

Table 8: Results of the PoS tagging subtask including non-competitive or late submissions (marked with *) and baseline systems (marked with [†]). If applicable, a subscript indicates the best run of the respective system (based on overall accuracy), which is listed in the table. The last column gives the official EmpiriST 2015 "podium" ranking. acc is given as a percentage for better readability.

gold tag	these tags are also accepted
EMOIMG	XY ITJ EMOASC
AKW	VVFIN VVIMP VVINF VVIZU VAFIN VAIMP VAINF VMFIN VMINF
HST	XY
ADR	XY NE
URL	XY
EML	XY
VVPPER	VVFIN VVIMP VVINF
VMPPER	VMFIN VMINF
VAPPER	VAFIN VAIMP VAINF
KOUSPPER	KOUS
PPERPPER	PPER
ADVART	ART
PTKIFG	ADV ADJD PTKMA PTKMWL
PTKMA	ADV ADJD PTKIFG PTKMWL
PTKMWL	ADV ADJD PTKIFG PTKMA
DM	KOUS ADV
ONO	ITJ VVFIN VVIMP VVINF
ADV	PTKIFG PTKMA PTKMWL DM
KOUS	DM
PIDAT	PIAT

Table 9: Mapping of extended tags for evaluation at the level of STTS 1.0.

uine CMC, there was only a modest improvement: 93.55% against STTS_IBK (vs. 91.82% baseline), and 94.62% against STTS 1.0 (vs. 92.96% baseline). It should be noted that the widely-used Stanford and TreeTagger tools performed substantially worse on tagging CMC than the COW baseline shown here.

Further evaluation of the results in future work should include a close examination and discussion of the performance of the tagger models with respect to the tag set extensions defined in STTS_IBK, as well as their performance on different genres and text sources. This will be the topic of a round table organized at the 3rd NLP4CMC workshop at KONVENS 2016.[17]

The results of the shared task can be considered a promising step towards better NLP tools for German CMC data, especially since all participants (except for UdS) have made their systems available to the community as open-source software. However, the adaptation of NLP tools to the linguistic peculiarities of CMC discourse—especially for PoS tagging—is still a challenging task. The resources developed for EmpiriST 2015 (gold standard and annotation guidelines) will remain available on the task Web site under a Creative Commons licence.[18] We hope that they will stimulate further advances in adapting NLP technologies to CMC discourse as well as in improving the annotation quality of German Web corpora.

Acknowledgments

We thank the *German Society for Computational Linguistics and Language Technology (GSCL)* for financial support, Stefanie Dipper and Marcel Bollmann (Ruhr-Universität Bochum) for providing the *CorA* tool for PoS annotations, our student annotators in Berlin, Darmstadt, Dortmund and Erlangen for their careful work and the members of the DFG network *Empirikom* for fruitful discussions in the design stage of the task.

References

Jannis Androutsopoulos. 2007. Neue Medien – neue Schriftlichkeit? *Mitteilungen des Deutschen Germanistenverbandes* 54(1):72–97.

Tetske Avontuur, Iris Balemans, Laura Elshof, Nanne van Noord, and Menno van Zaanen. 2012. Developing a part-of-speech tagger for Dutch tweets. *Computational Linguistics in the Netherlands Journal* 2:34–51.

Thomas Bartz, Michael Beißwenger, and Angelika Storrer. 2013. Optimierung des Stuttgart-Tübingen-Tagset für die linguistische Annotation von Korpora zur internetbasierten Kommunikation: Phänomene, Herausforderungen, Erweiterungsvorschläge. *Journal for Language Technology and Computational Linguistics (JLCL)* 28(1):157–198.

Michael Beißwenger. 2000. *Kommunikation in virtuellen Welten: Sprache, Text und Wirklichkeit*. Ibidem-Verlag.

Michael Beißwenger. 2013. Das Dortmunder Chat-Korpus. *Zeitschrift für Germanistische Linguistik* 41(1):161–164.

Michael Beißwenger, Sabine Bartsch, Stefan Evert, and Kay-Michael Würzner. 2013. Preparing a shared task on linguistic annotation of computer-mediated communication. Talk and poster presentation at the International Conference of the GSCL.

Michael Beißwenger, Sabine Bartsch, Stefan Evert, and Kay-Michael Würzner. 2015a. Richtlinie für die manuelle Tokenisierung von

---

[17]https://sites.google.com/site/nlp4cmc2016/

[18]https://sites.google.com/site/empirist2015/

Sprachdaten aus Genres internetbasierter Kommunikation. Empirist2015 Guideline document.

Michael Beißwenger, Thomas Bartz, Angelika Storrer, and Swantje Westpfahl. 2015b. Tagset und Richtlinie für das Part-of-Speech-Tagging von Sprachdaten aus Genres internetbasierter Kommunikation. EmpiriST2015 Guideline document.

Michael Beißwenger and Angelika Storrer. 2008. Corpora of computer-mediated communication. In Anke Lüdeling and Merja Kytö, editors, *Corpus Linguistics. An International Handbook*, Walter de Gruyter, Berlin and New York, volume 1 of *Handbücher zur Sprache und Kommunikationswissenschaft / Handbooks of Linguistics and Communication Science*, chapter Corpora of Computer-Mediated Communication, pages 292–308.

Marcel Bollmann, Florian Petran, Stefanie Dipper, and Julia Krasselt. 2014. CorA: A web-based annotation tool for historical and other nonstandard language data. In *Proceedings of the 8th Workshop on Language Technology for Cultural Heritage, Social Sciences, and Humanities (LaTeCH)*. Gothenburg, Sweden, pages 86–90.

David Crystal. 2001. *Language and the Internet*. CUP, Cambridge.

David Crystal. 2003. *English as a Global Language*. Cambridge University Press, second edition. Cambridge Books Online.

Christa Dürscheid. 2005. Normabweichendes Schreiben als Mittel zum Zweck. *Muttersprache: Vierteljahresschrift für deutsche Sprache / Gesellschaft für Deutsche Sprache (GfdS)* 115(1):40–53.

Eugenie Giesbrecht and Stefan Evert. 2009. Part-of-speech tagging – a solved task? An evaluation of POS taggers for the web as corpus. In Inaki Alegria, Igor Leturia, and Serge Sharoff, editors, *Proceedings of the Fifth Web as Corpus Workshop (WAC5), San Sebastián, Spain, 7 September, 2009*. pages 27–35.

Kevin Gimpel, Nathan Schneider, Brendan O'Connor, Dipanjan Das, Daniel Mills, Jacob Eisenstein, Michael Heilman, Dani Yogatama, Jeffrey Flanigan, and Noah A. Smith. 2011. Part-of-speech tagging for Twitter: Annotation, features, and experiments. In *Proceedings of the 49th Annual Meeting of the Association for Computational Linguistics: Human Language Technologies: Short Papers - Volume 2*. Association for Computational Linguistics, Stroudsburg, PA, USA, HLT '11, pages 42–47.

Martin Haase, Michael Huber, Alexander Krumeich, and Georg Rehm. 1997. *Internetkommunikation und Sprachwandel*, VS Verlag für Sozialwissenschaften, Wiesbaden, pages 51–85.

Susan C. Herring, editor. 1996. *Computer-Mediated Communication. Linguistic, Social and Cross-Cultural Perspectives*. Pragmatics and Beyond New Series 39. John Benjamins, Amsterdam and Philadelphia.

Susan C. Herring. 2010. Computer-mediated conversation part i: Introduction and overview. *Language@Internet* 7(2).

Susan C. Herring. 2011. Computer-mediated conversation part ii: Introduction and overview. *Language@Internet* 8(2).

Sepp Hochreiter and Jürgen Schmidhuber. 1997. Long short-term memory. *Neural Comput.* 9(8):1735–1780.

Andrea Horbach, Stefan Thater, Diana Steffen, M. Peter Fischer, Andreas Witt, and Manfred Pinkal. 2015. Internet corpora: A challenge for linguistic processing. *Datenbank-Spektrum* 15(1):41–47.

Tobias Horsmann and Torsten Zesch. 2016. LTL-UDE @ EmpiriST 2015: Tokenization and PoS tagging of social media text. In *Proceedings of the 10th Web as Corpus Workshop (WAC-X) and the EmpiriST Shared Task*. Association for Computational Linguistics, Berlin, pages 120–126.

Bryan Jurish and Kay-Michael Würzner. 2013. Word and Sentence Tokenization with Hidden Markov Models. *JLCL* 28(2):61–83.

Brian King. 2009. *Building and Analysing Corpora of Computer-Mediated Communication*, Continuum, London, volume Contemporary corpus linguistics, pages 301–320.

John D. Lafferty, Andrew McCallum, and Fernando C. N. Pereira. 2001. Conditional random fields: Probabilistic models for segmenting and labeling sequence data. In *Proceedings of the Eighteenth International Conference on Machine Learning*. Morgan Kaufmann Publishers Inc., San Francisco, CA, USA, ICML '01, pages 282–289.

Nikola Ljubešić, Darja Fišer, Tomaž Erjavec, Jaka Čibej, Dafne Marko, Senja Pollak, and Iza Škrjanec. 2015. Predicting the level of text standardness in user-generated content. In *Proceedings of Recent Advances in Natural Language Processing, Hissar, Bulgaria, Sep 7–9 2015.* page 371–378.

Tomas Mikolov, Ilya Sutskever, Kai Chen, Greg S Corrado, and Jeff Dean. 2013. Distributed representations of words and phrases and their compositionality. In *Advances in neural information processing systems.* pages 3111–3119.

Melanie Neunerdt, Bianka Trevisan, Michael Reyer, and Rudolf Mathar. 2013. Part-of-speech tagging for social media texts. In *Proceedings of the 25th Conference of the German Society for Computational Linguistics (GSCL 2013).* pages 139–150.

Olutobi Owoputi, Brendan O'Connor, Chris Dyer, Kevin Gimpel, and Nathan Schneider. 2015. Part-of-speech tagging for Twitter: Word clusters and other advances. Technical report, Technical report, Carnegie Mellon University (CMU-ML-12-107).

Jakob Prange, Andrea Horbach, and Stefan Thater. 2016. UdS-(retrain|distributional|surface): Improving POS tagging for OOV words in German CMC and web data. In *Proceedings of the 10th Web as Corpus Workshop (WAC-X) and the EmpiriST Shared Task.* Association for Computational Linguistics, Berlin, pages 97–105.

Thomas Proisl and Peter Uhrig. 2016. SoMaJo: State-of-the-art tokenization for German web and social media texts. In *Proceedings of the 10th Web as Corpus Workshop (WAC-X) and the EmpiriST Shared Task.* Association for Computational Linguistics, Berlin, pages 91–96.

Lawrence R. Rabiner. 1989. A tutorial on Hidden Markov Models and selected applications in speech recognition. *Proceedings of the IEEE* 77(2):257–286.

Ines Rehbein. 2013. Fine-grained pos tagging of German tweets. In *International Conference of the German Society for Computational Linguistics and Language Technology (GSCL2013), September 25-27, Darmstadt, Germany.*

Ines Rehbein, Emiel Visser, and Nadine Lestmann. 2013. Discussing best practices for the annotation of Twitter microtext. In *Proceedings of The Third Workshop on Annotation of Corpora for Research in the Humanities (ACRH-3).* pages 73–84.

Steffen Remus, Gerold Hintz, Darina Benikova, Thomas Arnold, Judith Eckle-Kohler, Christian M. Meyer, Margot Mieskes, and Chris Biemann. 2016. EmpiriST: AIPHES – robust tokenization and POS-tagging for different genres. In *Proceedings of the 10th Web as Corpus Workshop (WAC-X) and the EmpiriST Shared Task.* Association for Computational Linguistics, Berlin, pages 106–114.

Alan Ritter, Sam Clark, Mausam, and Oren Etzioni. 2011. Named entity recognition in tweets: An experimental study. In *Proceedings of the Conference on Empirical Methods in Natural Language Processing.* Association for Computational Linguistics, Stroudsburg, PA, USA, EMNLP '11, pages 1524–1534.

Jens Runkehl, Peter Schlobinski, and Torsten Siever. 1998. *Sprache und Kommunikation im Internet : Überblick und Analysen.* Westdt. Verl., Opladen [u.a.].

Roland Schäfer. 2015. Processing and querying large web corpora with the COW14 architecture. In Piotr Bański, Hanno Biber, Evelyn Breiteneder, Marc Kupietz, Harald Lüngen, and Andreas Witt, editors, *Proceedings of Challenges in the Management of Large Corpora 3 (CMLC-3).* UCREL, Lancaster, UK.

Roland Schäfer and Felix Bildhauer. 2012. Building large corpora from the web using a new efficient tool chain. In *Proceedings of the Eighth International Conference on Language Resources and Evaluation (LREC '12).* ELRA, Istanbul, Turkey, pages 486–493.

Anne Schiller, Simone Teufel, and Christine Stöckert. 1999. Guidelines für das Tagging deutscher Textcorpora mit STTS (Kleines und großes Tagset). University of Stuttgart: Institut für maschinelle Sprachverarbeitung.

Helmut Schmid. 1995. Improvements in part-of-speech tagging with an application to German. In *Proceedings of the ACL SIGDAT Workshop.*

Egon Stemle. 2016. bot.zen @ EmpiriST 2015 – a minimally-deep learning PoS-tagger (trained for German CMC and web data). In *Proceedings of the 10th Web as Corpus Workshop (WAC-X) and the EmpiriST Shared Task*. Association for Computational Linguistics, Berlin, pages 115–119.

Angelika Storrer. 2001. *Getippte Gespräche oder dialogische Texte? Zur kommunikationstheoretischen Einordnung der Chat-Kommunikation*, Walter de Gruyter, Berlin, New York, volume Sprache im Alltag. Beiträge zu neuen Perspektiven in der Linguistik. Herbert Ernst Wiegand zum 65. Geburtstag gewidmet, page 439–465.

Kristina Toutanova, Dan Klein, Christopher D. Manning, and Yoram Singer. 2003. Feature-rich part-of-speech tagging with a cyclic dependency network. In *Proceedings of the 2003 Human Language Technology Conference of the North American Chapter of the Association for Computational Linguistics*.

Swantje Westpfahl. 2013. STTS 2.0? Improving the tagset for the part-of-speech-tagging of German spoken data. In Manfred Levin, Lori und Stede, editor, *Proceedings of LAW VIII – The 8th Linguistic Annotation Workshop. Dublin, Ireland: Association for Computational Linguistics and Dublin City University*. Association for Computational Linguistics and Dublin City University, pages 1–10.

Swantje Westpfahl and Thomas Schmidt. 2013. Pos für(s) FOLK – Part of Speech Tagging des Forschungs- und Lehrkorpus Gesprochenes Deutsch. *Journal for Language Technology and Computational Linguistics* 28(1):139–153.

Heike Zinsmeister, Ulrich Heid, and Kathrin Beck. 2013. Das Stuttgart-Tübingen Wortarten-Tagset - Stand und Perspektiven. *Special Journal for Language Technology and Computational Linguistics* 28(1).

Heike Zinsmeister, Ulrich Heid, and Kathrin Beck. 2014. Adapting a part-of-speech tagset to non-standard text: The case of STTS. In *Proceedings of the Ninth International Conference on Language Resources and Evaluation (LREC'14)*. LREC 2014, pages 4097–4104.

SoMaJo: State-of-the-art tokenization for German web and social media texts

Thomas Proisl
FAU Erlangen-Nürnberg
Professur für Korpuslinguistik
Bismarckstr. 6
91054 Erlangen, Germany
thomas.proisl@fau.de

Peter Uhrig
FAU Erlangen-Nürnberg
Lehrstuhl für Anglistik, insbesondere Linguistik
Bismarckstr. 1
91054 Erlangen, Germany
peter.uhrig@fau.de

Abstract

In this paper we describe SoMaJo, a rule-based tokenizer for German web and social media texts that was the best-performing system in the EmpiriST 2015 shared task with an average F_1-score of 99.57. We give an overview of the system and the phenomena its rules cover, as well as a detailed error analysis. The tokenizer is available as free software.

1 Introduction

At first sight, tokenization is not only boring but also trivial. Humans have few problems with this task for at least two reasons: (1) They are experts at pattern-finding (see, for example, Tomasello, 2003). Thus, whether the form "your" in an English Facebook post is to be read as one unit (the possessive determiner) or as two (a common misspelling of "you're"), usually causes less problems due to the highly disambiguating grammatical context. (2) They are happy to accept meaningful units without having to determine the exact number of units. While most tokenization guidelines force us to treat "ice cream" as two tokens and "ice-cream" as one token, there often is no difference to native speakers – though it is possible to predict the spelling to some extent based on linguistic context, frequency, etc. (cf. Sanchez-Stockhammer, in preparation).

However, given the layered approach typically taken by NLP pipelines, no analysis of the grammatical context is available at the time when tokenization takes place since tokenization is one of the first steps in an NLP text processing pipeline, often only preceded by sentence splitting.[1] However,

tokenization is not fully independent of sentence splitting due to the ambiguity of some punctuation marks, most notoriously the baseline dot, which can for instance occur as (1) period/full stop to mark the end of a sentence, (2) marker of abbreviated forms, (3) decimal mark separating the integer from the fractional part of a number, (4) separator of host name, subdomain, domain, top-level domain in Internet addresses, (5) part of a so-called horizontal ellipsis ("..."). When all these restrictions are in place, tokenization immediately becomes more challenging as a task, also for humans. Thus whether the string "No." should be treated as one token or as two is impossible to decide out of context, since it could be a short answer to a question ("Would you like to join us for lunch?" – "No.") or it can be an abbreviation for "number" ("No. 6"). In the former case, tokenization should identify two tokens, in the latter only one. Thus the challenge for any tokenizer is to make use of the linguistic context to disambiguate potentially ambiguous forms even though no higher-level grammatical analysis (i.e. PoS-tagging, lemmatization or even syntactic or semantic analysis) is available. In a way, some of the work done by these high-level tools is thus duplicated in the tokenizer, e.g. identifying numbers, identifying punctuation, identifying proper names (in English) or nouns in general (in German) based on capitalization, where necessary for the tokenization.

Of course, an extremely large proportion of tokenization is indeed straightforward. A simple split on white space and common punctuation marks will result in an average F_1-score of 96.73 on the test data set used for the present task (cf. Section 4). However, the amount of work that is required to get closer to 100% is inversely proportional to the effect size of the improvements that can be achieved, which means that the bulk of this paper is devoted to the remaining 3.27%.

---

[1] In order to arrive at a sensible text corpus, there may of course be other preprocessing steps involved, such as boilerplate removal or duplicate detection.

57

Proceedings of the 10th Web as Corpus Workshop (WAC-X) and the EmpiriST Shared Task, pages 57–62,
Berlin, Germany, August 7-12, 2016. ©2016 Association for Computational Linguistics

The EmpiriST 2015 shared task on automatic linguistic annotation of computer-mediated communication / social media (Beißwenger et al., 2016) consists of two subtasks that deal with NLP for web and social media texts: (1) Tokenization and (2) part-of-speech tagging. We participated in the first subtask and developed a rule-based tokenizer that implements the EmpiriST 2015 tokenization guidelines (Beißwenger et al., 2015; EmpiriST team, 2015). Our system, SoMaJo, won the shared task and is freely available from PyPI, the Python Package Index.[2]

2 Related work

The most widespread approach to tokenization is probably the application of substitutions based on regular expressions, as examplified by the simple sed script for Penn-Treebank-style tokenization.[3] Typically, every piece of software that relies on tokenized input ships with its own tokenizer (usually rule-based), e. g. TreeTagger (Schmid, 1994; Schmid, 1995) or the Stanford Parser (Klein and Manning, 2003). There are, however, also systems that use supervised or unsupervised machine learning techniques, e. g. the maximum entropy tokenizer offered by the Apache OpenNLP project[4] or the HMM-based one presented by Jurish and Würzner (2013). For an overview of existing approaches to tokenization (and the related task of sentence splitting), see Jurish and Würzner (2013).

3 System description

3.1 General approach

SoMaJo is a rule-based tokenizer that applies a cascade of regular expressions to the input text to arrive at a tokenized version. In that process, recognized tokens that could be "problematic" further down the rule chain are replaced with unique pseudotokens. The major reason for why tokens could be problematic for subsequent rules is that they can contain certain characters that trigger those rules. URLs, for example, should be treated as single tokens and should not be split at dots, hyphens, slashes, etc. After all the rules have been applied, the original tokens are restored from the pseudotokens. Additionally, SoMaJo can output the token

class for each token, e. g. if it is a number, an XML tag, an abbreviation, etc.

3.2 Specifics

In this subsection, we will give a high-level overview of the most important rules, in the order in which they are applied. The ultimate reference to what the tokenizer does is of course its freely available source code.

- The identification of **XML tags** was performed with a regular expression taken from Goyvaerts (2012). XML tags are special because they are among the few tokens that can contain spaces. Spaces are normally unambiguous token delimiters, therefore we want to deal with XML tags as early as possible. Since there is no syntax check, non-XML conforming standalone tags without trailing slash, eg. "<br>" as used in traditional HTML/SGML will also be detected. Attributes without quotation marks – as allowed in SGML – are not covered.
- The regular expression for **email addresses** is a revised version of the pattern given in Goyvaerts (2012) available from Goyvaerts website,[5] where he claims that it covers "99% of the email addresses in use today". As discussed in Section 4.4, email address obfuscation was not taken into consideration in the original system, but a basic detection has now been incorporated for the release.
- The detection of **URLs** that include the protocol used is relatively straightforward. Our system currently detects "http", "https", "ftp", "svn", "doi" and treats strings with a leading "www." the same, even though it is not technically a protocol.

  URLs without a protocol and the "www" giveaway are detected based on a very conservative list of top-level-domains in order to minimize false positives that could occur when spaces at the end of a sentence are omitted, which often occurs in CMC, particularly in restricted-length messages such as the Twitter messages given in the training and test data. A small list of three-letter file extensions was also added to detect **file names** with internal dots.

- For **emoticons** it was possible to build on top of a list taken from the SentiKLUE polarity classifier (Proisl et al., 2013; Evert et al., 2014), which was extended based on websites with technology-mediated communication such as *Chat von gestern Nacht*[6] and complemented by a generic regular expression to account for further emoticons consisting of eyes, optional nose and/or tear and mouth.

- Further phenomena that are specific to **Twitter and chat** are also identified with relatively simple regular expressions and treated according to the tokenization guidelines. These include mentions ("@MimiSchmitz"), hashtags ("#lyrik") and actions words ("*kopfkratz*").

- In order to be able to distinguish between ad-hoc **combinations with plus signs ("+") or ampersands ("&")** such as "Thomas&Peter", and institutionalized combinations such as "Taylor&Francis", a lexicon of the latter was constructed based on a manually curated list of all Wikipedia page titles in the German Wikipedia that contain a plus sign and/or an ampersand, which results in a total of 643 items.

- Items written in **CamelCase**, i. e. single orthographic words with internal capitalization ("deineMutter"), had to be split up according to the tokenization guidelines unless they were proper names ("MySpace") or textual representations of emojis ("emojiQcatFaceWithWrySmile"). In order to distinguish the two cases, a lexicon of potential proper names (in a broad sense) and established forms was created based on a list of all words in Wikipedia page titles in the German Wikipedia that include an internal upper-case letter following at least one lower-case letter. The lexicon comprises 7,005 such items.

  However, the splitting of CamelCase can be switched off in our system since the behaviour propagated by the tokenization guidelines is in fact highly problematic in unstriced input. Thus CamelCase is used in certain wikis, in particular the original wiki software Wiki Wiki Web by Ward Cunningham[7] to create links to other pages and it is often found in naming conventions of programming languages such as Java or C#. So

if the input to tokenize contains computer-mediated communication from sources such as stackoverflow.com, it would be advisable to switch CamelCase splitting off. Furthermore, CamelCase splitting makes corpora useless for reasearch on non-standard graphemics.

An exception was also made for the German internal *I* as in "StudentInnen", which is never split up. URLs written in CamelCase, e. g. "ImmobilienScout24.de", are already recognized as a single token by the earlier rule identifying URLs.

- According to the tokenization guidelines, **abbreviations** representing multiple tokens (e. g. "d. h." for "das heißt") have to be split up unless they are established netspeak units such as "aka" or "cu". Thus three cases have to be distinguished: (1) Abbreviations that do not consist exclusively of single letters followed by a full stop have to be listed in a lexicon in order to not mistake them for sentence boundaries. For this, all 4,027 abbreviations listed in the German Wiktionary[8] on 10 February 2016 were downloaded and then manually checked for candidates that represented a single token (and did so unambiguously), which resulted in a total of 1,104 such abbreviations (e. g. "altröm" for "altrömisch"). (2) A further list of 29 multi-dot abbreviations that represent single tokens was created – 8 from the training data and the tokenization guidelines, 21 from the Wiktionary list of abbreviations mentioned above (e. g. "Dipl.-Ing." for "Diplomingenieur"). (3) A single letter followed by a full stop was always treated as an abbreviation, so single letters at the end of a sentence ("Ich kaufe ein E.") will be analysed erroneously. However, since such occurrences are rather rare, the decision to treat them as abbreviations will definitely lead to higher recognition rates.

- **Dates** had to be split up according to the tokenization guidelines so that day, month and year are treated as separate tokens. The matter is complicated by the fact that separators have to be in the same token as day or month ("05/15/2016" is tokenized as "05/ 15/ 2016" but "2016-05-15" is tokenized as "2016 -05 -15"), so mutliple regular expressions were needed to account for all typical cases.

[6]http://www.chatvongesternnacht.de
[7]http://c2.com/cgi/wiki?WikiWikiWeb

[8]https://de.wiktionary.org/

- Other combinations with **numbers** closely follow the tokenization guidelines, so indications of time (e. g. "12:30"), ordinal numbers and fractions are treated as one token as long as there is no space intervening.

  To be able to split numbers from their unit of measurement (e. g. "80kg"), a list of such units was compiled manually which is certainly far from complete and would need to be expanded particularly if CMC data from science domains is to be processed.

  Cardinal numbers were matched with both a dot or a comma as decimal mark since in CMC, the English format can often be found in German texts, despite the comma being the standard. Our number identifier further allows for signed and unsigned numbers and an optional exponent.

- Our treatment of **punctuation** is fairly standard. We allow for arbitrary combinations of question and exclamation marks, detect arrows, various styles of parentheses, quotation marks (including Unicode quotation marks and LaTeX-style quoation marks using backticks and apostrophes), ellipses (both as combinations of dots and as Unicode entities) and of course standard full stops.

4 Results and error analysis

4.1 Evaluation metrics

The performance of the systems participating in the shared task was evaluated using precision, recall and F_1-score (Jurish and Würzner, 2013, 72–73). These measures are based on the actual token boundaries (B_{actual}), i. e. the token boundaries in the gold standard, and the token boundaries identified by the system ($B_{\text{identified}}$). Correctly detected token boundaries that are both in the system output and in the gold standard are true positives, erroneously introduced token boundaries that are not in the gold standard are false positives and token boundaries in the gold standard that the system fails to detect are false negatives:

$$\text{tp} = |B_{\text{actual}} \cap B_{\text{identified}}|$$

$$\text{fp} = |B_{\text{identified}} \setminus B_{\text{actual}}|$$

$$\text{fn} = |B_{\text{actual}} \setminus B_{\text{identified}}|$$

Precision measures how many of the token boundaries that the system has detected are true token boundaries, recall measures how many of the true token boundaries have been found and the F_1-score is the harmonic mean of precision and recall:[9]

$$\text{precision} = \frac{|B_{\text{actual}} \cap B_{\text{identified}}|}{|B_{\text{identified}}|} = \frac{\text{tp}}{\text{tp} + \text{fp}}$$

$$\text{recall} = \frac{|B_{\text{actual}} \cap B_{\text{identified}}|}{|B_{\text{actual}}|} = \frac{\text{tp}}{\text{tp} + \text{fn}}$$

$$F_1 = \frac{2 \cdot \text{precision} \cdot \text{recall}}{\text{precision} + \text{recall}}$$

The ranking of the participating systems was based on macro-averaged F_1-scores, i. e. the arithmetic mean of the F_1-scores for the two datasets.

4.2 Ad-hoc baseline

As mentioned in Section 1, tokenization is not usually regarded as a terribly hard problem and depending on the task at hand, ad-hoc solutions centered around simple regular expressions often yield sufficiently good results. Therefore, we will use such a primitive ad-hoc tokenizer as a baseline. This simple tokenizer is a sed one-liner that ignores lines that look like they consist of an XML tag (because such lines are not part of the evaluation) and introduces token boundaries at whitespace and a couple of common punctuation symbols:

```
sed -re "/^<[^>]+>$/! {
    s/([.!?,;:+*()\"'-])/ \1 /g;
    s/\s+/\n/g }"
```

4.3 Results

Results for the baseline tokenizer, our submitted system and a revised version of our system fixing some of the most frequent types of errors (cf. next section) are summarized in Table 1.

For the CMC dataset with samples from different CMC genres, the submitted systems have F_1-scores ranging from 97.83 to 99.54, clearly outperforming the baseline tokenizer's F_1-score of 94.91. Our system outperformed all others with an F_1-score of 99.54 and a lead of 0.58 to the second-ranked system.

For the web corpus dataset with samples from text genres on the web, the F_1-scores of the submitted systems range from 99.39 to 99.77, still outperforming the baseline's 98.55 but by a much smaller margin. Our system ranks third with an F_1-score of 99.60 and a difference of 0.17 to the best-performing system.

---

[9]Note that the precision, recall and F_1-scores reported in this paper are all multiplied by 100 for better readability.

| | CMC | | | Web corpora | | | macro average |
	P	R	F	P	R	F	F
baseline	91.84	98.20	94.91	98.27	98.84	98.55	96.73
submission	99.52	99.56	99.54	99.57	99.64	99.60	99.57
revised	99.62	99.56	99.59	99.83	99.92	99.87	99.73

Table 1: Results

The averaged F_1-scores of the participating systems range from 98.61 to 99.57, with our submission leading the field by a 0.21 margin.

With some of the major remaining error sources fixed, the revised version of our system would also rank first on the web corpus dataset with an F_1-score of 99.87.

4.4 Error analysis

The submitted version of our system had 25 false positives and 23 false negatives in the CMC dataset and 33 false positives and 27 false negatives in the web corpus dataset. In the remainder of this section we will have a closer look at these errors, categorize them and fix the obvious ones. Results for the revised version of our system have been given in Section 4.3.

- 6 false positives and 3 false negatives are due to tokenization errors in the gold standard data. These errors have been pointed out to the task organizers and will be corrected in the next release of the data.
- 21 false negatives are due to our system not being aware of the en dash (–) that is used for example as *Streckenstrich* in "Herford–Lage–Detmold–Altenbeken–Paderborn".
- Our system was also not aware of file names containing slashes (/), which results in 8 false positives.
- Email address obfuscation using, for example, "[at]" and "[dot]" instead of the at (@) and dot (.) characters accounts for 8 false positives.
- 7 false positives are due to emoticons not in our lexicon (":!:", ":p" and ":;-))").
- The list of tokens containing an ampersand (&) was accidentally used case sensitively, resulting in 2 false positives.
- In some cases, a hyphen (-) is used as a *Bis-Strich* to indicate a range instead of the typographically correct en dash (–). This accounts for 12 false negatives and is difficult to fix since hyphens are normally used in compounds (*Bindestrichkomposita*) that should not be split up.
- 9 false positives are due to abbreviations that could also be words, e. g. "automat." or "zum."
- The ambiguity between a cardinal number at the end of a sentence and an ordinal number accounts for 3 false positives and 1 false negative.
- 5 false negatives and 7 false positives are due to tokens written without spaces between them and follow-up errors.
- Citations, e. g. "Storrer2007", are responsible for 2 false negatives and are difficult to distinguish from proper names like "Blume2000".
- Sometimes, two consecutive years are given as "1829/30" or "2009/2010". This accounts for 6 false negatives and is potentially problematic because of the ambiguity with fractions (that are single tokens) and term specifications like "WS05/06" that are tokenized as "WS 05/06", i. e. the two consecutive years are a single token.
- The remaining 8 false positives are due to other rare and unsystematic problems.

5 Conclusion

Tokenization is clearly one of the easier NLP problems, as should be obvious from the fairly good results that can be achieved even with the most primitive methods. Improving upon that baseline takes considerably more effort, however.

In this paper we presented SoMaJo, a rule-based tokenizer that won the EmpiriST 2015 shared task on automatic linguistic annotation of computer-mediated communication / social media. Since it is a rule-based system it is easy to maintain and adapt. Thanks to this flexibility it was easy to create a revised version of the system that incorporates insights from the error analysis and achieves even better results.

References

Michael Beißwenger, Sabine Bartsch, Stefan Evert, and Kay-Michael Würzner. 2015. Richtlinie für die manuelle Tokenisierung von Sprachdaten aus Genres internetbasierter Kommunikation. Guideline document from the Empirikom shared task on automatic linguistic annotation of internet-based communication (EmpiriST 2015). `https://sites.google.com/site/empirist2015/`.

Michael Beißwenger, Sabine Bartsch, Stefan Evert, and Kay-Michael Würzner. 2016. EmpiriST 2015: A shared task on the automatic linguistic annotation of computer-mediated communication, social media and web corpora. In *Proceedings of the 10th Web as Corpus Workshop (WAC-X)*, Berlin, Germany.

EmpiriST team. 2015. Ergänzungsdokument zu den Annotationsrichtlinien. Additional instructions and examples for selected PoS categories and tricky phenomena in CMC and social media data. `https://sites.google.com/site/empirist2015/`.

Stefan Evert, Thomas Proisl, Paul Greiner, and Besim Kabashi. 2014. SentiKLUE: Updating a polarity classifier in 48 hours. In *Proceedings of the 8th International Workshop on Semantic Evaluation (SemEval 2014)*, pages 551–555. ACL.

Jan Goyvaerts. 2012. *Regular Expressions Cookbook*. O'Reilly, Sebastopol, CA, 2nd edition.

Bryan Jurish and Kay-Michael Würzner. 2013. Word and sentence tokenization with Hidden Markov Models. *JLCL*, 28(2):61–83.

Dan Klein and Christopher D. Manning. 2003. Accurate unlexicalized parsing. In *Proceedings of the 41st Annual Meeting of the Association for Computational Linguistics*, pages 423–430.

Thomas Proisl, Paul Greiner, Stefan Evert, and Besim Kabashi. 2013. KLUE: Simple and robust methods for polarity classification. In *Proceedings of the 7th International Workshop on Semantic Evaluation (SemEval 2013)*, pages 395–401. ACL.

Christina Sanchez-Stockhammer. In preparation. *Determinants of English Compound Spelling*.

Helmut Schmid. 1994. Probabilistic part-of-speech tagging using decision trees. In *Proceedings of the International Conference on New Methods in Language Processing*, pages 44–49.

Helmut Schmid. 1995. Improvements in part-of-speech tagging with an application to German. In *Proceedings of the EACL SIGDAT-Workshop*, pages 47–50, Dublin.

Michael Tomasello. 2003. *Constructing a Language: A Usage-Based Theory of Language Acquisition*. Harvard University Press, Cambridge, MA.

UdS-(retrain|distributional|surface): Improving POS Tagging for OOV Words in German CMC and Web Data

Jakob Prange, Andrea Horbach, Stefan Thater
Department of Computational Linguistics
Saarland University
Saarbrücken Germany
`(jprange|andrea|stth)@coli.uni-saarland.de`

Abstract

We present in this paper our three system submissions for the POS tagging subtask of the Empirist Shared Task: Our baseline system *UdS-retrain* extends a standard training dataset with in-domain training data; *UdS-distributional* and *UdS-surface* add two different ways of handling OOV words on top of the baseline system by using either distributional information or a combination of surface similarity and language model information. We reach the best performance using the distributional model.

1 Introduction

Part-of-speech (POS) tagging is a fundamental sub-task in many linguistic tool-chains that provides necessary information for subsequent analysis steps such as lemmatization or syntactic parsing. Most recent approaches to POS tagging use statistical techniques and can provide excellent results – as long as the tagger is applied to the same kind of text it has been trained on. When applied out-of-domain, results tend to be significantly worse. This problem is particularly pronounced in the case of data from the domain of computer-mediated communication (CMC) such as posts in Internet fora or micro-posts from Twitter. POS taggers are usually trained on newspaper articles or other edited texts from professional writers, while CMC data often deviates on the lexical, orthographic (e.g., spelling errors, non-capitalization of German nouns) and grammatical level (e.g., sentences without subjects) and contains phenomena such as emoticons or action words that are not covered by standard POS tagsets (Bartz et al., 2014).

This paper describes our contribution to the Em-piriST 2015 Shared Task "Automatic Linguistic Annotation of Computer-Mediated Communica-tion/Social Media" where we participated in the subtask of adapting POS taggers to German CMC and Web data. All three of our submitted systems are at least partially based on a previous tagging system, that we developed in the BMBF funded project "Analyse und Instrumentarien zur Beobach-tung des Schreibgebrauchs im Deutschen."[1] We have shown that out-of-vocabulary (OOV) words are particularly problematic when a standard tagger is applied to out-of-domain CMC data. Therefore, our previous system focuses on OOV words in two ways: First, tagger accuracy can be improved sub-stantially by adding relatively small amounts of manually annotated in-domain (CMC) data to a standard training set (Horbach et al., 2014). This method is used in our *retrain* system that we con-sider as a baseline. A further, smaller but still significant improvement can be obtained by using an additional component based on distributional models (Prange et al., 2015) that predicts possible POS tags of words which are still OOV under the retrained model.

For the shared task, we modify our system in two ways: First, the annotation guidelines under-lying the training data used in our previous work differ in some details from the guidelines of the shared task. We re-annotate our previous training data to match the new annotation guidelines and use it in addition to the training data provided by the shared task. Second, we experiment with two different components for predicting POS tags of OOV words.

These experiments resulted in three individual systems: *UdS-retrain* uses different versions of ad-ditional in-domain training data to retrain a POS tagger and constitutes the basis tagger for the other two systems. *UdS-distributional* adds a compo-nent to predict the POS tag for OOV words based

---

[1] www.schreibgebrauch.de

Proceedings of the 10th Web as Corpus Workshop (WAC-X) and the EmpiriST Shared Task, pages 63–71,
Berlin, Germany, August 7-12, 2016. ©2016 Association for Computational Linguistics

on distributional information similar to (Prange et al., 2015); *UdS-surface* uses a combination of surface similarity and language model perplexity to normalize OOV words in a preprocessing step.

Almost all of our system configurations outperform a baseline trained on the TIGER corpus (Brants et al., 2004) alone on both datasets (with the exception of surface run 1 on Web); the improvement is especially pronounced on the CMC subcorpus. We achieve the best results on both corpora with the distributional system (87.33% on CMC and 93.55% on Web). An oracle experiment shows that the different models do not subsume each other and perform differently so that there might be room for further benefits through model combinations.

The plan for the paper continues as follows: We give a short overview of our previous work in Section 2 and describe the various data and tagsets used in our experiments in Section 3. We describe the architecture of our three systems in Section 4 and provide our results in Section 5. Section 6 provides additional analyses and experiments to better understand our results. We conclude in Section 7.

2   Our Previous Work

In previous work, we experimented with various ways to adapt statistical POS taggers to German CMC data. This section briefly summarizes the approach by Prange et al. (2015), as it was the basis for our distributional system and conceptually also inspired the surface system. It uses the *HunPos* tagger (Halácsy et al., 2007) and combines two approaches to adapt it to German CMC data.

In a first step, the tagger is (re-)trained on data which combines the standard TIGER corpus (Brants et al., 2004) with manually annotated in-domain CMC data, the *Schreibgebrauch* dataset (Horbach et al., 2015). This in-domain data was collected from forum posts of a German online cooking community (*www.chefkoch.de*), the *Dortmunder Chat-Korpus* (Beißwenger, 2013) and microposts from Twitter.[2] In total, the dataset contains approx. 34 000 tokens and has been independently annotated by three trained undergraduate students of computational linguistics using an extension of a preliminary version of the "STTS 2.0" tagset proposed by Bartz et al. (2014): Our original motivation for adapting POS taggers was to support

the monitoring of German orthography; therefore, we added two additional POS tags for cases where the author incorrectly wrote two words as a single token (ERRTOK) or incorrectly separated a single word into two tokens (ERRAW).

Tagging accurracy is increased substantially (+11% on chat data) when using the annotated in-domain data as additional training data (Horbach et al., 2015). A major reason for this is that the original tagger performs relatively poorly on OOV words, and adding in-domain data to the training set decreases the amount of OOV tokens. Yet, a substantial amount of OOV tokens remains even after re-training the tagger.

Prange et al. (2015) therefore use a second component that aims at learning candidate POS tags for OOV tokens. The two key observations underlying this second component are that (i) in-vocabulary (IV) words are tagged with high accurracy and (ii) distributionally similar words tend to belong to the same lexical class and thus have the same POS label. We tagged the complete *chefkoch* dataset and trained a distributional model on the automatically annotated dataset. For each OOV word, we compute the 20 most similar in-vocabulary words, which by assumption carry reliable POS information. This candidate set is then ranked using a combination of different string similarity measures and the POS tags of the words in the candidate set are propagated to the OOV word. This results in a POS lexicon for OOV tokens, which can be directly applied to the *HunPos* tagger to guide the search process during tagging.

3   Data and Tagset

As do potentially most other participating systems we use the TIGER corpus (Brants et al., 2004) as one of the standard corpora for the task of German POS tagging as a basis, and make use of the training data provided by the shared task (*EmpiriST train*); additionally, we also use the Schreibgebrauch dataset. In contrast to previous approaches on this dataset, we use both the training and the test section for training. Table 1 shows the size and composition of all datasets.

The standard tagset for German POS tagging (here referred to as STTS 1.0) (Schiller et al., 1999) has been extended recently to account for phenomena not present in standard newswire text. The EmpiriST Shared Task datasets are annotated with a version of the STTS 2.0 tagset (Beißwenger et

---

[2] The dataset is available at http://www.coli.uni-saarland.de/projects/schreibgebrauch/

Dataset	Appr. size (in tokens)	Domain	Tagset
TIGER	900 000	newspaper text	STTS 1.0
EmpiriST-train CMC	5 000	Chat, Twitter, Wikipedia talk, blog comments, whatsapp	STTS 2.0
EmpiriST-train Web	5 000	monologic Internet texts	STTS 2.0
Schreibgebrauch	34 000	Forum, Chat, Twitter	STTS 2.0* & STTS 2.0

Table 1: Datasets used in our models

al., 2015) that differs slightly from the tagset used in our previous studies to annotate the *Schreibgebrauch* corpus (we call it STTS 2.0* here to distinguish it from the shared task tagset). Since we want to use both datasets to re-train the tagger, we re-annotated (in part automatically) our Schreibgebrauch corpus as follows:

- Certain particles in conceptually oral utterances that had been tagged as adverbs ADV in our data received their own tags in the EmpiriST datasets as 1) intensifier, focus and gradation particles (PTKIFG), 2) modal and downtoner particles (PTKMA) or 3) particles as part of multi-word lexemes (PTKMWL). We manually re-examined the Schreibgebrauch annotations of adverbs and adapted the tag where necessary.

- Action words like *freu* are annotated with the tag AKW in the EmpiriST data, while the Schreibgebrauch corpus uses AW. Also, the "*" which is often used to indicate an action word is taken to be part of the action word in the EmpiriST datasets, while it is a separate token in the Schreibgebrauch corpus (*/AWIND breit/ADJD grins/AW */AWIND). We automatically changed AW to AKW and replaced AWIND by $((*/$(freu/AKW */$().

- The EmpiriST datasets distinguish between ASCII emoticons and emoticons represented as images, while the Schreibgebrauch corpus tags all emoticons as EMOASC even if they are represented as images. Also, the dataset uses the standard PAV instead of the tag PROAV as used in the TIGER corpus and our annotations. We used a simple regular expression to automatically identify image emoticons in the Schreibgebrauch corpus and re-annotated them as EMOIMG, and replaced PROAV by PAV.

- The Schreibgebrauch corpus uses two tags to annotate tokens which are incorrectly tokenized by the author. In cases where a word like "Umkleidekabinen" is incorrectly split into two tokens by the author ("Umkleide Kabinen"), the first token is tagged as ERRAW. In cases where two separate words are incorrectly written as a single token ("alldas"), the token is annotated as ERRTOK. Instances of ERRTOK are automatically re-tagged as XY and all tokens tagged as ERRAW were removed following the observation that these tokens are mainly premodifiers.

Since tokens which need to be re-annotated as a disourse marker DM cannot be identified systematically using simple regular expressions, we checked and re-annotated only occurrences of ADV and KOUS. We did not (re-)annotate EMLs; we conjecture that they do not occur in our data.

4 Our Systems

We entered three different systems into the competition that tackle the tagging problem in different ways: a simple retraining approach (UdS-retrain), which enriches a standard training set with additional in-domain training data and is used as a baseline; and two systems that additionally target specifically OOV words: a distributional approach that exploits the observation that similar words tend to have the same POS tag (UdS-distributional) and an approach based on surface similarity that aims at detecting and correcting potential spelling mistakes (UdS-surface). We also compare our models against another baseline that is trained on the TIGER corpus only. In all of our systems, we use the *HunPos* tagger (Halácsy et al., 2007).

4.1 UdS-retrain

Following previous work (Horbach et al., 2014; Kübler and Baucom, 2011), we adapt the tagger by retraining it on a dataset that combines the standard

corpus	run1	run2	run3	run4
TIGER	✓	✓	✓	✓
EMPIRIST - same domain	✓	✓	✓	✓
EMPIRIST - other domain			✓	✓
Schreibgebrauch - original	✓			
Schreibgebrauch - adapted			✓	✓

Table 2: Training corpora for each of our system runs

TIGER corpus with additional in-domain data: the *Schreibgebrauch* corpus and the shared task training sets.

Since the annotated in-domain training data is very small compared to the size of the TIGER corpus, we boost the in-domain data by adding it 5 times to give it more weight. Furthermore, we duplicated the TIGER corpus and used both the original version as well as a version obtained by automatically converting it to the new German orthography, to account for the fact that writers in German CMC data might be using both the old and the new German orthography.

We submitted runs for three different configurations of the UdS-retrain system, depending on the corpora used to train the model:

- **run 1** uses a model trained on TIGER, the EmpiriST training data for the specific subcorpus (CMC and Web) and the original *Schreibgebrauch* training data without any tagset adaptations.

- **run 2** is like run 1, but uses a version of the *Schreibgebrauch* training data adapted to the STTS 2.0 version used in the shared task datasets.

- **run 3** is like run 2, but uses both the CMC and web training data sets, independent of the text type the model is applied to.

4.2 UdS-distributional

This system closely follows Prange et al. (2015). As described above in Section 2, the system induces a POS lexicon that lists suitable POS tags for OOV words, i.e., words that do not occur in the training data. This POS lexicon is used by the *HunPos* tagger to limit the search space when the tagger sees an OOV word.

We use the UdS-retrain model (run-2) to tag about half a billion tokens from the German online cooking platform *www.chefkoch.de* and train a distributional model that uses POS 5-grams as features, weighted using pointwise mutual information (PMI). This distributional model is used to find, for each OOV word in the test set, the 20 distributionally most similar IV words. From this candidate set, we extract one or more POS tags and store them in the POS lexicon as possible tags of the OOV word.

We submitted three system runs, that differ in how the POS tags to be added to the POS lexicon are selected:

- **run 1:** The distributional model returns a list of the distributionally most similar words together with their POS tag. The tags are then ranked using different ranking algorithms based on surface similarity between the original words and its distributional neighbours (Levenshtein and 2 variants of Jaro-Winkler distance) and the position and frequency of each POS tag in the list (ranking by frequency, ratio between frequency and first position in the list, sum of inverse ranks at which a tag occurs). Each ranker contributes one top-ranked POS tag, among which we take a majority vote.

- **run 2:** This setting is a variant of the one above, where we use up to three POS tags from the list of top-ranked tags proposed by the different rankers: If the list contains at least three tags and the most frequent tag occurs less than 4 times in the candidate list, we also include the second most frequent tag in the POS lexicon. If the list contains 4 or more entries, we also include the third best entry. In doing so, we treat the frequency of each tag in the list as a confidence threshold and include more candidates if our confidence in the best one is low.

- **run 3:** the best-performing configuration from (Prange et al., 2015), where we linearly combine the two best-performing rankers from run-1: Levenhstein distance and the frequency-position-ratio.

4.3 UdS-surface

This approach explores an alternative to the distributional model; like the former, it explicitly addresses OOV words. In contrast to the former, however, we rely here on the assumption that many OOV words are spelling errors (or voluntary misspellings) that are on the surface very similar to the word they stand for, similar to approaches by Han et al. (2012) and Gadde et al. (2011). In this approach, we first filter the OOV words that are likely to be typos and then rank their potential replacements using language models. We thus construct a normalized version of the sentence and feed it to the tagger.

In order to make sure that we select primarily such candidates for normalization that are indeed misspellings and not just words unknown to the tagger, we use the spellchecker *aspell* in its standard configuration to identify words that are likely misspellings (in contrast to known words or words for which aspell has no suggestions for corrections). For these words we collected lists of potential replacements candidates in three different ways (described below). We then use a language model using the SRILM toolkit (Stolcke, 2002) built on raw texts from *www.chefkoch.de*, rank the different versions for each sentence and select the one with the lowest perplexity.

We tested the following three configurations of the system.

- **run 1:** We use a variant of Jaro-Winkler similarity[3] and consider only replacement candidates from the annotated training data with a surface similarity above a certain threshold. In the first run we set the threshold to 0.8.

- **run 2:** In the second run, we use a more restrictive threshold and only select tokens with a similarity above 0.95.

- **run 3:** In this setting we only select the candidates with the highest similarity (several if they have the same similarity score).

5 Shared Task Results

This section presents the results for our submitted runs.

5.1 Shared task runs

Table 3 shows that all of our systems' configurations clearly outperform the baseline for both CMC

---

³Standard Jaro-Winkler uses the length of common prefixes to compute a similarity score; we also consider a variant that uses common suffixes instead, with the idea that a shared suffix might indicate the same POS tag

Run	CMC	Web
TIGER baseline	71.15	91.19
UdS-retrain 1	85.48	92.71
UdS-retrain 2	86.40	92.79
UdS-retrain 3	86.43	92.71
UdS-distributional 1	87.26	93.51
UdS-distributional 2	87.33	93.55
UdS-distributional 3	87.29	93.01
UdS-surface 1	84.58	91.19
UdS-surface 2	86.45	92.43
UdS-surface 3	85.36	92.01

Table 3: Evaluation results of our system runs

and Web corpora ($\alpha < 0.001$ according to a McNemar test), except for surface run 1; the distributional model works best for both subcorpora. This is plausible, given that the model builds on UdS-retrain as its baseline and has – compared to UdS-surface – a more unbiased approach towards OOV words; it does not expect them to be necessarily typos. The model can find replacements whenever an OOV word is frequent enough in the large background corpus for the model. Within the three variants of our distributional models, we see very little variance in performance.

For the retraining approach, we can see that the adaptation of our project corpus to the new tagset gives a performance boost of about 1 percent for the CMC dataset (statistically significant, $\alpha < 0.001$), but not for the Web corpora. This is not surprising as the CMC dataset contains much more phenomena covered by new tags, some of which have systematically different tags in our original version of our own training data: 479 CMC test tokens (out of 5234) received a gold tag from STTS 2.0 (285 tokens from the subset that would have been tagged differently in our STTS 2.0* version compared to our adapted version), compared to 94 tokens (out of 7568) from the Web dataset (87 tokens that differ between tagset versions).

The UdS-surface system outperforms the retrain approach only slightly for the CMC dataset (statistically not significant), and not for the Web Corpora. We suspect a higher frequency of typos in the CMC dataset. The Web corpora dataset seems much more well-formed, so that we might have there a higher percentage of OOV words that are erroneously replaced, although the word is not a typo but just a lexical gap, i.e. does not occur in the tagger lexicon.

5.2 Performance on OOV Words

All of our systems focus on improving the performance of words that are OOV for a standard tagger. We therefore evaluate the performance on OOV and IV words separately. Table 4 shows the performance on these words, if we take the TIGER baseline as a reference as to whether a word is known or not. Consequently, all retrain, distributional and surface runs have the same OOV words as TIGER and thus the numbers for the performance on OOV are directly comparable.

We can see that we reach the vast majority of our improvements over the TIGER baseline on OOV words; the performance on IV words also improves by 5 to 6%, due to both a better context that helps to disambiguate words with several possible POS tags (e.g. ART vs. PREL) and additional lexicon entries for words that were already known in TIGER but with different or fewer POS tags. For instance, a word like *essen* (verb – to eat) might also occur in in-domain training data as the erroneously not-capitalized version of the noun *Essen* (meal).

Adding a component for handling OOV words reduces the number of words for which our model has no additional information about the POS tag. For the distributional models, there are only about 4% of tokens for which we do not have any predictions about distributional neighbours. For the surface models, between 3 and 10 percent of all tokens are not replaced by a similar word and thus are treated as OOV by the tagger.

6 Discussion and Analysis

This section presents additional experiments and analyses that aim at shedding light on the differences between the individual systems.

6.1 Experiment 1: How different are our systems?

One interesting question is how different our individual systems really are: Do they subsume each other, or are there opportunities for improvements by combining them? To address this question, we evaluate as an oracle condition how good a combined tagger would be. To this end, we evaluate a condition where we take everything as correct that is correctly done by at least one configuration of one of our systems. This evaluation is thus an upper bound of what an optimal combination of all our apporaches might be able to reach. We do that within individual systems and across all three systems (see Table 5). We also evaluate for how many tokens all systems get it right (*all correct* in the table). We can see that we only profit slightly from combining different variations for a single system, and – as expected – more substantially from combining the three models corresponding to three different approaches.

The *all correct* evaluation shows that even the system with the worst performance (surface-1) is better than only those cases that all systems have correct, i.e. even this system contributes something and is not subsumed by the others.

In order to understand the remaining problems better, we looked at the remaining hard cases, i.e., tokens that none of our system configurations were able to tag correctly. Tables 6 and 7 show the most frequent mistaggings and the confusions for those POS tags that occur at least 10 times in a dataset.

We can see that we especially struggle with the new adverb derivates; we assume that to be because of their low frequencies, and because the lexical items appear often with the ADV tag in TIGER. Other hard cases are more typical POS confusion phenomena such as NN vs. NE, ADJD vs. ADV, VVINF vs. VVFIN etc.

6.2 Experiment 2: The influence of our manually annotated data

All of our submitted systems use the Schreibgebrauch data in some way. We have observed in previous work that adding this data improved performance, compared to a model trained on newspaper data, by a large amount Therefore, we want to check, in the next experiment, what our results would be if we had used only the in-domain training data provided by the shared task for each subcorpus.

We see in table 8 that the CMC subcorpus profited substantially from the additional *Schreibgebrauch* corpus (up to +2.96%); for Web, however, the performance did not change. We attribute that to the domain differences between Web and CMC.

7 Conclusion

In this paper we described our contributions to the EmpiriST 2015 Shared Task on automatic linguistic annotation of computer-mediated communication/social media. We entered three systems into

Run	CMC			Web		
	IV	OOV	%OOV	IV	OOV	%OOV
TIGER baseline	83.39	28.95	22.83	94.44	71.07	14.20
UdS-retrain 1	88.88	73.97	22.83	95.16	77.86	14.20
UdS-retrain 2	89.82	74.81	22.83	95.23	78.05	14.20
UdS-retrain 3	89.90	74.73	22.83	95.10	78.23	14.20
UdS-distributional 1	89.73	78.91	22.83	95.27	82.88	14.20
UdS-distributional 2	89.75	79.16	22.83	95.29	83.07	14.20
UdS-distributional 3	89.80	78.83	22.83	95.26	79.44	14.20
UdS-surface 1	88.66	70.79	22.83	94.93	68.56	14.20
UdS-surface 2	89.40	76.49	22.83	95.12	76.19	14.20
UdS-surface 3	88.66	74.23	22.83	94.99	73.95	14.20

Table 4: Evaluation results split into OOV and IV words according to the TIGER baseline.

	CMC	Web
oracle - retrain	87.03 (86.43)	93.05 (92.79)
oracle - distributional	87.62 (87.33)	93.70 (93.55)
oracle - surface	87.52 (86.45)	93.59 (92.43)
oracle - all	89.78 (87.33)	94.94 (93.55)
all correct - all	81.14 (84.58)	89.14 (91.19)

Table 5: Results for an oracle condition experiment. In parentheses is the performance of the best run that contributed to the oracle experiment and the worst run for the *all correct* condition.

tag	freq	out of	3 most frequent confusions
PTKIFG	59	72	ADV (413), ADJD (71), PIS (21),
$(	43	343	$. (306), XY (45), KON (36),
PTKMA	42	74	ADV (325), ADJD (23), PTKIFG (20),
NE	33	230	NN (121), ADR (89), FM (19),
$.	32	358	$((282), NN (3), ITJ (2),
NN	32	696	NE (90), ADJA (69), ADJD (30),
ADJD	30	187	ADV (152), VVPP (63), ADJA (27),
ITJ	17	99	ONO (45), AKW (31), NN (25),
URL	16	16	NE (37), CARD (27), XY (18),
AKW	15	60	VVFIN (45), NN (28), NE (12),
VVFIN	14	183	VVINF (73), NN (18), ADJD (13),
PTKVZ	12	40	APPR (54), ADV (27), ADJD (18),
ADR	12	48	NE (36), NN (32), ADV (18),
ADV	12	268	ADJD (36), PTKVZ (18), PIAT (14),
ADJA	11	149	NE (38), NN (25), FM (15),
VVIMP	11	20	VVFIN (27), NE (24), ADV (18),
KOKOM	11	21	APPR (45), KOUS (27), FM (16),
PDS	10	51	ART (45), PRELS (19), PDAT (9),

Table 6: Most frequent mistagged gold standard tags for CMC. We show the frequency of the mistagged word compared to the overall occurrence of that word. Misstagging numbers are higher, as they refer to the sum of misstaggings by all nine tagging models.

tag	freq	out of	3 most frequent confusions
PTKIFG	53	61	ADV (424), ADJD (53),
VVFIN	36	250	VVINF (172), VVPP (116), NN (11),
NN	27	1661	NE (121), ADJA (57), FM (18),
NE	26	252	NN (190), ADJD (9), URL (8),
$(	23	263	NN (68), XY (45), $. (30),
FM	18	43	NE (76), NN (20), VAFIN (18),
ADJD	17	223	ADV (101), ADJA (17), NE (14),
ADJA	14	498	FM (27), NN (25), ADJD (18),
APPR	13	583	ADV (36), KOKOM (36), KON (36),
VVINF	13	125	VVFIN (81), NN (36),
PTKMWL	13	14	ADV (108), ADJD (9),
VVIMP	10	12	VVFIN (59), VVPP (13), ADJD (9),
VAFIN	10	208	VAINF (90),

Table 7: Most frequent mistagged gold standard tags for Web

	CMC	Web
retrain run 1/2	83.44	92.71
retrain - run 3	83.65	92.84
distrib - run 1	84.89	93.38
distrib - run 2	85.00	93.39
distrib - run 3	84.94	92.88
surface - run 1	82.25	91.05
surface - run 2	84.05	92.36
surface - run 3	82.98	91.66

Table 8: Results for versions of our systems that have been trained without our additionally annotated training data.

the competition: *UdS-retrain* uses manually annotated in-domain CMC data in addition to a standard newspaper corpus (TIGER) to train the tagger, *UdS-distributional* additionally learns possible POS tags of OOV words not covered by the training set and *UdS-surface* normalizes OOV words prior to tagging using surface similarity measures and a language model.

Our results confirm findings made in previous work: A big improvement over a standard tagger trained on newspaper texts is obtained by UdS-retrain (+15% on CMC); a further improvement is obtained by UdS-distributional (+1.8% on CMC), while UdS-surface does not lead to significantly better results (+0.05% on CMC; -0.4% on Web).

The distributional system is closely based on previous work by Prange et al. (2015). This previous system learns only one possible POS tag for OOV words. Here, our attempt was to learn several possible POS tags and let the tagger decide which of these candidate tags is most appropriate in a certain context (run 2). However, the differences from runs 1 and 3 are very small and statistically not significant.

While UdS-surface improves tagging accuracy of OOV words (compared to UdS-retrain on CMC), the accuracy on IV words decreases, which suggests that this approach is not accurate enough to improve tagging results. More specifically, we often erroneously correct words that are OOV but not spelling errors.

From our oracle experiments, we see that the combination of our taggers has the potential to be better than each tagger individually. None of our systems explores "low hanging fruits" such as using regular expressions to identify addressing terms, email addresses or emoticons, which might also be integrated in future work.

Acknowledgments

This work is part of the BMBF-funded project "Analyse und Instrumentarien zur Beobachtung des Schreibgebrauchs im Deutschen". We thank our student assistants Maximilian Wolf and Sophie Henning for the annotations used in this study as well as the anonymous reviewers for their helpful comments on this paper.

References

Thomas Bartz, Michael Beißwenger, and Angelika Storrer. 2014. Optimierung des Stuttgart-Tübingen-Tagset für die linguistische Annotation von Korpora zur internetbasierten Kommunikation: Phänomene, Herausforderungen, Erweiterungsvorschläge. *Journal for Language Technology and Computational Linguistics*, 28(1):157–198.

Michael Beißwenger, Thomas Bartz, Angelika Storrer, and Swantje Westpfahl. 2015. Tagset und Richtlinie für das Part-of-Speech-Tagging von Sprachdaten aus Genres internetbasierter Kommunikation. Guideline-Dokument aus dem Projekt "GSCL Shared Task: Automatic Linguistic Annotation of Computer-Mediated Communication / Social Media" (EmpiriST2015). Technical report.

Michael Beißwenger. 2013. Das Dortmunder Chat-Korpus. *Zeitschrift für germanistische Linguistik*, 41(1):161–164.

Sabine Brants, Stefanie Dipper, Peter Eisenberg, Silvia Hansen, Esther Koenig, Wolfgang Lezius, Christian Rohrer, George Smith, and Hans Uszkoreit. 2004. TIGER: Linguistic interpretation of a German Corpus. *Journal of Language and Computation, Special Issue*, 2(4):597–620.

Phani Gadde, L. Venkata Subramaniam, and Tanveer A. Faruquie. 2011. Adapting a WSJ trained part-of-speech tagger to noisy text: preliminary results. In *Proceedings of the 2011 Joint Workshop on Multilingual OCR and Analytics for Noisy Unstructured Text Data*, page 5. ACM.

Péter Halácsy, András Kornai, and Csaba Oravecz. 2007. HunPos: An open source trigram tagger. In *Proceedings of the 45th Annual Meeting of the ACL on Interactive Poster and Demonstration Sessions*, ACL '07, pages 209–212, Stroudsburg, PA, USA. Association for Computational Linguistics.

Bo Han, Paul Cook, and Timothy Baldwin. 2012. Automatically constructing a normalisation dictionary for microblogs. In *Proceedings of the 2012 joint conference on empirical methods in natural language processing and computational natural language learning*, pages 421–432. Association for Computational Linguistics.

Andrea Horbach, Diana Steffen, Stefan Thater, and Manfred Pinkal. 2014. Improving the performance of standard part-of-speech taggers for computer-mediated communication. In Josef Ruppenhofer and Gertrud Faaß, editors, *Proceedings of the 12th Edition of the Konvens Conference, Hildesheim, Germany, October 8-10, 2014*, pages 171–177. Universitätsbibliothek Hildesheim.

Andrea Horbach, Stefan Thater, Diana Steffen, Peter M. Fischer, Andreas Witt, and Manfred Pinkal. 2015. Internet corpora: A challenge for linguistic processing. *Datenbank Spektrum*, 15(1):41–47.

Sandra Kübler and Eric Baucom. 2011. Fast domain adaptation for part of speech tagging for dialogues. In Galia Angelova, Kalina Bontcheva, Ruslan Mitkov, and Nicolas Nicolov, editors, *RANLP*, pages 41–48. RANLP 2011 Organising Committee.

Jakob Prange, Stefan Thater, and Andrea Horbach. 2015. Unsupervised Induction of Part-of-Speech Information for OOV Words in German Internet Forum Posts. In *Proceedings of the 2nd Workshop on Natural Language Processing for Computer-Mediated Communication / Social Media (NLP4CMC 2015)*.

Anne Schiller, Simone Teufel, Christine Stöckert, and Christine Thielen. 1999. Guidelines für das Tagging deutscher Textcorpora mit STTS. Technical report, IMS-CL, University of Stuttgart.

Andreas Stolcke. 2002. SRILM - An Extensible Language Modeling Toolkit. pages 901–904.

Babler - Data Collection from the Web to Support Speech Recognition and Keyword Search

Gideon Mendels   **Erica Cooper**   **Julia Hirschberg**
Columbia University, New York, USA
gm2597@columbia.edu   {ecooper, julia}@cs.columbia.edu

Abstract

We describe a system to collect web data for Low Resource Languages, to augment language model training data for Automatic Speech Recognition (ASR) and keyword search by reducing the Out-of-Vocabulary (OOV) rates – words in the test set that did not appear in the training set for ASR. We test this system on seven Low Resource Languages from the IARPA Babel Program: Paraguayan Guarani, Igbo, Amharic, Halh Mongolian, Javanese, Pashto, and Dholuo. The success of our system compared with other web collection systems is due to the targeted collection sources (blogs, twitter, forums) and the inclusion of a separate language identification component in its pipeline, which filters the data initially collected before finally saving it. Our results show a major reduction of OOV rates relative to those calculated from training corpora alone and major reductions in OOV rates calculated in terms of keywords in the training development set. We also describe differences among genres in this reduction, which vary by language but show a pronounced influence for augmentation from Twitter data for most languages.

1   Introduction

Collecting data from the web for commercial and research purposes has become a popular task, used for a wide variety of purposes in text and speech processing. However, to date, most of this data collection has been done for English and other High Resource Languages (HRLs). These languages are characterized by having extensive computational tools and large amounts of readily available web data and include languages such as French, Spanish, Mandarin, and German. Low Resource Languages (LRLs), although many are spoken by millions of people, are much less likely and much more difficult to mine, due largely to the smaller presence these languages have on the web. These include languages such as Paraguayan Guarni, Igbo, Amharic, Halh Mongolian, Javanese, Pashto, and Dholuo, inter alia.

In this paper we describe a new system which addresses the problem of collecting large amounts of LRL data from multiple web sources. Unlike current HRL collection systems, Babler provides a targeted collection pipeline for social networks and conversational style text. The purpose of this data collection is to augment the training data used by Automatic Speech Recognition (ASR) to create language models ASR and for Keyword Search (KWS) for LRLs. The more specific goal is to reduce the Out-of-Vocabulary (OOV) rates for languages when the amount of data in the training set is small and thus words in the test set may not occur in the training set. Web data can add many additional words to the ASR and KWS lexicon which is shown to improve performance over WER and KW hit rate. Critically, this web data must be in a genre close to that of the ASR training and test sets which is the main reason we developed a pipeline that focuses on conversational style text. In this paper we describe the properties which LRL web collection requires of systems, compare ours with other popular web collection and scraping software, and describe results achieved for reducing Word Error Rate (WER) for ASR and OOVs and improvements in the IARPA Babel keyword search task.

In Section 2 we describe previous research in web collection for speech recognition and keyword search. In Section 3 we briefly describe the

Proceedings of the 10th Web as Corpus Workshop (WAC-X) and the EmpiriST Shared Task, pages 72–81,
Berlin, Germany, August 7-12, 2016. ©2016 Association for Computational Linguistics

IARPA Babel project and we describe its language resources. In Section 4 we describe the components of our web collection systems. In Section 5 we identify the web sources we use. In Section 6 we compare our system to other tools for web data collection. In Section 7 we describe subsequent text normalization used to prepare the collection material for language modeling. In Section 8 we describe results of adding collected web data to available Babel training data in reducing OOV rates. We conclude in Section 9 and discuss future research.

2 Previous Research

A number of tools and methodologies have been proposed for web scraping use in building web corpora for speech and NLP applications. Baroni and Bernardini (2004) developed BootCat to generate search engine queries in an iterative process in order to create a corpus typically for specific domains. De Groc et al (2011) optimized the query generation process by graph modeling the relationship between queries, documents and terms. This approach improved mean precision by 25% over the BootCat method. Hoogeveen and Pauw (2011) used a similar query generation method but incorporated language identification as part of their pipeline. In text-based research, web resources have been mined by researchers to collect social media and review data for sentiment analysis ((Wang et al., 2014);(C. Argueta and Chen, 2016)), to improve language identification (Lui et al., 2014), to find interpretations of compound nominals (Nicholson and Baldwin, 2006), to find variants of proper names (Andrews et al., 2012), to provide parallel corpora for training Machine Translation engines, to develop corpora for studies of code-switching (Solorio et al., 2014), to predict chat responses in social media to facilitate response completion (Pang and Ravi, 2012), inter alia. In each case the data collected will differ depending upon the application.

However, in speech research, web data collection has been largely focused on improving ASR and KWS, where insufficient data may be available from existing training corpora. Until recently, most attempts at data augmentation from the web have been confined to HRLs such as English, French, and Mandarin. In ASR research, improved performance has been achieved by supplementing language model training data with web data in different domains (Iyer et al., 1997), particularly when that data closely matches the genre of the available training material and the task at hand (Bulyko et al., 2003). While earlier work focused on English, (Ng et al., 2005) extended this approach to the recognition of Mandarin conversational speech and Schlippe et al 2013 explored the use of web data to perform unsupervised language model adaptation for French Broadcast News using RSS feeds and Twitter data. Creutz et al. (2009) presented an efficient method for selecting queries to extract useful web text for general or user-dependent vocabularies. Most of this research has used perplexity to determine improvement resulting from the addition of web text to the original language model corpus (Bulyko et al., 2007) although (Sarikaya et al., 2005) have also proposed the use of BLEU scores in augmenting language model training data for Spoken Dialogue Systems.

In recent years, the use of web data has begun to be used to improve OOV rates for ASR and KWS performance on LRLs in the IARPA Babel project (Harper, 2011) which presents major new challenges. Web data for these languages is typically much scarcer than for HRLs, particularly in genres that are similar to the telephone conversations used in this project; since many of these LRLs are spoken with significant amounts of *code-switching*, which must be identified during web scraping, collecting data for Babel LRLs is much more complex than for other languages. Language ID is thus also an important component of LRL web data collection.

(Gandhe et al., 2013) used simple web query word seeding from the Babel lexicon on Wikipedia data, news articles and results from 30 Google queries for five of the Babel Base Period languages: Cantonese, Pashto, Tagalog, Turkish and Vietnamese. This approach improved OOV rates by up to 50% and improved Actual Term Weighted Value (ATWV) (Fiscus et al., 2007) by 0.0424 in the best case (larger values of ATWV represent improved performance), compared to a baseline system trained only on the Babel Limited Language Pack data which was provided for the task of recognition and search; each corpus consisted of ten hours of transcribed conversational speech. On average, ATWV was improved by 0.0243 across all five languages. (Zhang et al., 2015) used automatically generated query terms followed by simple language identification techniques to reduce OOV rates for Babel Very Limited Language Packs (three hours of transcribed telephone conversations) on Cebuano, Kazakh, Kurdish, Lithuanian, Telugu and Tok Pisin. Using a variety of web genres, they managed to halve the OOV on the development set and to improve keyword spotting by an absolute 2.8 points of ATWV.

In our work, (Mendels et al., 2015), working on the same data and using a variety of additional web genres including blogs, TED talks, and online news sources obtained from keyword searches seeded by the 1000 most common words in each language, together with BBN-collected movie subtitles, all filtered by several language ID methods, we reduced OOV rates by 39-66% and improved Maximum Term Weighted Value (MTWV) by 0.0076-.0.1059 absolute points over the best language models trained without web data. In this paper, we describe an enhanced version of our system for collecting LRL data from the web, including collection of Paraguayan Guarani, Igbo, Amharic, Halh Mongolian, Javanese, Pashto, and Dholuo.

3 The Babel Program

The work presented here has been done within the context of the IARPA Babel program (Harper, 2011), which targets rapid development of speech processing technology in LRLs, focusing on keyword search in large speech corpora from ASR transcripts. The Babel program currently provides language packs for 24 languages: IARPA-babel101-v0.4c Cantonese 205b-v1.0a, 102b-v0.5a Assamese, 103b-v0.4b Bengali, 104b-v0.4a Pashto, 105b-v0.4 Turkish, 106-v0.2f Tagalog, 107b-v0.7 Vietnamese, 201b-v0.2b Haitian Creole, 202b-v1.0d Swahili, 203b-v3.1a Lao, 204b-v1.1b Tamil, 205b-v1.0a Kurmanji Kurdish, 206b-v0.1e Zulu, 207b-v1.0b Tok Pisin, 301b-v1.0b Cebuano, 302b-v1.0a Kazakh, 303b-v1.0a Telugu, 304b-v1.0b Lithuanian, 305b-v1.0b Paraguayan Guarani, 306b-v2.0c Igbo, 307b-v1.0b Amharic, 401b-v2.0b Halh Mongolian, 402b-v1.0b Javanese, and 403b-v1.0b Dholuo. We describe our system and evaluate it on the last six languages (the current phase languages) as well as Pashto. This data was collected by Appen and is released in three subsets: Full Language Packs (FLPs), consisting of 80 hours of transcribed (primarily) telephone conversations between two speakers and recorded on separate channels under a variety of recording conditions; Limited Language Packs (LLPs) with 10 hours of transcribed speech; and Very Limited Language Packs (VLLPs) with 3 hours of transcribed speech from the FLP corpus. We evaluate here on the LLP lexicons (derived from the 10 hour transcripts) for the seven languages examined. The speakers are diverse in terms of age and dialect and the gender ratio is approximately equal. A main goal of the Babel program is determining how speech recognition and keyword search technology can be developed for LRLs using increasingly smaller data sets for training. This makes data augmentation via web collection increasingly important. The major goal of the program is determining how quickly ASR and KWS systems can be developed for new languages when little transcribed speech data is initially available for use.

4 Web Data Collection

A major constraint on our data collection effort is that we must collect and process as much data as possible in a given (very short) amount of time. This constraint is designed to simulate a situation in which speech processing tools for a new language for which ASR and keyword search tools are not already available and must be created quickly. With that requirement in mind we designed a highly customizable, multi-threaded pipeline for the task (Figure 1). The pipeline consists of the following components:

1. Seeding language models

2. Search Producer

3. Job Queue

4. Scraper

5. Language identification

6. Database

We first provide an overview of the source-independent components (shown in Figure 1) and then describe in detail how we collect data from each source.

4.1 Seeding Language Models

The first component in the pipeline depicted in Figure 1 is responsible for generating keywords for seeding searches. Independent of the actual

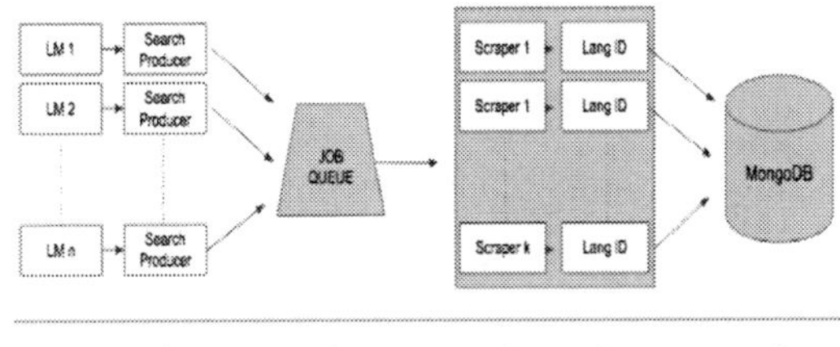

Figure 1: Data Collection Pipe Line

search provider (e.g. Bing API, Twitter API), this component is based on pre-computed unigram language models for each of the languages we want to collect. The unigram model provides the search query as explained below in Section 4.2. We compute the frequency of each token in the dataset and then remove all tokens shorter than 4 characters or tokens that occur in a standard English word list (SIL, 1999). The primary reason for removing these tokens is to reduce the number of English search results in later steps. We discovered that a query containing an English word is likely to produce mainly English results, even if that word is shared with another language, due to the heavy preponderance of English material on the web. The data for the unigram models is obtained from the Babel program; also from the Leipzig corpora (Quasthoff et al., 2006), a multilingual corpus collected from the web; and from the Crubadan project (Scannell, 2007), another multilingual corpus providing trigram counts for more than 2000 languages and dialects. Our system also supports generating bigram and trigram queries which improves accuracy of the target language results but lowers recall.

4.2 Search Production

The search production component of our systems polls a keyword from the seeding model and generates a search query. Different search providers are implemented based on the same interface to allow flexibility in adding additional search providers later. Our system currently supports Bing search API, DuckDuckGo API, Google Search, Twitter API and Topsy API.

4.3 Job Queue

The search producer described in Section 4.2 adds jobs to the queue. Each job contains the URL or data that should be inspected by the scraper. Using a concurrent blocking queue in a producer-consumer design pattern, we allow the search producer and the scraper components to work concurrently and independently, thus reducing the overhead of waiting for HTTP requests.

4.4 Scraper

This component is the heart of the pipeline and is responsible for fetching a data source, extracting the data from that source and passing it further down the pipeline.

4.5 Language Identification

Raw data that is collected is examined using our language identification multi-classifier, majority vote approach. Lui and Baldwin (2014) showed that using a majority vote over three independent language classifiers consistently outperforms any individual system, so we use the following classifiers:

- LingPipe - A language identification classifier built from LingPipe (http://alias-i.com/lingpipe/), and described in Mendels et al. (2015)

- TextCat - We implemented the TextCat algorithm (Cavnar et al., 1994) using precomputed counts from the Crubadan Project. (Scannell, 2007)

- Google's Compact Language Detector 2 [1] - CLD2 is a Nave Bayesian classifier that supports 83 languages. We implemented a Java native interface to the original CLD2 distribution.

4.6 Database

We use MongoDB, a noSQL document-oriented database system, to store the filtered data. MongoDB allows us to process the data easily via its built in *map-reduce* component. Using MongoDB provided significant improvements compared to saving documents as text files; for example, in a single task of counting the number of tokens in the entire data set we found that MongoDB was approximately three orders of magnitude faster than using ext4 FS on Ubuntu. By overriding MongoDB internal id field we also solve the issue of duplicates, which we encounter in many sources, especially Twitter data, where tweets are often

---

[1]https://github.com/CLD2Owners/cld2

retweeted. To avoid saving duplicates or laboriously checking the entire dataset, we compute the SHA256 hash code for each data source and save that as the internal id field. Since this field is defined as unique over the entire MongoDB collection we avoid duplicates by definition.

5 Web Sources

5.1 Blogs - By Rich Site Summary (RSS)

RSS feeds are structured XML feeds that usually contain the latest posts from a blog. Since the data is completely structured, the task essentially involves simply fetching and parsing the XML file and extracting the correct node. We collect blog data from `blogspot.com` and `wordpress.com`. Once the search producer polls a keyword from the unigram model it constructs a Bing search query of the following form `site:blogspot.com unigram NOT lang:en`. The query consists of a domain filter, a keyword and a language filter that removes all results classified as English by Bing. The result from this query is a list of blog posts that contain the keyword. We classify the raw text using our language identifier and, if it matches the language we seek, we save the blog post.

In some cases RSS feeds are either unavailable or contain only the first paragraph of a blog post. In such cases it is necessary to separate the actual content of the post from ads, menus and other boilerplate data. To collect these posts we explored two methods for boilerplate removal:

- DiffBot, a commercial service that builds a structured representation of an HTML page by rendering it and breaking it down into its component parts using computer vision techniques.

- A pre-trained ML model (Kohlschütter et al., 2010) that uses shallow text features such as number of words and text density to separate content from boilerplate.

5.2 Forums

For web forums, we target forums created using phpBB, an open-source forum/bulletin management system. Once the search producer polls a keyword from the unigram model, it constructs a Bing search query of the following form: `Powered by phpBB AND unigram NOT lang:en`. Many phpBB forums follow the same Document Object Model (DOM) structure, for which we have written a custom scraper based on Cascading Style Sheets (CSS) style queries. Once a thread is found to be a match, we crawl the entire forum for additional threads

5.3 Twitter By Query

We poll a keyword from the unigram model and produce a search query on the Twitter and Topsy.com APIs. Both APIs are the same in terms of content but using both facilitates provides a higher throughput. The tweets in the search results are cleaned from mentions, urls, hashtags and emojis prior to language identification.

5.4 Twitter By User

An independent service revisits all the user pages from which we have collected tweets successfully in the language desired and crawls through their public history to find more tweets from the same user. This is based on the assumption that a user who tweets in a specific language will be more likely to have more tweets in that language.

5.5 TED Talks

TED.com is a website that is devoted to spreading ideas, usually in the form of short, powerful talks. Many of the talks are offered with user-translated subtitles. We use CSS queries and simple URL manipulation to download all the subtitles.

5.6 News

In some cases we have also implemented custom CSS query-based scrapers for news sites. This approach provides data with very little noise but requires implementing a manual scraper for each page.

5.7 Wikipedia

Our system also supports downloading and processing Wikipedias XML dumps, which are available for many LRLs.

6 Comparison to Other Data Collection Tools

Most tools for bootstrapping corpora-building from the web were designed for languages with a large presence in the web and for building corpora for a specific topics and terminology. Keyword search and ASR language modeling in telephone conversations collected for LRLs requires a different type of corpus. We aim to build a topic independent, conversational corpus with very little noise in the form of HTML, JavaScript and out-of-language tokens. With this in mind, our system was designed in three main parts.

6.1 Query Generation and Sources

Topic and terminology-oriented corpora-building requires robust query generation (similar to our search producer step). It is preferable to fetch a specific subset of the documents available from the search engine. BootCat (Baroni and Bernardini, 2004) randomly generate ngram queries from the unigram seeding model. GrawlTCQ (De Groc et al., 2011) further develops the query generation process by modeling the links between documents, terms and queries. CorpusCollie (Hoogeveen and Pauw, 2011) uses a similar approach but also removes tokens that are considered to be stop-words in other languages.

Our system queries only documents from specific sources that are most suitable for our corpus: blogs, forums, twitter and subtitles rather than the entire web. This choice is dictated by the fact that the ASR language modeling and keyword search tasks that we target involve conversational telephone speech: thus, more "conversational" text is most useful. Furthermore, when working with LRLs, we optimize the initial query generation process for recall and not precision, which explains our use of basic unigrams. Since there are very few resources available, we filter documents using language identification rather than by query design. Nonetheless we have also implemented support for bigram and trigram seeding models in cases where it would be desirable.

6.2 Language Identification and Boilerplate Removal

BootCat (Baroni and Bernardini, 2004) and GrawlTCQ (De Groc et al., 2011) have no language identification support or boilerplate removal. CorpusCollie (Hoogeveen and Pauw, 2011) uses regular expressions based filtering to remove boilerplate. For example if an HTML element contains © it is likely to be boilerplate. Rule based methods are language dependent and considered to be less robust than a machine learning models, as have been shown by Kohlschütter et al. (2010). Our system uses state of the art boilerplate removal and language identification as part of the pipeline.

6.3 Performance

Our system uses multithreading to reduce the overhead of the many HTTP requests required in web data collection. Furthermore all the tools described above use the operating system file system to manage collected documents. As shown in section 4 we have found that using a production level database system is preferable in both performance and scale.

7 Text Normalization

As previously noted, we are collecting web data for the purpose of including it in the language models for ASR that will be used to transcribe data for a spoken keyword search task. Due to the noisy nature of text found on the web, we must clean our collected data to make it appropriate for this task. Our text normalization proceeds in three distinct steps:

- Pre-normalization: a first pass in which non-standard punctuation is standardized;

- Sentence segmentation: which is accomplished using the Punkt module of NLTK (Kiss and Strunk, 2006); and

- Post normalization: in which sentence-by-sentence cleaning of any out-of-language text and standardization of numerals is done.

7.1 Pre-normalization

During pre-normalization, we first remove list entries and titles, since those generally are not full sentences. We replace non-standard characters with a standard version: these include ellipses, whitespace, hyphens, and apostrophes. Hyphens and apostrophes are removed as extraneous punctuation, except word-internal cases such as hyphenated words or contractions. Finally, any characters not part of the language's character set, the Latin character set, numerals, or allowed punctuation are removed. This cleans special characters such as symbols from the data. Latin characters are preserved, even for languages which use a different alphabet, to enable more accurate removal of entire sentences containing foreign words and URLs during post-normalization.

7.2 Sentence Segmentation

We perform sentence tokenization using the Punkt module of NLTK. Punkt uses a language-independent, unsupervised approach to sentence boundary detection. It learns which words are abbreviations as opposed to sentence-final words, based on three criteria: First, abbreviations appear as a tight collocation of a truncated word and a final period. Second, abbreviations tend to be very short. Third, abbreviations sometimes contain internal periods. Once the abbreviations in the training corpus are learned and identified, periods after non-abbreviation words can be designated as sentence boundaries. Then, Punkt performs additional classification to detect abbreviations that are also ends of sentences, ellipses at the ends of sentences, initials, and ordinal numbers. Punkt does not require knowledge of upper and lower case letters, so it is well-suited to languages or data which may not use them.

7.3 Post-normalization

Our final pass, post-normalization, examines the segmented data sentence-by-sentence. First, any sentences in languages which do not use the Latin script but that nonetheless contain words in the Latin alphabet are removed. We also remove sentences containing URLs and put abbreviations into a standard form, using underscores instead of periods. Finally, we replace numerals with their written-out form, where possible, based on the Language Specific Peculiarities document (LSP) provided by Appen Butler Hill to Babel participants.

This type of normalization, while specific to our application, should be reasonable for use in other tasks as well, especially where language modeling is the target.

8 Experiments and Results

Our goal in collecting web data is to supplement language models for ASR and KWS by increasing the lexicon available from the ASR training corpus in order to reduce the number of OOV words available for ASR and KWS. That is, if new words can be added to the lexicon from sources similar in genre to the training and test data, then there is a greater chance that these words can be identified in ASR and KWS on the test corpus. For evaluation purposes here, we calculate OOV reduction by comparing the web-data-augmented lexicon with each of the Babel LLP lexicons for the six Babel OP3 languages – Pashto, Paraguayan Guarani, Igbo, Amharic, Halh Mongolian, and Javanese in Table 1. "LLP" refers to the original

Language	Lexicon	OOV KW Rate %	OOV Hit Rate %	Voc. Size (K)
Pashto	LLP	24.18	7.35	6.2
	+web	7.44	1.51	2461.6
	%rel.ch	-69.21	-79.39	39693.8
Para- guayan Guarani	LLP	34.84	6.65	9.1
	+web	32.00	5.75	40.3
	%rel.ch	-8.17	-13.66	339.93
Igbo	LLP	30.50	6.52	6.7
	+web	21.74	3.43	50.5
	%rel.ch	-28.71	-47.39	650.1
Amharic	LLP	34.67	9.96	11.6
	+web	32.96	9.27	84.1
	%rel.ch	-4.91	-6.91	627.4
Halh Mongo lian	LLP	32.95	15.67	8.5
	+web	5.37	0.44	2427.6
	%rel.ch	-83.71	-97.16	28450.1
Javanese	LLP	33.61	14.37	5.7
	+web	4.35	0.17	1723.2
	%rel.ch	-87.06	-98.78	30037.3
Dholuo	LLP	31.61	22.26	7.2
	+web	25.46	3.12	48.0
	%rel.ch	-19.45	-85.99	561.6

Table 1: OOV Reduction on Unnormalized Data

lexicon that was distributed with the Limited Language Pack for each language, and "+web" is the union of all of the words in the LLP lexicon and all of the words that we found in the web data. The "%rel.ch" row shows the percent relative change in OOV rate when the web data is added to the lexicon. "OOV KW Rate %" shows the percentage of KWS development queries containing an out-of-vocabulary tokens, both before and after our web data is added to the lexicon. "OOV Hit Rate %" is a similar measure, except that each query term is weighted by the number of times that it actually appears in the development transcripts; in this metric, keywords that appear more often have a greater impact. Finally, "Voc. Size (K)" shows the size of the vocabulary (in thousands of words), before and after adding web data. We see that, for each language, the percentage of OOV queries is significantly reduced; in particular, most Halh Mongolian and Javanese OOV keywords missing from the original lexicons are in fact added to the lexicon by the web data collection.

While text normalization is important if we are to use the web data for training a language model for ASR, we must also consider the extent to which normalization processes data may in fact remove useful words. Table 2 shows OOV reduction when adding the normalized web data collected. Surprisingly, using the normalized web data to augment the vocabulary actually helps in some instances over using the unnormalized data.

Language	Lexicon	OOV KW Rate %	OOV Hit Rate %	Voc. Size (K)
Pashto	LLP	24.18	7.35	6.2
	+web	5.73	0.75	801.9
	%rel.ch	-76.32	-89.74	12863.6
Para-guayan Guarani	LLP	34.84	6.65	9.2
	+web	31.35	5.64	22.8
	%rel.ch	-10.02	-15.21	149.1
Igbo	LLP	30.50	6.52	6.7
	+web	20.98	3.33	28.1
	%rel.ch	-31.21	-48.91	317.8
Amharic	LLP	34.67	9.96	11.6
	+web	9.54	1.59	646.7
	%rel.ch	-72.48	-83.99	5495.4
Halh Mongolian	LLP	32.95	15.67	8.5
	+web	5.28	0.44	1190.1
	%rel.ch	-83.96	-97.19	13896.8
Javanese	LLP	33.61	14.37	5.7
	+web	4.10	0.15	950.1
	%rel.ch	-87.81	-98.94	16516.7
Dholuo	LLP	31.61	22.26	7.3
	+web	25.22	3.10	24.0
	%rel.ch	-20.23	-86.07	231.1

Table 2: OOV Rate on Normalized Data

Language		Blogs	Forums	TED	Tweets
Pashto	KW	-64.59	-64.48	3.77	-73.20
	Hits	-79.57	-79.57	-8.00	-87.65
Para-guayan Guarani	KW	-4.70	-4.70	n/a	-6.44
	Hits	-8.09	-8.44		-10.39
Igbo	KW	-3.47	-0.42	-0.14	-30.37
	Hits	-9.97	0.29	-0.18	-47.86
Amharic	KW	-66.09	-60.44	-4.30	-61.30
	Hits	-76.42	-72.61	-6.35	-76.12
Halh Mongolian	KW	-73.11	-72.98	-28.16	-82.32
	Hits	-95.16	-95.33	-74.94	-96.86
Javanese	KW	-77.26	-73.12	n/a	-83.17
	Hits	-97.16	-96.42		-97.82
Dholuo	KW	0.0	0.0	n/a	-20.23
	Hits	0.0	0.0		-86.07

Table 3: OOV Rates for Languages by Genre

This is probably because the removal of special characters and punctuation attached to words results in exact matches for keywords.

Finally, we are interested in seeing the individual contribution of each of the web data genres we collected. Table 3 shows the percent relative reduction in OOVs for both OOV keywords and OOV hit rate in the development data when adding our normalized web data, by language and by genre. It is apparent that the genre that best reduces OOVs varies by language, but tweets were the most generally useful, resulting in the largest OOV reduction for Pashto, Igbo, Halh Mongolian, Javanese, and Dholuo. In fact, tweets were the only useful genre for Dholuo. Paraguayan Guarani saw the largest OOV reduction from forum posts, and Amharic from blogs.

9 Conclusions and Future Research

We have presented a system for collecting conversational web text data for Low Resource Languages. Our system gathers data from a variety of text sources (blogs, forums, Twitter, TED talks) which have proven to be useful for substantially reducing OOV rates for language models based on telephone conversations in a KWS task. Despite the noisy and highly variable nature of text found on the web, by including language identification and text normalization as part of our pipeline, we can be much more confident that the data we collect is likely to be in the target language. Our results have reduced OOV rates for KWS in LRLs significantly, resulting in significantly higher KWS scores. Our future work will explore additional sources for conversational web data, such as Facebook pages and other public social media. We also plan to release our system in the near future as an open source tool for the entire research community.

10 Acknowledgements

This work is supported by the Intelligence Advanced Research Projects Activity (IARPA) via Department of Defense U.S. Army Research Laboratory (DoD/ARL) contract number W911NF-12-C-0012. The U.S. Government is authorized to reproduce and distribute reprints for Governmental purposes notwithstanding any copyright annotation thereon. Disclaimer: The views and conclusions contained herein are those of the authors and should not be interpreted as necessarily representing the official policies or endorsements, either expressed or implied, of IARPA, DoD/ARL, or the U.S. Government.

References

Nicholas Andrews, Jason Eisner, and Mark Dredze. 2012. Name phylogeny: A generative model of string variation. In *Proceedings of the 2012 Joint Conference on Empirical Methods in Natural Language Processing and Computational Natural Language Learning*, pages 344–355. Association for Computational Linguistics.

Marco Baroni and Silvia Bernardini. 2004. Bootcat: Bootstrapping corpora and terms from the web. In *LREC*.

Ivan Bulyko, Mari Ostendorf, and Andreas Stolcke. 2003. Getting more mileage from web text sources for conversational speech language modeling using class-dependent mixtures. In *Proceedings of the 2003 Conference of the North American Chapter of the Association for Computational Linguistics on Human Language Technology: companion volume of the Proceedings of HLT-NAACL 2003–short papers-Volume 2*, pages 7–9. Association for Computational Linguistics.

Ivan Bulyko, Mari Ostendorf, Manhung Siu, Tim Ng, Andreas Stolcke, and Özgür Çetin. 2007. Web resources for language modeling in conversational speech recognition. *ACM Transactions on Speech and Language Processing (TSLP)*, 5(1):1.

F. H. Calderon C. Argueta and Y-S. Chen. 2016. ultilingual emotion classifier using unsupervised pattern extraction from microblog data. *JIntelligent Data Analysis*, 29(6).

William B Cavnar, John M Trenkle, et al. 1994. N-gram-based text categorization. *Ann Arbor MI*, 48113(2):161–175.

Mathias Creutz, Sami Virpioja, and Anna Kovaleva. 2009. Web augmentation of language models for continuous speech recognition of sms text messages. In *Proceedings of the 12th Conference of the European Chapter of the Association for Computational Linguistics*, pages 157–165. Association for Computational Linguistics.

Clément De Groc, Xavier Tannier, and Javier Couto. 2011. Grawltcq: terminology and corpora building by ranking simultaneously terms, queries and documents using graph random walks. In *Proceedings of TextGraphs-6: Graph-based Methods for Natural Language Processing*, pages 37–41. Association for Computational Linguistics.

Jonathan G Fiscus, Jerome Ajot, John S Garofolo, and George Doddington. 2007. Results of the 2006 spoken term detection evaluation. In *Proc. SIGIR*, volume 7, pages 51–57. Citeseer.

Ankur Gandhe, Long Qin, Florian Metze, Alex Rudnicky, Ian Lane, and Matthias Eck. 2013. Using web text to improve keyword spotting in speech. In *Automatic Speech Recognition and Understanding (ASRU), 2013 IEEE Workshop on*, pages 428–433. IEEE.

Mary Harper. 2011. Iarpa solicitation iarpa-baa-11-02. *IARPA BAA*.

D. Hoogeveen and G. De Pauw. 2011. corpuscollie-a web corpus mining tool for resource-scarce languages. In *Proceedings of Conference on Human Language Technology for Development. Alexandria, Egypt*, pages 44–49.

Rukmini Iyer, Mari Ostendorf, and Herb Gish. 1997. Using out-of-domain data to improve in-domain language models. *Signal Processing Letters, IEEE*, 4(8):221–223.

Tibor Kiss and Jan Strunk. 2006. Unsupervised multilingual sentence boundary detection. *Computational Linguistics*, 32(4):485–525.

Christian Kohlschütter, Peter Fankhauser, and Wolfgang Nejdl. 2010. Boilerplate detection using shallow text features. In *Proceedings of the third ACM international conference on Web search and data mining*, pages 441–450. ACM.

Marco Lui and Timothy Baldwin. 2014. Accurate language identification of twitter messages. *EACL 2014*, pages 17–25.

Marco Lui, Ned Letcher, Oliver Adams, Long Duong, Paul Cook, Timothy Baldwin, and NICTA Victoria. 2014. Exploring methods and resources for discriminating similar languages. *COLING 2014*, page 129.

Gideon Mendels, Erica Cooper, Victor Soto, Julia Hirschberg, Mark Gales, Kate Knill, Anton Ragni, and Haipeng Wang. 2015. Improving speech recognition and keyword search for low resource languages using web data. *Proc. Interspeech, Dresden, Germany*.

Tim Ng, Mari Ostendorf, Mei-Yuh Hwang, Man-Hung Siu, Ivan Bulyko, and Xin Lei. 2005. Web-data augmented language models for mandarin conversational speech recognition. In *ICASSP (1)*, pages 589–592.

Jeremy Nicholson and Timothy Baldwin. 2006. Interpretation of compound nominalisations using corpus and web statistics. In *Proceedings of the Workshop on Multiword Expressions: Identifying and Exploiting Underlying Properties*, pages 54–61. Association for Computational Linguistics.

Bo Pang and Sujith Ravi. 2012. Revisiting the predictability of language: Response completion in social media. In *Proceedings of the 2012 Joint Conference on Empirical Methods in Natural Language Processing and Computational Natural Language Learning*, pages 1489–1499. Association for Computational Linguistics.

Uwe Quasthoff, Matthias Richter, and Christian Biemann. 2006. Corpus portal for search in monolingual corpora. In *Proceedings of the fifth international conference on language resources and evaluation*, volume 17991802.

Ruhi Sarikaya, Agustin Gravano, and Yuqing Gao. 2005. Rapid language model development using external resources for new spoken dialog domains.

Kevin P Scannell. 2007. The crúbadán project: Corpus building for under-resourced languages. In *Building and Exploring Web Corpora: Proceedings of the 3rd Web as Corpus Workshop*, volume 4, pages 5–15.

SIL. 1999. English wordlists. `http://www01.sil.org/linguistics/wordlists/english/`. Accessed: 2015-09-30.

Thamar Solorio, Elizabeth Blair, Suraj Maharjan, Steven Bethard, Mona Diab, Mahmoud Gohneim, Abdelati Hawwari, Fahad AlGhamdi, Julia Hirschberg, Alison Chang, et al. 2014. Overview for the first shared task on language identification in code-switched data. In *Proceedings of The First Workshop on Computational Approaches to Code Switching*, pages 62–72. Citeseer.

Yu Wang, Tom Clark, Eugene Agichtein, and Jeffrey Staton. 2014. Towards tracking political sentiment through microblog data. *ACL 2014*, page 88.

Le Zhang, Damianos Karakos, William Hartmann, Roger Hsiao, Richard Schwartz, and Stavros Tsakalidis. 2015. Enhancing low resource keyword spotting with automatically retrieved web documents. In *Sixteenth Annual Conference of the International Speech Communication Association*.

A Global Analysis of Emoji Usage

Nikola Ljubešić
Dept. of Knowledge Technologies
Jožef Stefan Institute
Jamova cesta 39
SI-1000 Ljubljana, Slovenia
`nikola.ljubesic@ijs.si`

Darja Fišer
Faculty of Arts
University of Ljubljana
Aškerčeva cesta 2
SI-1000 Ljubljana, Slovenia
`darja.fiser@ff.uni-lj.si`

Abstract

Emojis are a quickly spreading and rather unknown communication phenomenon which occasionally receives attention in the mainstream press, but lacks the scientific exploration it deserves. This paper is a first attempt at investigating the global distribution of emojis. We perform our analysis of the spatial distribution of emojis on a dataset of ∼17 million (and growing) geo-encoded tweets containing emojis by running a cluster analysis over countries represented as emoji distributions and performing correlation analysis of emoji distributions and World Development Indicators. We show that emoji usage tends to draw quite a realistic picture of the living conditions in various parts of our world.

1 Introduction

Emojis, pictograms that have recently gained a worldwide momentum, are considered to be a further development of emoticons, pictorial representations of facial expressions using punctuation marks. While the first days of emoticons go as far as the 19th century (Fitzgerald, 2016), emojis were developed in the late 1990s by Shigetaka Kurita for Japanese mobile phone providers. The difference between emoticons and emojis is that, while emoticons primarily express emotional states, emojis offer a wider spectrum of concepts such as animals, plants, weather, sports, food etc.

Emojis have been present in the Unicode standard for some time now, with the first Unicode characters explicitly intended as emoji added to Unicode 5.2 in 2009. At that point a set of 722 characters was defined as the union of emoji characters used by Japanese mobile phone carriers (Davis and Edberg, 2015). Additional emoji characters followed in later updates, so that the current version 8.0 comprises 1624 emoji characters (Unicode Consortium, 2016). The current popularity of emojis is primarily due to the inclusion of emoji characters on the iOS and Android mobile platforms.

So far, emojis have primarily attracted mainstream media interest, the most prominent being the Word of the Year nomination handed by Oxford University Press in 2015 for the "Face With Tears of Joy" 😂 emoji. For this nomination Oxford University Press partnered with the company SwiftKey which is the author of the currently most detailed analysis of Emoji usage around the world (SwiftKey, 2015).

Despite their popularity, however, emojis are still a poorly researched communication phenomenon as only a few study have focused on it.

Kralj Novak et al. (2015b) inspect the sentiment of emojis by manually annotating 70,000 tweets written in 13 European languages. Their work has resulted in the Emoji Sentiment Ranking lexicon (Kralj Novak et al., 2015a) consisting of 751 emoji characters with their corresponding sentiment distribution. The data the sentiment distributions were calculated on are also available for download (Mozetič et al., 2016).

Pavalanathan and Eisenstein (2016) investigate the relationship between emojis and emoticons, showing that Twitter users who adopt emojis tend to reduce their usage of emoticons in comparison with the matched users who do not adopt emojis.

In this paper we will try to answer the following questions:

1. How popular are emojis in different parts of the world?

2. Does emoji usage differ in various parts of the world?

Proceedings of the 10th Web as Corpus Workshop (WAC-X) and the EmpiriST Shared Task, pages 82–89,
Berlin, Germany, August 7-12, 2016. ©2016 Association for Computational Linguistics

3. Does emoji usage in specific parts of the world reflect local living conditions?

We will answer these questions by performing the following analyses over large collections of geo-encoded tweets:

- estimating the probability of emoji occurrence in a tweet given the country,

- clustering countries represented as emoji probability distributions,

- calculating correlation between World Development Indicators and distributions of specific tweets across countries.

The remainder of the paper is structured as follows: Section 2 describes the two datasets used in the analyses while the remaining sections address our three questions: Section 3 gives an analysis of the popularity of emojis in different parts of the world, Section 4 gives an analysis of the spatial distribution of specific tweets, while in Section 5 we present the results of our correlation analysis over specific emojis and the World Development Indicators.

2 The datasets

2.1 Data collection

Our analyses in this paper are performed on two datasets of tweets collected through the Public Twitter Stream API[1].

The first dataset consists of tweets that have longitude and latitude encoded, regardless of whether they contain emojis. This dataset's sole purpose was to estimate the probability of an emoji occurrence in a specific part of the world. This dataset was collected during a period of 21 days and contains 12,451,835 tweets. We refer to this dataset as the *Twitter dataset*.

The second dataset consists of tweets that have longitude and latitude encoded and that contain emojis. The purpose of this dataset was to estimate the probability distribution of specific emojis in different parts of the world. Since we need more data to estimate the probability of an occurrence of a specific emoji than the probability of the overall emoji occurrence, this dataset was collected throughout a much longer period of 5

months (and is still running) and currently contains 17,458,001 tweets. We refer to this dataset as the *Emoji dataset*.

2.2 Removing overrepresented users

A frequent problem when analysing data from social networks is the problem of bias towards users with higher productivity, especially since the most productive users tend to be bots with a frequent and specific, if not static, content production.

We apply three methods of removing users with frequent or temporally regular activity. All three methods are run on our Emoji dataset which contains tweets of 2,623,645 users. The identified overrepresented users are then removed both from the Twitter and the Emoji dataset.

The first method removes users who produced on average more than 10 tweets with emojis per day. With that approach we removed 42 users, the user with the highest emoji productivity posting on average 509 tweets per day, the second one posting 72 tweets per day.

Given that most of our later analyses are based on comparing emoji distributions on country level, our second method removes tweets of users that have contributed more than 10% of the tweets that contain emojis in a specific country. Through this procedure we assure that the emoji distribution in a specific country is not heavily influenced by a single user.

We perform this procedure in an iterative manner, removing in each iteration all users that contribute to a specific country more than 10% of all its data points. After each iteration the distributions of user contributions given the country are recalculated. We should note that with this procedure we remove all users from countries that had ten or fewer contributors. With this method we removed 260 users.

The third method focuses primarily on removing bots by calculating the time between two postings and removing all users for which the three most frequent time spans between postings, calculated in seconds, cover more than 90% of their overall production. This method removed overall 16 users from our datasets.

While the precision of all the three presented methods is very high, our assumption is that we still suffer from recall issues. Our plan is to focus on the problem of removing overrepresented / non-human users in more detail in future work.

[1] https://dev.twitter.com/streaming/public

3 Overall emoji popularity

The analyses in this section are primarily focused on how popular emojis are on Twitter. The first part of the analyses looks at the world as a whole, while the second one focuses on the distribution across countries.

Given that for these analyses we need both tweets with and without emojis, we perform all analyses in this section on our Twitter dataset.

3.1 Global analysis

Emojis are present in nearly a quarter of the tweets in the dataset (19.6%) and are used by well over a third of the users (37.6%). In this and the following analyses that are focused on users we take under consideration only the users with 100 or more tweets in our dataset as for the remaining users we do not have enough data gathered to produce stable estimates. There are 8,489 such users in our Twitter dataset.

While we have already reported that 62.4% of the users do not use emojis, investigating the probability distribution of using emojis in a tweet among the remaining users shows that half of them use emojis in up to 10% of the tweets while 75% use them in not more than 30% of the tweets. However, the distribution shows a surprisingly thick tail: while 5% of emoji users insert them in every second tweet, 2% of users post less than one emoji-less tweet in ten.

In the following analyses we investigate the differences between the emoji-using and emoji-abstaining users regarding their number of tweets, the number of tweets they have favourited, their number of followers and friends (users that a user follows). We compare the distributions of the four variables among the two types of users with the Wilcoxon test as neither of the variables is normally distributed. The null hypothesis assumes that the median of the two distributions is zero. We always perform a one-tailed test.

By performing our tests on the median we additionally eliminate the impact of outliers which is very beneficial given that our procedures for removing highly active and temporally regular users described in Section 2.2 were focused on emoji-producing users only.

The emoji-producing users have significantly more followers (median 595 vs. 402) and friends (median 438 vs. 288), produce more tweets (median 18280 vs. 12020) and favourite more tweets (median 1760 vs. 1). All the obtained p-values lie in the range $p < 0.001$. One should bear in mind that all the users taken under consideration are highly active on Twitter, producing in the time span of 21 days on average five or more tweets per day.

We have also investigated the dependence of the amount of emojis a user produces and the remaining four variables we have at our disposal, but none of the correlations were strong enough to be worth reporting.

Finally, looking into the number of emojis per tweet we find that single emojis occur in 45% of the emoji-containing tweets, two emojis make for 25% of the tweets, three emojis 15%, four emojis 7%, five emojis 3% and tweets with more than five emojis make 5% of all emoji-containing tweets. This distribution shows that in more than half of the tweets emojis occur with other emojis which makes a co-occurrence analysis as a method for obtaining an insight in the meaning of emojis (or rather the similarity of their meanings) very appealing.

3.2 Per-country analysis

In this subsection we investigate the popularity of emojis on a per-country basis. We quantify the emoji popularity in a specific country by calculating the percentage of geo-encoded tweets that contain emojis. By calculating the percentage of the tweets containing emojis, and not the overall amount of the emojis produced on Twitter, we neutralise the differences in popularity of Twitter among different countries.

Emoji density by country is given in Figure 1. The highest density of tweets can easily be observed in Indonesia (46.5% of tweets containing emojis) and the neighbouring third-ranking Philippines (34.6%). In South America the king of emojis, overall ranking second, is Paraguay (37.6%), followed by Argentina, overall ranking sixth (30.7%). In Africa emojis are most popular in the north, with Algeria ranking fourth (33.5%), Egypt ranking seventh (30.4%) and Libya ranking eight (29.7%). In the Arab peninsula Qatar comes first (overall ranking fifth, 32.6%), followed by UAE (ranking 10th, 27.1%). The two highest ranking European countries are Latvia (24.4%) and Spain (24.1%), followed by the Czech Republic, Portugal and the Russian Federation. Interestingly, Japan, the home of emojis, is ranked 163rd

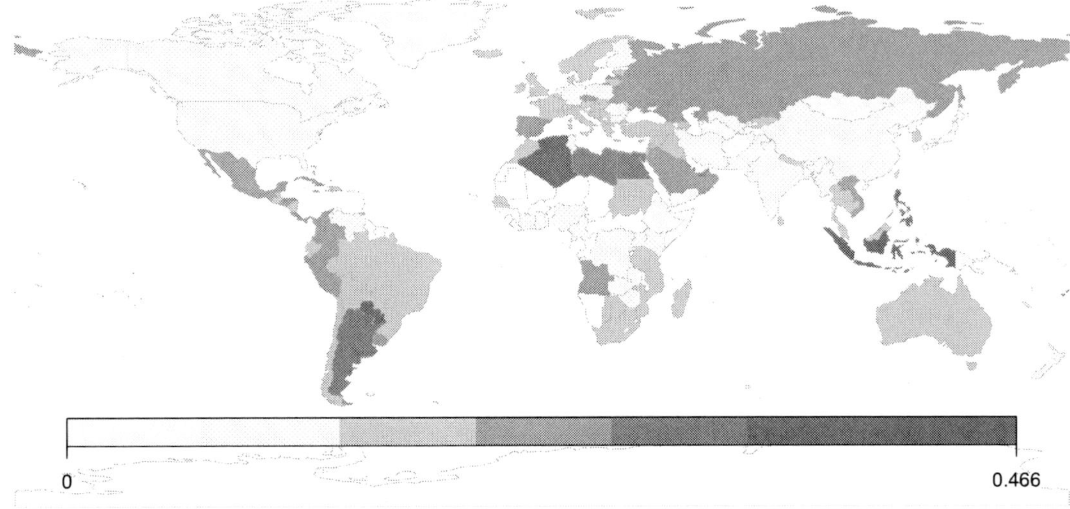

Figure 1: Emoji density per country measured as the percentage of tweets containing emojis

with only 7% of tweets containing emojis. The United States of America, the country responsible for making the pictograms widely popular, is just doing slightly better, ranking 152nd with 10% of tweets containing emojis. The highest ranking North American state is Mexico (21.8%) in 37th position.

Regarding the density of tweets on the continent level, Asia has the highest density with 26.3% tweets containing emojis, South America comes second with 20.9%, followed by Europe (16.7%), Africa (14.9%), Australia (13.7%) and North America (11.5%).

One has to stress right here that although the dataset used for estimating this distribution is rather large, it is still collected from one source only and therefore reflects the sociodemographic specificities of Twitter users of a specific country. Investigating the reliability of these estimates calculated on one social network only is left for future work.

4 Popularity of specific emojis

In this section we move from analysing the overall popularity of emojis to analysing the popularity of specific emojis. Again we start with a global analysis, continuing with a per-country one.

This set of analyses is performed on the Emoji dataset as here we are not interested in the probability of emoji occurrence, but the probability of specific emojis among all of them. To estimate these probabilities we do not require tweets that do not contain emojis.

4.1 Global analysis

The overall frequency distribution of emojis shows that the most frequent emoji on Twitter since December 2015, with around 2.6 million occurrences in our Emoji dataset, is the "Face with tears of joy" 😂, representing 6.7% of all emoji occurrences. The second most frequent emoji is the "Smiling face with heart-shaped eyes" 😍 (3.72%), on third place we find the "Emoji modifier Fitzpatrick type-1-2" ▨[2] (2.3%), position 4 is taken by "Smiling face with smiling eyes" 😊 (2.1%), and position 5 by "Face throwing a kiss" 😘 (2.1%).

We give a full list of encountered emojis with their frequency and popularity across countries in a separate publication we call *The Emoji Atlas*.[3]

4.2 Per-country analysis

In this set of analyses we are interested in how popular specific emojis are in individual countries. We therefore calculate the probability distribution of specific emojis for each country. We discard all the countries having less than 5000 data

---

[2]There are 5 emoji modifiers that define the skin tone of the emoji. In our analyses we consider these modifiers to be entities by themselves to achieve better generalisation both among modifiers and emojis.

[3]http://nlp.ffzg.hr/data/emoji-atlas/

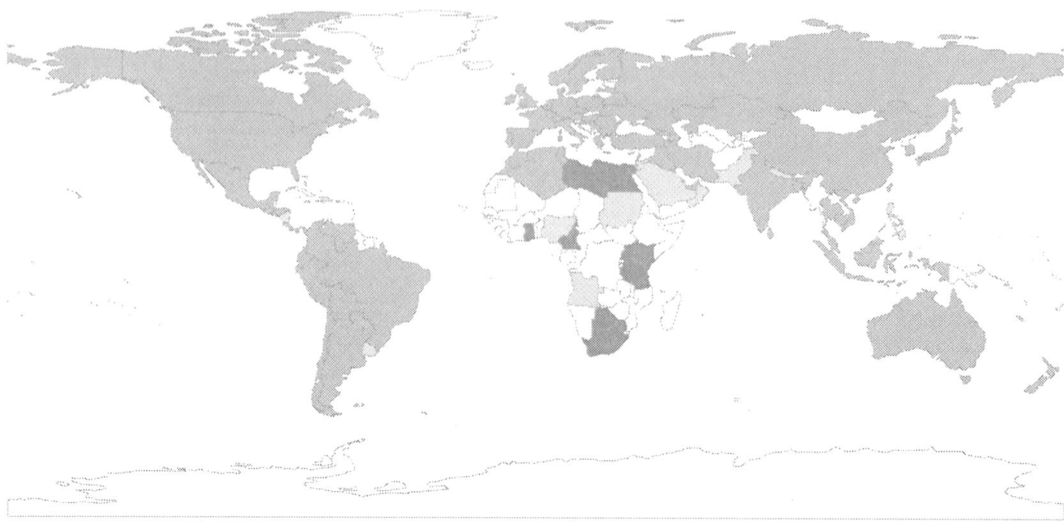

Figure 2: Results of the k-means algorithm on countries represented through the emoji probability distribution

points from our analyses as the estimated distribution of the 1282 emojis found in our data below this threshold would be quite unreliable. While defining this frequency threshold we were not only lead by the number of variables to be determined, but also by the percentage of countries left for our analysis, aiming at a decent global coverage. By applying the defined threshold we were left with 108 out of 233 countries from which we collected tweets in the 5-month period.

To obtain a first insight into the similarities and differences of emoji distributions among countries we ran the K-means clustering algorithm on countries, each country represented by the emoji probability distribution only. We ran the algorithm multiple times on different numbers of clusters and concluded for the 4-cluster division as presented in Figure 2 to be most explanatory. Additionally, this clustering result has proven to be very stable.

We refer to the light red cluster covering North America, Western Europe, the Russian Federation, and Australia as the "first world" cluster.

We call the blue cluster, covering most of South America, India and China, Eastern Europe, Morocco, Algeria and Tunisia the "second world" cluster.

The light blue cluster covering three African states (Angola, Nigeria and Sudan), Jordan, Saudi Arabia, Yemen, Pakistan, Nepal and the Philippines is referred to as the "third world" cluster.

The lilac cluster covering the remaining African states with enough coverage we call the "fourth world" cluster.

While most of the clustering decisions, besides a few that should be inspected more carefully (like Chile belonging to the "first world" cluster), are self-explanatory, we were quite puzzled by the clustering algorithm to pick out Angola, Nigeria and Sudan from the Sub-Saharan Africa and attach them to the cluster of less-fortunate Arab and Asian states. A short online search pointed to their common attribute: they have oil. The question remains whether the shift in the emoji distribution is due to better living conditions of the local population in comparison to most other African states or to the impact of the oil exploiters on the Twitter emoji production.

We analyse the difference between each cluster and the remaining world by calculating one arithmetic mean emoji vector for the cluster in question and another arithmetic mean emoji vector for the remaining clusters. We then subtract the cluster vector from the remaining world vector and inspect the 20 lowest dimensions, i.e. emojis that are most distinctive for the cluster in question. The twenty most distinctive emojis per cluster are given in Table 1.

Interestingly, different to all other clusters, the most distinctive emojis in the "first world" cluster are not face emojis, the first one occurring on

cluster	most distinctive emojis
"first world"	
"second world"	
"third world"	
"fourth world"	

Table 1: Twenty most distinctive emojis by cluster

position 19, the "Sleeping face" emoji . The two most distinctive emojis in the "first world" cluster are Emoji modifiers Fitzpatrick type 1-2 and 3 . The list is continued with a series of weather conditions like the sun and snow , natural occurrences like "Palm tree" , different types of flowers ("Cherry blossom" , "Hibiscus"), "Sparkles" , and celebration symbols such as "Party popper" and "Christmas tree" . The interesting feature of this cluster is that it lacks direct emotions represented by face emojis that make the most distinctive emojis in all the remaining clusters.

The most distinctive "second world" cluster emojis are a series of happy faces like "Face throwing a kiss" , "Smiling face with sunglasses" , "Smiling face with open mouth and smiling eyes" , "Smiling face with heart-shaped eyes" , "Winking face" and "Kissing face with closed eyes" . They are interrupted with a "Kiss mark" , "Thumbs up sign" , "Sparkling heart" etc.

The 20 emojis most typical of the "third world" cluster contain some happy faces such as "Smiling face with heart-shaped eyes" and "Face with tears of joy" , but also unhappy ones, such as "Loudly crying face" , "Sleepy face" , "Unamused face" and "Expressionless face" . Here the "Person with folded hands" makes its first appearance in our analyses.

Besides two rather happy emojis, "Face with tears of joy" and "Smiling face with open mouth and cold sweat" , the "fourth world" cluster is specific for a series of unhappy faces such as "Loudly crying face" , "Unamused face" , "Crying face" and "Weary face" . In addition to these face emojis the "Fire" , "Person raising both hands in celebration" and "Dancer" emojis are very distinctive as well. A series of emojis depicting people's hands like "Raised hand" , "White down pointing backhand index" , "White right pointing backhand index" and "White up pointing backhand in-

dex" are also very specific. The list then continues with a series of music-related emojis like "Multiple musical notes" , "Headphone" , "Microphone" and "Musical note" (the last two not making the top 20 emojis), the Emoji modifiers Fitzpatrick type 5 and 6 and "Person with folded hands" .

While skin modifiers make the list of most distinctive emojis in three out of four clusters, their presence does not significantly affect the clustering results as the same cluster structure was obtained when these modifiers were removed from our dataset.

To wrap-up, the "first world" cluster seems emotionally empty (or at least inexplicit) with almost no face emojis and only two general celebratory emojis, the "second world" cluster is highly positive with most distinctive emojis being the happy face emojis. The dominating emojis in the "third world" cluster are a series of unhappy faces and the praying emoji, while the "fourth world" cluster adds a series of hand symbols (for which we do not have an explanation yet) and rather basic symbols like fire, dance, music and celebration.

The already mentioned *Emoji Atlas* contains a full list of countries with their corresponding emoji distributions as well as a full list of emojis with their country distributions. We are confident that this resource will be of great use for less technically-oriented researchers who do not have the opportunity to compile and process such big datasets. Additionally, as we continue to run the data collection procedure, we will regularly update the resource and, with time, add the temporal component as well.

5   Emojis and development indicators

In the last set of experiments we look into the correlation between the spatial representation of each emoji and a selection of World Development Indicators of the World Bank.[4] Our spatial repre-

---

[4] http://data.worldbank.org

sentation of an emoji consists of probabilities of the emoji given a country which makes it comparable to the World Development Indicators since they are calculated by country as well.

For this initial analysis we have selected World Development Indicators for which we were intuitively expecting results with a straight-forward explanation: "Life expectancy at birth, total (years)", "Total tax rate (% of commercial profits)", "Trade in services (% of GDP)" and "GDP per capita (current US$)". Future work should include a wider set of Indicators.

For each indicator we calculate the Pearson correlation coefficient with each of the emojis and rank them by absolute value, inspecting all emojis with a correlation higher than 0.4.

We again remove data from countries with less than 5000 tweets with emojis as we consider the probability distribution of 1282 emojis calculated on such little data to be insufficient for a good estimate.

5.1 Life expectancy

The first indicator we take into account is the "Life expectancy at birth, total (years)" indicator.[5]

The emoji with absolutely the highest correlation with this indicator is the frequently mentioned "Face with tears of joy" emoji 😂 (-0.675), surprisingly with a negative sign, meaning that the higher the life expectancy, the lower the usage of the emoji. We have already observed this emoji to be heavily used in our "third world" and "fourth world" clusters.

The second and fourth absolutely highest correlations are the Emoji modifiers Fitzpatrick type 3 (0.596) and type 1-2 (0.578), both occurring more frequently as life expectancy rises. The third position is taken by the "Confused face" emoji 😕 (-0.585), the fifth by the "Person with folded hands" 🙏 (-0.549), both occurring, as expected, more frequently as life expectancy shrinks.

"Dog face" 🐶 and "Hot beverage" ☕ are following emojis with positive correlation, while the strong ones with negative correlation are "Dancer" 💃, "Fire" 🔥, "Baby symbol" 🚼 and "Person raising both hands in celebration" 🙌, all of which have a correlation coefficient higher than 0.5 which is considered to be a strong correlation.

5.2 Tax rate

The second indicator we consider is the "Total tax rate (% of commercial profits)" indicator.[6]

The only two emojis with a correlation above 0.4 are "Thumbs down sign" 👎 (0.467) and "Pouting face" 😡 (0.461).

5.3 Trade

Our third indicator is the "Trade in services (% of GDP)" indicator.[7]

The three emojis with the highest correlation to this indicator are "Slot machine" 🎰 (0.626), "Game die" 🎲 (0.584) and "Speedboat" 🚤 (0.579). Interestingly, there are no emojis with a high and negative correlation with this indicator.

5.4 GDP per capita

Our last indicator is the "GDP per capita (current US$)" indicator.[8]

The three emojis with the strongest correlation are "Emoji modifier Fitzpatrick type-3" 🟫 (0.593), "Fork and knife with plate" 🍽 (0.592) and "Bottle with popping cork" 🍾 (0.565). Further positively strongly correlating emojis are "Airplane" ✈ and "Cooking" 🍳.

The emojis with the strongest negative correlation are "Unamused face" 😒 (-0.428) and "Crying face" 😢 (-0.419).

6 Conclusion

In this paper we presented a worldwide spatial study of emoji usage by analysing a large dataset of geo-encoded tweets containing emojis. We depicted the popularity of emojis on Twitter around the world showing that they are most popular in South-Eastern Asia and South America, while in the USA (that technically enabled the rise of emojis) and Japan (the origin of emojis) the usage frequency on Twitter is multiple times lower.

Inspecting the specificities of the countries regarding the usage of different emojis, our country clustering results differentiate between the "first world" cluster the most distinctive features of which are rather emotionally empty, the "second world" cluster which is specific for highly positive emotions, the "third world" cluster which

[6]http://data.worldbank.org/indicator/
IC.TAX.TOTL.CP.ZS
[7]http://data.worldbank.org/indicator/
BG.GSR.NFSV.GD.ZS
[8]http://data.worldbank.org/indicator/
NY.GDP.PCAP.CD

[5]http://data.worldbank.org/indicator/
SP.DYN.LE00.IN

contains both positive and negative emotions, and the "fourth world" cluster which is predominantly negative with additional, rather basic concepts like fire, dance, music and hand gestures.

Finally, by performing a correlation analysis between emoji distributions across countries and a series of the World Development Indicators we have shown that emojis with the strongest correlation clearly describe the indicator in question which allows us to conclude that emoji usage is indicative of the living conditions in different parts of the world.

However, all our results are to be perceived by having in mind that only one social network was used for building our datasets which opens the natural question of data representativeness as (1) not all people use a specific social network and (2) different sociodemographic groups use the same social network in different countries. Nevertheless, this study objectively depicts the state in our social network of choice.

Our future work goes in three directions. The first one is investigating the impact of using only one social network on the final results.

The second direction goes towards the understanding of the meaning of emojis and using them for tasks like sentiment identification, emotion detection etc. For unsupervised modelling of the emoji meaning we primarily consider distributional models and emoji co-occurrence. We also wish to investigate semantic shifts of emojis across space. By continuous data collection, the temporal dimension becomes a relevant focus of interest with a series of similar research questions.

The third direction is aimed at understanding how emojis are included in natural language syntax.

Acknowledgments

The research leading to these results has received funding from the Swiss National Science Foundation grant IZ74Z0 160501 (ReLDI), and the Slovenian Research Agency within the national basic research project "Resources, Tools and Methods for the Research of Nonstandard Internet Slovene" (J6-6842, 2014-2017).

References

Mark Davis and Peter Edberg. 2015. Unicode emoji. Technical report, Unicode Consortium. http://unicode.org/reports/tr51/.

Britney Fitzgerald. 2016. Did Abraham Lincoln pioneer emoticons? 1862 speech may offer clues. http://www.huffingtonpost.com/2012/09/19/abraham-lincoln-emoticons_n_1893411.html.

Petra Kralj Novak, Jasmina Smailović, Borut Sluban, and Igor Mozetič. 2015a. Emoji Sentiment Ranking 1.0. Slovenian language resource repository CLARIN.SI.

Petra Kralj Novak, Jasmina Smailović, Borut Sluban, and Igor Mozetič. 2015b. Sentiment of Emojis. *PLoS ONE*, 10(12).

Igor Mozetič, Miha Grčar, and Jasmina Smailović. 2016. Twitter sentiment for 15 European languages. Slovenian language resource repository CLARIN.SI.

Umashanthi Pavalanathan and Jacob Eisenstein. 2016. Emoticons vs. Emojis on Twitter: A Causal Inference Approach. In *AAAI Spring Symposium on Observational Studies through Social Media and Other Human-Generated Content*.

SwiftKey. 2015. SwiftKey Emoji Report, April 2015. Technical report. https://goo.gl/9QXoEn.

The Unicode Consortium. 2016. Full emoji data. http://unicode.org/emoji/charts/full-emoji-list.html.

Genre classification for a corpus of academic webpages

Erika Dalan
University of Bologna
erika.dalan@unibo.it

Serge Sharoff
University of Leeds
s.sharoff@leeds.ac.uk

Abstract

In this paper we report our analysis of the similarities between webpages that are crawled from European academic websites, and comparison of their distribution in terms of the English language variety (native English vs English as a lingua franca) and their language family (based on the country's official language). After building a corpus of university webpages, we selected a set of relevant descriptors that can represent their text types using the framework of the Functional Text Dimensions. Manual annotation of a random sample of academic pages provides the basis for classifying the remaining texts on each dimension. Reliable thresholds are then determined in order to evaluate precision and assess the distribution of text types by each dimension, with the ultimate goal of analysing language features over English varieties and language families.

1 Introduction

English is increasingly regarded as the language of international communication in professional and institutional settings. In particular, it is the main language used by the European universities to communicate to their audience outside of their own country. English language communication is both a strategic choice for enhancing competitiveness and prestige, with the ultimate goal of attracting international students, and a transparency requirement imposed by the European Higher Education Area (EHEA).[1] At the same time, one can expect that the strategies used for communication vary according to culture and language factors. For instance, British and Irish universities may

adopt specific practices that differ from the ones of their counterparts on the continent, which are likely to be using ELF, English as Lingua Franca (Mollin, 2006). Differences may occur on at least two levels. First, on the higher level of genres and second, on the level of language patterns that are used to fulfil specific communicative functions. As regards the former, and with reference to university websites, related work has mainly focused on single genres, rather than the whole website. Some of these genres include *About us* pages (Caiazzo, 2011), Academic Course Descriptions or ACDs (Gesuato, 2011), international student prospectuses (Askehave, 2007), module descriptions (Bernardini et al., 2010) and mission statements (Morrish and Sauntson, 2013). Fewer studies have described university websites as a stand-alone unit, probably because of their high variability in terms of text types and genres. Based on a case study carried out on a small sample of universities (Dalan, 2015), both native English and ELF websites comprise five main textual functions - i.e. desctiptions, narratives, instructions, information and opinions – and a set of more structured genres such as FAQs, news and news archives, forums, descriptions of research projects, personal homepages (PHPs) and many others. Furthermore, some texts belong to proper academic domains (e.g. research papers and abstracts), others to institutional domains (the vast majority of running text) and others are derived from professional settings following the marketization of higher education (e.g. testimonials and *Why choose us* pages).

This wealth of genres and text types makes university websites a sort of a colony of genres that deserves to be further studied in terms of its textual functions.

As for language choices, Saichaie (2011) has investigated university websites using critical dis-

---

[1] http://www.ehea.info/.

Proceedings of the 10th Web as Corpus Workshop (WAC-X) and the EmpiriST Shared Task, pages 90–98,
Berlin, Germany, August 7-12, 2016. ©2016 Association for Computational Linguistics

course analysis. By analysing a sample of 12 US colleges, he notes a standardisation in the use of promotional language practices, in such a way that generic images tend to be delivered, regardless of how prestigious universities are. Ferraresi and Bernardini (2013) conducted a case study on the use of modal and semi-modal verbs by academic institutions in Europe and noted that native English texts show higher frequencies of modal verbs as compared to ELF university webpages. Modals of permission, possibility and ability seem to be used more widely in native texts as compared to ELF texts. It is still unclear whether these observations may be related to other variables as well, such as the set of genres mentioned above. Different institutional practices between native English and ELF countries may influence the quality and quantity of pages associated with specific functions. Therefore, finding a reliable method for classifying academic pages may help overcome or minimize biases related to genre variability. Automatic classification of university web-based genres is a fundamental preliminary step for comparing native English and ELF language patterns, as well as a thriving research area in itself that needs to be further explored.

In this paper, we will discuss the methods used for corpus collection (Section 2), a typology used for classifying our texts (Section 3), present the experimental setup (Section 4), analyse the results (Section 5) and discuss further research directions (Section 6).

2 Corpus collection

As mentioned in the Section 1, the final aim of this corpus is to compare communicative strategies of ELF and native English countries in university websites. Due to a lack of standards and best-practices as regards translation, localisation or drafting of online contents in English within the ELF community (Costales, 2012; Palumbo, 2013), only high-ranked universities are considered for inclusion in the corpus, in the attempt of obtaining a golden sample. Furthermore, texts in the gold standard are more easily comparable considering that these universities are evidently involved in the international scene. Therefore, a few design criteria were defined to collect a sample of academic webpages. Criteria for corpus building include the full list of European countries and a selection of universities based on the total number of universi-

ties per country listed in the QS World University Rankings.[2] The top 30% of universities in each country was chosen, fixing a maximum of ten. The procedure for text collection followed the pipeline described in the acWaC project (Bernardini and Ferraresi, 2013), including post-processing techniques developed in the WaCky project (Baroni and Bernardini, 2006). Corpus building consists of three steps: a) retrieving a list of seed URLs, i.e. university English homepages; b) crawling university websites starting from the list of URLs; c) post-processing data, annotation and indexing.

As concerns the first step, due to the relatively limited number of universities included in this corpus, English homepages of ELF universities were identified manually. The list of URLs was then used to run a crawl of university websites, starting from homepages down to level two, by following webpages internal links. The third step includes boilerplate removal, de-duplication and language identification. The whole process discarded 10% of universities overall, either because homepages could not been fetched or because they were removed during language identification processes. A set of metadata was also defined, in order to account for internal categorisation and to register contextual information. The list of metadata comprises:

- webpage URL and university English homepage;
- university extended name and main domain;
- QS World University overall ranking and QS World University score associated with the number of international students;
- status (public/private) and size (s/m/l/xl), as registered in the ranking;
- family of the country official language (e.g. Germanic in Norway and Romance in Italy);
- variety of English (either native in the UK and Ireland or ELF);
- level of crawling (from 0 to 2, where 0 is the homepage).

The final corpus contains approximately 20M tokens and 35K texts produced in 91 universities, 78 of which represent ELF countries whereas 13 represent the countries with native English. Table 1 and Table 2 provide descriptive statistics of the final corpus, split by language variety and

---

[2]http://www.topuniversities.com/qs-world-university-rankings

	ELF	Native EN	Total
Tokens	9,375,739	11,813,692	21,189,431
Texts	17,383	17,562	34,945
Universities	78	13	91
Countries	27	2	29

Table 1: Corpus statistics by English language variety (ELF and native English).

language family (Table 2 refers to ELF countries only).

3 Text typology

The webpages in the corpus can express several functions at the same time. For example, typical *About us* pages include informative descriptions, 'Description of a thing' according to the Web text classification scheme (Egbert et al., 2015), as well as promotional materials ('Informational Persuasion'). In order to deal with such variation we adapted the typology based on Functional Text Dimensions (FTD) (Forsyth and Sharoff, 2014) by selecting the following dimensions relevant to the academic webpages collected for this study:

A7, instruct To what extent does the text aim at teaching the reader how something works?

A8, hardnews To what extent does the text appear to be an informative report of events recent at the time of writing?

A9, legal To what extent does the text lay down a contract or specify a set of regulations?

A12, compuff To what extent does the text promote a product or service?

A14, scitech To what extent does the text serve as an example of academic research?

A16, info To what extent does the text provide information to define a topic?

A21, narrate To what extent does the text describe a chronologically ordered sequence of events?

Application of this procedure leads to a compact description of each text as scoring on some of the dimensions. For example, some *About us* webpages are strictly informational (**A16**),[3] some

are narrative (**A21**),[4] while others combine information with promotion.[5]

We have annotated a subset of 897 webpages, randomly sampled from the main corpus. Due to limited resources, annotation was done by one annotator only. However, other studies which used the FTD annotation categories listed above demonstrated reasonable interannotator agreement levels, with Krippendorff's α ranging from 0.78 to 0.97 for different FTDs (Sharoff, 2015).

Sampling was done by selecting the ten pages for each university randomly.[6] To balance the lack of information required to perform a stratified sample and the need for a representative sample of most text types, we have manually analysed URLs to make sure that specific portions of the website did not dominate over other portions. If URLs were skewed towards a portion of a website (e.g. www.bg.ac.rs/en/bodies/), more pages were taken from other uncovered sections. Each webpage was annotated using a scale from 0 to 2, with 0 meaning that the descriptor is not present at all, 0.5 meaning that it is present to a small extent, 1 meaning that it is partly present and 2 meaning that it is strongly characterised by a specific descriptor. This four-value scale has proven successful in a number of experiments (Forsyth and Sharoff, 2014) and was deemed an acceptable trade-off between precision and confidence for annotation. In order to get cleaner text types for training purposes, pages containing two or more text types in separate areas were split into different texts. On the other hand, proper hybrid pages, i.e. those fulfilling multiple functions simultaneously, were given a strong value in each applicable attribute. This resulted in a training corpus of 931

---

[3]https://www.cam.ac.uk/public-engagement/about-us

[4]http://www.sci.u-szeged.hu/english/brief-history/about-us

[5]http://wwwf.imperial.ac.uk/business-school/

[6]Given that the corpus includes 91 universities, there should be at least 910 pages to code. However, two universities comprise less than 10 pages overall. Specifically, University of Rome Tor Vergata in Italy and University of Innsbruck in Austria contain two and five pages respectively.

Country	Language Family	Tokens	Texts
Germany	Germanic	1,269,884	2,674
Switzerland	Germanic-Romance	807,456	1,845
Netherlands	Germanic	801,244	1,767
Denmark	Germanic	779,139	1,382
Finland	Uralic	771,860	1,263
Sweden	Germanic	680,928	1,258
France	Romance	633,523	1,155
Italy	Romance	620,940	1,059
Spain	Romance	603,882	941
Russia	Slavic	530,522	722
Belgium	Germanic-Romance	408,088	657
Norway	Germanic	283,059	554
Austria	Germanic	185,224	352
Czech Republic	Slavic	183,370	324
Estonia	Uralic	176,162	299
Portugal	Romance	117,919	234
Slovenia	Slavic	95,309	161
Latvia	Baltic	72,568	123
Poland	Slavic	63,443	111
Romania	Romance	58,915	111
Hungary	Uralic	55,437	96
Belarus	Slavic	46,291	83
Serbia	Slavic	40,606	81
Lithuania	Baltic	36,552	44
Ukraine	Slavic	30,632	39
Greece	Hellenic	14,881	30
Slovakia	Slavic	7,905	18

Table 2: Corpus statistics by country and language family (ELF countries only).

texts. Drawing on experience from earlier annotation experiments, this number is sufficiently large to contain a representative picture of variation in academic webpages.

The annotation process produced a numeric data matrix in which each row corresponds to an observation and each column corresponds to a functional descriptor. Many texts score on several dimensions. Legal and instructional texts tend to be more recognizable, whereas informative, promotional and narrative pages show a higher degree of overlapping. Texts dealing with academic research very often score on the hardnews dimension as well, since they are often presented in the form of news bites.

The annotation matrix is used to retrieve a set of positive and negative examples for each FTD, to be used as a training set for experimenting automatic classification of the entire corpus. The amount of the positive examples for each FTD in the training corpus is listed in Table 3.

4   Automatic genre classification

Classification of texts according to their genres can be achieved by extracting a range of higher-level features, such as combinations of POS tags, parse trees or rhetorical relations (Santini et al., 2010). However, lower-level features based on character n-grams offer a surprisingly efficient method for detecting genres without requiring heavy linguistic resources (Kanaris and Stamatatos, 2007). In a comparative evaluation, their performance can exceed what is achieved by resource-heavier approaches. For example, pure n-grams can successfully generalise dates (*.*day* for *yesterday, today, Friday*), which are typical in reporting, nominalisations (*.*tion*) or passives (*.*ed by*), which are typical in scientific discourse (Sharoff et al., 2010).

The frequencies of character n-grams can be directly used as features in algorithms of Machine Learning. However, many classification methods use kernels as a mechanism for comparing the similarity between objects described by the features in order to build a model separating their classes. String Kernels (Lodhi et al., 2002) is one of such methods, which measures the similarity between webpages represented as the distance between their character n-grams.

In this study, we experimented with classification using Support Vector Machines (Smola and Schölkopf, 2004) or Relevance Vector Machines (Tipping, 2001). The advantage of RVM is the ability to produce a small number of Support Vectors, leading to better learning generalisation in the case of relatively sparse data, for example, only 25 positive examples have been identified for **A9** (legal texts). The task is to predict whether a webpage features strongly in each FTD. The commonly used F1 measure is reported in Table 3 with cross-validation for detecting the FTDs.

Once we produced reliable classifiers for each dimension, we applied them to the entire corpus of academic webpages. To establish which pages score on each dimension with minimal noise outside the training set, we experimented with reliable thresholds to achieve the desired precision. Table 3 shows the composition of the corpus in terms of the number of pages for which the predicted score is greater than or equal to each threshold and the corresponding percentage in the final corpus as opposed to the manually annotated training corpus described in Section 3.

On the whole, post-hoc evaluation shows that classification by n-grams is highly efficient in terms of precision, considering that at least 80% of pages above the threshold perfectly or widely match each specific dimension. Note that the proportion of pages that score on one dimension exclusively is very close to the one obtained from manual annotation, except for A16 dimension. The latter, however, diverges from other dimensions in that any university webpage tends to contain some degree of informational content, which may lead this dimension to be considered as a 'safety margin' and, eventually, to be over-represented in human annotation. Overall, approximately 50% of pages in the training set and 40% in the final corpus were classified as scoring high on one function, which is an encouraging result if we consider that online content is increasingly

evolving, producing new genres and hybrid pages (Santini, 2007; Bruce, 2011).

5 Differences between language varieties

We also calculated the relative frequencies of pages that score above each threshold in order to assess their distribution across language varieties (ELF and native English) and language families (as registered in our metadata). Native English and ELF texts are equally distributed over all dimensions, apart from A16, which seems slightly more typical of ELF texts.

Looking more closely at the distribution of texts by language family (Figure 1) at least one aspect becomes immediately clear. Instructional (A7) and promotional (A12) functions are the only ones showing a medium-to-high number of pages; moreover, promotional texts are detected even in those countries that include very few pages in the original corpus, such as the Baltic and Hellenic ones, counting 144 and 30 texts respectively (Table 2). Although this may be partly related to automatic selection of pages during crawling and postprocessing, the high relative frequency of promotional pages may suggest that when it comes to providing contents in English language, promotional texts are given priority over plain information, and in some cases, over instructional pages as well. A12 texts comprise very typical promotional genres, such as the ones already mentioned above (*Why choose us* pages, *About us* pages, mission statements, *Welcome* pages), as well as other texts belonging to various website sections, for instance research projects, visiting students and international strategies, descriptions of university facilities and departments, student life, sport and many others. Hard-news pages (A8) are also spread over the majority of language families, whereas legal texts (A9) appear to be relatively rare. Legal pages are slightly more frequent in Ireland and the UK where they tend to be associated with privacy policies.[7] Moving on to the A16 dimension, i.e. plain information, Romance languages seem to be separated from ELF Germanic, ELF Germanic-Romance and native English texts;[8] the former are placed between the second and fourth quartile, whereas the latter are spread below the second quartile. Greece does not include any informational pages, while Uralic and Slavic coun-

---

[7] http://www.ucc.ie/en/ocla/comp/data/dataprotection/
[8] Native English texts are of Germanic origin as well.

	A7	A8	A9	A12	A14	A16	A21
% in training set	8.4	5.0	3.2	8.5	6.3	13.6	5.5
F-measure	0.95	0.92	0.96	0.85	0.93	0.79	0.94
% in final corpus	13.9	6.3	0.5	10.2	3.9	3.3	1.1
N. of pages	4,737	2,168	190	3,492	1,353	1,127	383

Table 3: Manual annotation of the training set and final corpus.

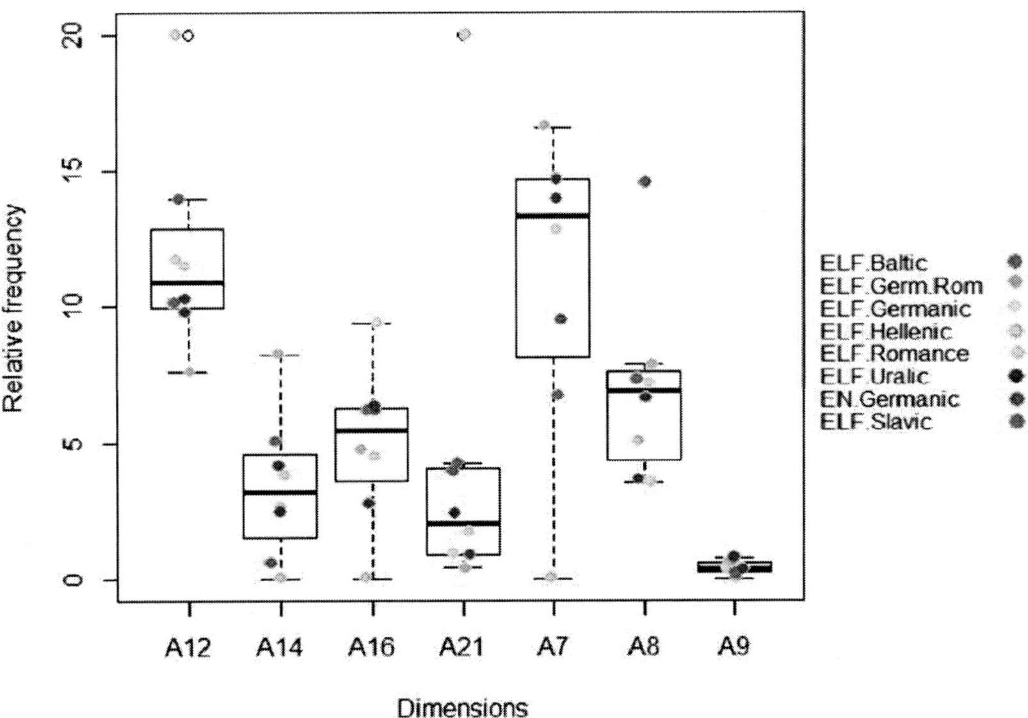

Figure 1: Distribution of texts by language variety and language family.

tries are closer to the Romance ones. Examples of informational texts include lists of items,[9] descriptions of university services and administrative offices.[10]

Pages reporting academic research (A14) are less evenly distributed. Switzerland is the country with the highest number of texts representing academic research, whereas Hellenic and Baltic countries have next to no pages in the corpus on this dimension. Finally, narrative texts - i.e. pages describing chronologically ordered events - place themselves between legal and research pages, showing higher frequencies in Slavic, Uralic and Baltic regions, and a very high peak in Greece. Genres from this dimension include university history in Greece,[11] the description of historical figures in Romania,[12] Professors academic careers in Ukraine and the description of university museums in Estonia.[13]

By exploiting URL strings, one can also detect typical website sections in order to analyse a) how language is used in the same dimensions across English varieties and families and b) how language is used across different dimensions. For instance, when searching the string *why* among pages that score highly on the A12 dimension, 78 texts are retrieved overall, each of them matching the genre *Why choose us*. Although no systematic analysis of language features has been performed yet, some interesting patterns emerge when analysing these pages by language variety. Besides native English and ELF dissimilarities that have already been observed in previous studies (Bernardini et al., 2010) - e.g. a larger use of second person pronouns by native English universities - from the point of view of content, *Why choose us* texts produced in Ireland and the UK make more frequent references to *help* and *support*, as compared to ELF pages. On the other hand, in ELF texts there is repeated mention of the *international* and *European* perspective that seems to be less common among native English countries. As far as the second type of analysis is concerned, searching the string *mission* among texts that score highly on A16 and A12 dimensions will yield two completely different text types. Example 1 and Example 2 below are two excerpts of mission statements taken, respectively, from the University of Vienna[14] and from Imperial College London.[15] As predicted by automatic classification, Example 1 scores highly on the A16 dimension, whereas Example 2 scores on the A12 dimension.

(1) The International Office serves as an information hub and service facility in the field of internationalisation and international relations at the University of Vienna. We support and advise members of the university in all international agendas, in particular in relation to requests for bilateral cooperation projects. The International Office is also involved in the implementation of the internationalization strategy of the University of Vienna.

(2) The Graduate School plays a key role in delivering the postgraduate student experience as well as with postgraduate education, policy and strategy development. The Graduate School enriches the postgraduate student experience by delivering a tailored programme of professional skills training which enhances the professional impact and helps to ensure personal ambitions are realised.

Although both texts are placed on the same website section named *mission* or *our mission*, from an internal perspective they are different. Example 1 adopts language patterns that usually characterise administrative texts (*serves as, in relation to requests, implementation of*), whereas Example 2 employs positive loaded words that are very typical of evaluative language (*key, enrich, enhance, ambitions realised*) and mission statements as well (Morrish and Sauntson, 2013). Besides confirming the performance of classification based on n-grams, these two examples raise some issues related to the efficiency of reflexive categories (Sinclair and Ball, 1996), especially when university webpage titles refer to genre, rather than topic.

---

[9] http://www.bsu.by/en/main.aspx?guid=134021

[10] http://www.unibo.it/en/university/campuses-and-structures/urp-public-relations-office/services-urp

[11] http://www.ntua.gr/history_en.html

[12] http://150.uaic.ro/personalitati/biologie/ioan-borcea/?lang=en

[13] http://www.univ.kiev.ua/en/geninf/adm/Zacusilo/

[14] http://zid.univie.ac.at/en/about-us/vision-mission/

[15] https://www.imperial.ac.uk/study/pg/graduate-school/about-us/mission-statement-/

6 Conclusions and further research

This paper reports an experiment on automatic classification and analysis of a corpus of university webpages in terms of genres by using string kernels with the aim of exploring the distribution of genres across English varieties and English language families. Classification by n-grams has proven successful in terms of precision. Post-hoc evaluation showed that more than 80% of pages above the reliability thresholds match the predicted dimension.

Instructional and promotional webpages have the largest share in our corpus across all language varieties, such as English native and ELF. However, variation is higher when considering each language family. In a few cases, variation may be related to country-specific aspects and how universities wish to present themsleves internationally, for instance Greece focusing on university history and Switzerland showing the highest number of texts related to academic research. Universities located in a country where the official language is of Romance origin exhibit the highest number of plain information, partially due to the descriptions of university offices and services. The informational dimension seems to be quite uncommon in ELF-Germanic and Native English texts, where it reaches its lowest levels, i.e. Ireland, the UK, Belgium and Denmark.

Automatic classification of university web genres enables comparison of genres across dimensions and language varieties. Although findings have not been generalised to the full set of our data, they form the basis for future systematic analysis across text types, genres and English language varieties in university websites. In the future, we plan to carry out clustering to identify hybrid texts and genre categories that score on more than one functional dimension simultaneously, such as info-promotional pages and news describing academic research. Other plans include investigating the relation between text types and other linguistic or contextual information, such as university world ranking. Finally, this work also carries applied implications for developing and improving communicative strategies based on the analysis of typical features of highly-ranked universities, as suggested by the examples provided at the end of the previous section.

Acknowledgments

We are grateful to Silvia Bernardini for her extensive comments on the earlier drafts.

References

Inger Askehave. 2007. The impact of marketization on higher education genres: The international student prospectus as a case in point. *Discourse Studies*, 9:723–742.

Marco Baroni and Silvia Bernardini, editors. 2006. *Wacky! Working papers on the Web as Corpus*. GEDIT, Bologna.

Silvia Bernardini and Adriano Ferraresi. 2013. The academic Web-as-Corpus. In *Proceedings of the 8th Web as Corpus Workshop*, Lancaster.

Silvia Bernardini, Adriano Ferraresi, and Federico Gaspari. 2010. Institutional academic English in the European context: a web-as-corpus approach to comparing native and non-native language. In *Professional English in the European context: The EHEA challenge*, pages 27 – 53. Peter Lang, BERNA.

Ian Bruce. 2011. Evolving genres in online domains: the hybrid genre of the participatory news article. In Alexander Mehler, Serge Sharoff, and Marina Santini, editors, *Genres on the Web: Text, Speech and Language Technology*. Springer.

Luisa Caiazzo. 2011. Hybridization in institutional language: Exploring we in the 'about us' page of university websites. In Srikant Sarangi, Vanda Polese, and Giuditta Caliendo, editors, *Genre(s) on the move. Hybridization and discourse change in specialized communication*, pages 243–260. Edizioni Scientifiche Italiane, Napoli.

Alberto Fernndez Costales. 2012. The internationalization of institutional websites: The case of universities in the European Union. In A. Pym and D. Orrego-Carmona, editors, *Translation Reasearch Projects 4*. Intercultural Studies Group, Terragona.

Erika Dalan. 2015. Classifying university websites: A case study. Poster session presented at Corpus Linguistics 2015, Lancaster, July.

Jesse Egbert, Douglas Biber, and Mark Davies. 2015. Developing a bottom-up, user-based method of web register classification. *Journal of the Association for Information Science and Technology*.

Richard Forsyth and Serge Sharoff. 2014. Document dissimilarity within and across languages: a benchmarking study. *Literary and Linguistic Computing*, 29:6–22.

Sara Gesuato. 2011. Course descriptions: Communicative practices of an institutional genre.

In Srikant Sarangi, Vanda Polese, and Giuditta Caliendo, editors, *Genre(s) on the move. Hybridization and discourse change in specialized communication*, pages 221–241. Edizioni Scientifiche Italiane, Napoli.

Ioannis Kanaris and Efstathios Stamatatos. 2007. Webpage genre identification using variable-length character n-grams. In *Proceedings of ICTAI*.

Huma Lodhi, Craig Saunders, John Shawe-Taylor, Nello Cristianini, and Chris Watkins. 2002. Text classification using string kernels. *Journal of Machine Learning Research*, 2:419–444.

Sandra Mollin. 2006. English as a lingua franca: A new variety in the new expanding circle? *Nordic Journal of English Studies*, 5(1):41–57.

Liz Morrish and Helen Sauntson. 2013. Business-facing motors for economic development: an appraisal analysis of visions and values in the marketised uk university. *Critical Discourse Studies*, 10(1):61–80.

Giuseppe Palumbo. 2013. Divided loyalties? Some notes on translating university websites into English. *CULTUS*, 6:95–109.

Kem Saichaie. 2011. *Representation on college and university websites: An approach using critical discourse analysis*. Ph.D. thesis, University of Iowa.

Marina Santini, Alexander Mehler, and Serge Sharoff. 2010. Riding the rough waves of genre on the web. In Alexander Mehler, Serge Sharoff, and Marina Santini, editors, *Genres on the Web: Computational Models and Empirical Studies*. Springer, Berlin/New York.

Marina Santini. 2007. Characterizing genres of web pages: Genre hybridism and individualization. In *Proceedings of the 40th Annual Hawaii International Conference on System Sciences*, pages 71 – 81, Washington, DC, USA. IEEE Computer Society.

Serge Sharoff, Zhili Wu, and Katja Markert. 2010. The Web library of Babel: evaluating genre collections. In *Proc. of the Seventh Language Resources and Evaluation Conference, LREC 2010*, Malta.

Serge Sharoff. 2015. Approaching genre classification via syndromes. In *Proc Corpus Linguistics*, Lancaster.

John Sinclair and Jackie Ball. 1996. Preliminary recommendations on text typology. Technical Report EAG-TCWG-TTYP/P, Expert Advisory Group on Language Engineering Standards document.

Alex J Smola and Bernhard Schölkopf. 2004. A tutorial on support vector regression. *Statistics and computing*, 14(3):199–222.

Michael E Tipping. 2001. Sparse Bayesian learning and the Relevance Vector Machine. *Journal of Machine Learning Research*, 1:211–244.

On Bias-free Crawling and Representative Web Corpora

Roland Schäfer
Freie Universität Berlin
Habelschwerdter Allee 45
14195 Berlin, Germany
roland.schaefer@fu-berlin.de

Abstract

In this paper, I present a specialized open-source crawler that can be used to obtain bias-reduced samples from the web. First, I briefly discuss the relevance of bias-reduced web corpus sampling for corpus linguistics. Then, I summarize theoretical results that show how commonly used crawling methods obtain highly biased samples from the web. The theoretical part of the paper is followed by a description my feature-complete and stable *ClaraX* crawler which performs so-called Random Walks, a form of crawling that allows for bias-reduced sampling if combined with methods of post-crawl rejection sampling. Finally, results from two large crawling experiments in the German web are reported. I show that bias reduction is feasible if certain technical and practical hurdles are overcome.

1 Corpus Linguistics, Web Corpora, and Biased Crawling

Very large web corpora are necessarily derived from crawled data. Such corpora include COW (Schäfer and Bildhauer, 2012), LCC (Goldhahn et al., 2012), UMBC WebBase (Han et al., 2013), and WaCky (Baroni et al., 2009). A crawler software (Manning et al., 2009; Olston and Najork, 2010) recursively locates unknown documents by following URL links from known documents, which means that a set of start URLs (the *seeds*) has to be known before the crawl. Diverse crawling strategies differ primarily in how they queue (i. e., prioritize) the harvested links for download. A typical real-world goal is to optimize the queueing algorithm in a way such that many good corpus documents are found in the shortest possible time, in order to save on bandwidth and

processing costs (Suchomel and Pomikálek, 2012; Schäfer et al., 2014).

Such an efficiency-oriented approach is reasonable if corpus size matters most. However, the goals of corpus construction might be different for many corpora intended for use in corpus linguistics. Especially in traditional corpus linguistics, where forms of *balanced* or even *representative* corpus design (Biber, 1993) are sometimes advocated as the only viable option, web corpora are often regarded with reservation, partly because the sources from which they are compiled and their exact composition are unknown (Leech, 2007). Other corpus linguists are more open to web data. For example, in branches of cognitively oriented corpus linguistics where the *corpus-as-input* hypothesis is adopted—e. g., Stefanowitsch and Flach (2016 in press)—, nothing speaks against using large web corpora. Under such a view, corpora are seen as reflecting an average or typical input of a language user. Consequently, the larger and thus more varied a corpus is, the better potential individual differences between speaker inputs are averaged out.

Even under such a more open perspective, corpus designers should make sure that the material used for a web corpus is not heavily biased. Naive crawling can lead to very obvious biases. For example, Schäfer and Bildhauer (2012, 487) report that in two large-scale crawls of the *.se* top-level domain, the Heritrix crawler (Mohr et al., 2004) ended up downloading 75% of the total text mass that ended up in the final corpus from a single blog host. The final corpus was still 1.5 billion tokens large, and seemingly large size does thus *not* prevent heavy crawling bias in web corpora, as the Swedish web most certainly does not consist of 75% blogs.

Apart from such immediately visible problems (which, admittedly, can be solved by relatively simple countermeasures) there are structural and

Proceedings of the 10th Web as Corpus Workshop (WAC-X) and the EmpiriST Shared Task, pages 99–105,
Berlin, Germany, August 7-12, 2016. ©2016 Association for Computational Linguistics

hard to detect biases introduced by all variants of the ubiquitously used *breadth-first search* (BFS) crawling algorithm.[1] As theoretical work has shown, BFS is biased towards web pages that have a high *in-degree*, i. e., pages to which many other pages link (Achlioptas et al., 2005; Kurant et al., 2010; Maiya and Berger-Wolf, 2011). It follows that crawling algorithms used for corpus construction so far do not give each page the same chance of being sampled. They do not perform *uniform random sampling*, and it is mathematically impossible to correct for BFS bias post-hoc.

Although the problem has been mentioned sporadically in the web-as-corpus literature, for example by Ciaramita and Baroni (2006, 131) or Schäfer and Bildhauer (2013, 29–34), nobody has ever tried to investigate whether such fundamental biases pose a problem. As of today, it is simply unclear whether even corpus linguists of the more permissive type (w. r. t. corpus composition) can rely on web corpora as being good samples of the whole text mass on the web.[2] Thus, retrieving unbiased (and thus technically speaking *representative*) samples from the web is not only important for fundamental research, but it might ultimately help to improve the acceptance of web corpora in corpus linguistics. I want to point out that the term *representative(ness)* in the remainder of this paper is used in a purely statistical—i. e., sampling-theoretic—way: a web corpus is representative of the documents on the web if each page had the same chance of being sampled.[3]

In this paper, I mainly describe the features and configurability of an open-source crawler which can be used for bias-corrected sampling from the web. I also show some preliminary results from the analysis of large experimental crawls in the German-speaking segment of the web. In Section 2, I briefly discuss crawling algorithms which allow for the (partial) correction of crawling biases. The system description of the crawler follows in Section 3. Finally, I present the experimental results in Section 4.

2 Methods for Bias Correction

In the theoretical literature, algorithms for bias-free crawling have been proposed. When considering such algorithms, it is vital to understand that the web forms a *directed graph* and that all crawlers implement a strategy by which they explore this graph. The web pages are the *nodes* of the graph, and each link from one page to another forms an *edge*. Any web crawler moves from node (page) to node by following edges (links), and it consequently implements a graph search algorithm (like BFS). The web graph is *directed* (and not *undirected*) because links cannot be followed backwards.[4]

It has been suggested by Henzinger et al. (2000) and Rusmevichientong et al. (2001) that bias-free samples can be obtained from directed graphs by applying Random Walk algorithms (RW) instead of BFS. See also the summary in Schäfer and Bildhauer (2013, 29–34). A RW jumps from page to page by randomly selecting exactly one outgoing link, following it, and discarding all others. No additional restrictions are imposed on the walker's search path, and thus revisits of pages seen before are conceptually desired.[5] A subtype of the RW algorithm reserves a certain probability at each step of jumping to a random URL instead of following a link.[6] Fundamental results show that RW crawling is also biased, but in a way that we can correct for.

---

[1]The simplest BFS prioritizes harvested links in the order that they were harvested. Optimizations usually depart slightly from BFS and add mechanisms by which those links receive higher priority which promise to lead to better content according to some metrics.

[2]I want to point out in passing that Google searches are most likely not an appropriate method of obtaining unbiased samples from the web, especially because we have no way of knowing how Google selects and sorts search results. Biber and Egbert (2016, 9) call their corpus based on Google queries 'representative' but at the same time admit that the sampling method does not guarantee representativeness. See Kilgarriff (2006) or Schäfer and Bildhauer (2013, 6–7) for summaries of why Google is not a good choice for sampling corpus documents.

[3]While such samples might ultimately not be the optimal samples for certain specific research questions, they are clearly required in order to establish a basis for any further (informed/stratified) sampling. A common example in introductory statistics courses teaches students that obtaining a sample for an opinion poll at the convention of a single party is useless for predicting the outcome of an election, no matter how large the sample is. It would be highly biased without any chance of correcting the bias through additional stratification. The work presented here will ultimately help to make

sure that our web corpus sampling procedures do not suffer similar fatal biases.

[4]Technically, because a page i can have n_{ij} links pointing to any page j (with $n_{ij} \in \mathbb{N}_0$), the web graph is a *network*, and n_{ij} is the *weight* of the edge between i and j.

[5]This is very different in efficiency-oriented crawling, where a lot of effort is invested into avoiding revisits.

[6]For all practical applications, the random URL has to be taken from a very large database of known (thus pseudo-random) links.

Essentially, RWs sample pages with a probability that is dependent on their *PageRank*. The PageRank (Brin and Page, 1998) is a well known metric and essentially a generalization of the indegree. See the accessible summary in Bryan and Leise (2006). While the exact PageRank of each page can only be calculated if the whole graph is known, Henzinger et al. (2000) show that a page's PageRank can be estimated from the number of times a long RW revisits the page. Bias correction is then just a matter of applying a form of *rejection sampling* to all pages visited by the RW (the *biased sample*): by sampling pages from the biased sample with a probability inverse to their estimated PageRank, one can create an *unbiased sample*. Rusmevichientong et al. (2001) show that Henzinger's rejection sampling method, while strongly alleviating the bias, does not remove it completely because the PageRank estimation is inexact. They suggest a modified algorithm which increases the precision of the estimation by performing additional independent RWs originating from each node of the original RW (for mathematical details see their paper).

The crawler described in Section 3 can be used for both types of bias correction. However, preliminary results reported in Section 4 show that only Henzinger's algorithm might be feasible for web crawling, and even that only with certain modifications.

3　An Experimental Random Walker

In this section, I describe a highly configurable experimental crawler called *ClaraX* that performs random walks through the web graph: a *walker* rather than a crawler. I call it *experimental* because it is intended for experiments and fundamental research, not for the construction of large web corpora. The software is feature-complete and stable, compiles on GNU/Linux and OSX, and it is made available (including the source code) under a maximally permissive 2-clause BSD open-source license.[7]

3.1　Crawling Architecture

The basic crawling strategy implemented in the walker is a simple RW. In other words, the walker walks from document to document, always following a single randomly selected outgoing link from the current document, discarding all other

links. Consequently, it starts with a single seed URL. A *random jump probability* can be specified, in which case a file with a list of seed URLs must be passed. The walker will then jump to a random link from the list instead of following a link from the current page with the specified probability. The walker implements all essential crawler functionality. This includes

- URL scope restriction via regex
- URL block regexes
- politeness restrictions (including *robots.txt*)
- obfuscation through User-Agent forging and randomized waits
- web page caching
- HTTP time-out control
- crawl step limit/maximal path length

The basic URL selection scheme is simply random selection of one link from each page (see Section 2). However, for practical reasons, the walker can be configured to follow

- links to entirely different hosts
- links to different virtual hosts (such as *www.host.com* and *forum.host.com*)
- links to the exact same host
- any combination of the above

Further URL selection is implemented based on the integrated post-processing described in Section 3.2. If the walker jumps to a page which turns out to be too short, too bad in terms of text quality, written in the wrong language, etc., then the walker can be set to discard this step and try another random link from the *previous* page. This effectively allows users to define sub-graphs of the web graph which the walker should explore.

Finally, the walker offers ways of dealing with dead ends. A dead end is reached when a page does not contain any links, or if all outgoing links from a page have been tried but none of the linked documents fulfilled the defined criteria. Since a RW always follows a single non-branching path through the web graph, it cannot continue from such a page. In this case, a *forced jump* to another seed URL can be performed, or the walk can be terminated. Alternatively, the walker can *backtrack*. This means that it follows its own path backwards and tries alternative paths.[8]

---

[7]https://github.com/rsling/texrex

[8]Theoretically, the walker would ultimately find the longest possible path beginning at the initial seed URL by

3.2 Built-in Processing and Output Formats

The walker integrates a full post-processing tool chain consisting of diverse modules, such as an HTML stripper, a UTF-8 converter and NFC normalizer, a boilerplate detector, and a language detector/text quality evaluator based on frequencies of function words. The post-processing modules are re-used from the previously developed *texrex* software (Schäfer and Bildhauer, 2012; Schäfer et al., 2013; Schäfer, 2016b; Schäfer, 2016a). The walker documents the progression of the RW in a short and a long file format. Python scripts are available which convert these files to JSON, allowing anyone to easily read in the data. Also, the original HTML documents are stored in a subset of the ISO WARC file format.[9] Furthermore, a processed clean corpus is stored in the simple (but fully well-formed) XML that is also used for the COW corpora. Finally, in order to locate near-duplicate documents in the resulting corpus, w-shingles (Broder, 2000) are stored in separate files for later analysis with included tools.

4 First Experiments

In this section, I present results from two experiments performed using the walker described in Section 3. For both experiments, the walker was configured to:

- walk only within the top-level domains .*at*, .*ch*, and .*de*, which are associated with countries where German is the (or one of the) major official languages
- only proceed if the documents found were written in German
- obfuscate the fact that it was a crawler, transmitting a false User-Agent header and not respecting *robots.txt*
- be very polite with a minimal wait of 10 seconds between requests to a host
- use a list of over 15 million seed URLs extracted from the large German DECOW14 web corpus

In other words, the experiments relate to the sub-segment of the web that can be called the *German-speaking web.*

---

using backtracking. Given the size and complexity of the web graph, however, backtracking can only be used effectively combined with a relatively low maximal desired path length.

[9]`http://www.iso.org/iso/catalogue_`
`detail.htm?csnumber=44717`

Steps	Host
91,442	www.vsw-news.de
40,806	pauls-blog.over-blog.de
35,787	fielders-choice.de
34,411	www.my-bikeshop.de
34,091	www.bremer-treff.de
24,769	www.deutscher-werkbund.de
24,114	www.vau-niedersachsen.de
24,096	www.icony.de
22,299	www.discover.de
20,093	www.dewezet.de

Table 1: The 10 longest RW segments spent on a single host during the first experiment

Exper.	Runtime	Steps	Hosts	St./Host
1	12.75d	1,093,047	1,227	890.83
2	25.36d	2,090,443	204,053	10.25

Table 2: Key figures for the two experiments

4.1 Link Structures on the Web

The first experiment was a baseline experiment intended to establish how web pages and web hosts link to each other, allowing an estimation of the feasibility of any subsequent sampling experiments. The walker was configured to follow *any* link, including host-internal links. The essential numbers are reported in Table 2. While the average number of steps made before the walker jumped to a new web host was as low as 16.42, the walk often bounced back and forth between two or three hosts which strongly linked to each other, leading to an average 890.83 documents per host in the whole experiment. The 10 longest single-host segments of the RW are shown in Table 1.

These results are not surprising because it is known that web hosts strongly link internally, and that there is strong linking within clusters of hosts, not necessarily but often for purposes of search engine optimization. What this experiment establishes is that we cannot perform naive RWs jumping from page to page and expect bias correction algorithms to work in any real-world web corpus creation scenario. Link structures between single pages are so pathologically biased that we would have to crawl for much longer than feasible. What seems more appropriate than page-level bias correction is host-level bias correction, to which I turn in the next section.

4.2 Host Walking and Bias Reduction

The first experiment showed that just following any link makes RWs practically useless. In the second experiment, the walker was therefore configured to follow only links leading to *different hosts*. This changes the interpretation of the web graph as explored by the walker: it is viewed as a graph composed of hosts (not pages) as nodes. Furthermore, the random jump probability was set to 0.1, making sure that the walker could not get stuck between neighboring hosts of a link farm, etc. The essential figures are reported in Table 2. Compared to the first experiment, the average number of pages per host drops dramatically from 890.83 to 10.25.

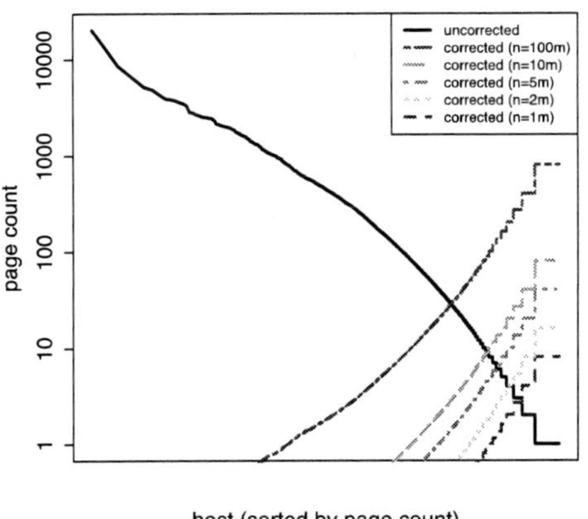

Figure 1: Number of pages (y) visited in the second experiment per host (x), sorted in decreasing order, and the theoretically expected document counts when applying Henzinger's rejection sampling method depending on the targeted bias-reduced corpus size, given as n; log-log axes

I then projected the expected corpus sizes and the per-host probabilities for the rejection sampling process. The logic behind these projections is that aggressive rejection sampling can easily lead to a situation where hosts with a high Page-Rank receive a near-zero probability of being sampled from the crawl and making it into the final corpus. Figure 1 shows the expected page counts per host in the biased and bias-corrected corpora if a final corpus of a specific size is desired. The lines for the bias-corrected corpora show the expected number of pages per host that would be retained after naive and aggressive bias-correction.

For example, if we target a bias-reduced corpus of 1 million documents, most of the very prominent hosts from the original RW receive an extremely low probability of being sampled from the walk. On the other hand, hosts which had a very low document count in the original RW would have to contribute more documents than we actually have. If we perform the rejection sampling such that hosts which were visited only once during the original RW contribute (on average) one document to the bias-corrected corpus, we can only keep approximately 125,000 documents in total, in which case the 108,523 most prominent hosts are (on average) not represented at all in the bias-corrected corpus. In other words, a RW with 2 million steps is too short for aggressive rejection sampling, which only goes to show how strong the bias in the original walk is.

5 Outlook

The type of experiment described in Section 4.2 appears suitable for the creation of web corpora which are representative samples of the population of web documents. However, we obviously need to run much longer RWs, and we need to perform simulations on artificial graphs in order to test how well less aggressive (but more practically feasible) bias-reduction works, which would enable us to retain more documents in the rejection sampling step.

Apart from implementing these steps, I will also explore the effects of bias reduction on the composition of web corpora through automatic classification of the documents in the resulting corpora, for example by content and register.[10] This will finally make it possible to compare different methods of crawling (BFS as used for the COW corpora and bias-corrected RWs) in terms of the linguistically relevant effects on corpus composition that they might have.

Acknowledgments

My research presented here was funded by the German Research Council (Deutsche Forschungsgemeinschaft, DFG) through grant SHA/1916-1 *Linguistic Web Characterization*.

---

[10] See also Schäfer and Bildhauer, this volume.

References

Dimitris Achlioptas, Aaron Clauset, David Kempe, and Cristopher Moore. 2005. On the bias of traceroute sampling: or, power-law degree distributions in regular graphs. In *Proceedings of the thirty-seventh annual ACM symposium on Theory of computing*, STOC '05, pages 694–703, New York, NY, USA. ACM.

Marco Baroni, Silvia Bernardini, Adriano Ferraresi, and Eros Zanchetta. 2009. The WaCky Wide Web: A collection of very large linguistically processed web-crawled corpora. *Language Resources and Evaluation*, 43(3):209–226.

Douglas Biber and Jesse Egbert. 2016. Using grammatical features for automatic register identification in an unrestricted corpus of documents from the open web. *Journal of Research Design and Statistics in Linguistics and Communication Science*, 2:3–36.

Douglas Biber. 1993. Representativeness in corpus design. *Literary and Linguistic Computing*, 8(4):243–257.

Sergey Brin and Lawrence Page. 1998. The anatomy of a large-scale hypertextual web search engine. In *Proceedings of the 7th International World Wide Web Conference*, pages 107–117. Elsevier Science.

Andrei Z. Broder. 2000. Identifying and filtering near-duplicate documents. In R. Giancarlo and D. Sanko, editors, *Proceedings of Combinatorial Pattern Matching*, pages 1–10, Berlin.

Kurt Bryan and Tanya Leise. 2006. The $25,000,000,000 eigenvector: The linear algebra behind Google. *SIAM Review*, 48(3):569–581.

Massimiliano Ciaramita and Marco Baroni. 2006. Measuring web-corpus randomness: A progress report. In Marco Baroni and Silvia Bernardini, editors, *WaCky! Working papers on the Web as Corpus*, pages 127–158. GEDIT, Bologna.

Dirk Goldhahn, Thomas Eckart, and Uwe Quasthoff. 2012. Building Large Monolingual Dictionaries at the Leipzig Corpora Collection: From 100 to 200 Languages. In *Proceedings of the Eight International Conference on Language Resources and Evaluation (LREC'12)*, Istanbul, Turkey, May. European Language Resources Association (ELRA).

Lushan Han, Abhay L Kashyap, Tim Finin, James Mayfield, and Johnathan Weese. 2013. UMBC_EBIQUITY-CORE: Semantic Textual Similarity Systems. In *Proceedings of the Second Joint Conference on Lexical and Computational Semantics*. Association for Computational Linguistics.

Monika R. Henzinger, Allan Heydon, Michael Mitzenmacher, and Marc Najork. 2000. On near-uniform URL sampling. In *Proceedings of the 9th International World Wide Web conference on Computer Networks: The International Journal of Computer and Telecommunications Networking*, pages 295–308. North-Holland Publishing Co.

Adam Kilgarriff. 2006. Googleology is bad science. *Computational Linguistics*, 33(1):147–151.

Maciej Kurant, Athina Markopoulou, and Patrick Thiran. 2010. On the bias of BFS (Breadth First Search). In *International Teletraffic Congress (ITC 22)*.

Geoffrey Leech. 2007. New resources or just better old ones? The Holy Grail of representativeness. In Marianne Hundt, Nadja Nesselhauf, and Carolin Biewer, editors, *Corpus linguistics and the web*, pages 133–149. Rodopi, Amsterdam and New York.

Arun S. Maiya and Tanya Y. Berger-Wolf. 2011. Benefits of bias: towards better characterization of network sampling. In *Proceedings of the 17th ACM SIGKDD international conference on Knowledge discovery and data mining*, KDD '11, pages 105–113, New York, NY, USA. ACM.

Christopher D. Manning, Prabhakar Raghavan, and Hinrich Schütze. 2009. *An Introduction to Information Retrieval*. CUP, Cambridge.

Gordon Mohr, Michael Stack, Igor Ranitovic, Dan Avery, and Michele Kimpton. 2004. Introduction to Heritrix, an archival quality web crawler. In *Proceedings of the 4th International Web Archiving Workshop (IWAW'04)*.

Christopher Olston and Marc Najork. 2010. *Web Crawling*, volume 4(3) of *Foundations and Trends in Information Retrieval*. now Publishers, Hanover, MA.

Paat Rusmevichientong, David M. Pennock, Steve Lawrence, and C. Lee Giles. 2001. Methods for sampling pages uniformly from the World Wide Web. In *In AAAI Fall Symposium on Using Uncertainty Within Computation*, pages 121–128.

Roland Schäfer and Felix Bildhauer. 2012. Building large corpora from the web using a new efficient tool chain. In Nicoletta Calzolari (Conference Chair), Khalid Choukri, Thierry Declerck, Mehmet Uğur Doğan, Bente Maegaard, Joseph Mariani, Asuncion Moreno, Jan Odijk, and Stelios Piperidis, editors, *Proceedings of the Eight International Conference on Language Resources and Evaluation (LREC'12)*, pages 486–493, Istanbul, Turkey. European Language Resources Association (ELRA).

Roland Schäfer and Felix Bildhauer. 2013. *Web Corpus Construction*. Synthesis Lectures on Human Language Technologies. Morgan and Claypool, San Francisco.

Roland Schäfer, Adrien Barbaresi, and Felix Bildhauer. 2013. The good, the bad, and the hazy: Design decisions in web corpus construction. In Stefan Evert, Egon Stemle, and Paul Rayson, editors, *Proceedings of the 8th Web as Corpus Workshop (WAC-8)*, pages 7–15, Lancaster. SIGWAC.

Roland Schäfer, Adrien Barbaresi, and Felix Bildhauer. 2014. Focused web corpus crawling. In Felix Bildhauer and Roland Schäfer, editors, *Proceedings of the 9th Web as Corpus workshop (WAC-9)*, pages 9–15, Stroudsburg. Association for Computational Linguistics.

Roland Schäfer. 2016a. Accurate and efficient general-purpose boilerplate detection for crawled web corpora. *Language Resources and Evaluation.* Online first: DOI 10.1007/s10579-016-9359-2.

Roland Schäfer. 2016b. CommonCOW: Massively huge web corpora from CommonCrawl data and a method to distribute them freely under restrictive EU copyright laws. In Nicoletta Calzolari (Conference Chair), Khalid Choukri, Thierry Declerck, Marko Grobelnik, Bente Maegaard, Joseph Mariani, Asuncion Moreno, Jan Odijk, and Stelios Piperidis, editors, *Proceedings of the Tenth International Conference on Language Resources and Evaluation (LREC 2016)*, pages 4500–4504, Portorož, Slovenia. European Language Resources Association (ELRA).

Anatol Stefanowitsch and Susanne Flach. 2016, in press. A corpus-based perspective on entrenchment. In Hans-Jörg Schmid, editor, *Entrenchment and the psychology of language: How we reorganize and adapt linguistic knowledge.* De Gruyter, Berlin.

Vít Suchomel and Jan Pomikálek. 2012. Effcient Web crawling for large text corpora. In Adam Kilgarriff and Serge Sharoff, editors, *Proceedings of the seventh Web as Corpus Workshop*, pages 40–44.

EmpiriST: AIPHES
Robust Tokenization and POS-Tagging for Different Genres

Steffen Remus[†§] and **Gerold Hintz**[†§] and **Darina Benikova**[‡§] and **Thomas Arnold**[†§] and **Judith Eckle-Kohler**[†§] and **Christian M. Meyer**[†§] and **Margot Mieskes**[*§] and **Chris Biemann**[†§]

[†]**Computer Science Dept.**
Technische Universität Darmstadt

[‡]**Computer Science and Applied Cognitive Science Dept.**
Universität Duisburg-Essen

[*]**Information Science**
University of Applied Sciences, Darmstadt

[§]**Research Training Group AIPHES**
Heidelberg University and
Technische Universität Darmstadt

[§]`www.aiphes.tu-darmstadt.de`

Abstract

We present our system used for the AIPHES team submission in the context of the EmpiriST shared task on "Automatic Linguistic Annotation of Computer-Mediated Communication / Social Media". Our system is based on a rule-based tokenizer and a machine learning sequence labelling POS tagger using a variety of features. We show that the system is robust across the two tested genres: German computer mediated communication (CMC) and general German web data (WEB). We achieve the second rank in three of four scenarios. Also, the presented systems are freely available as open source components.

1 Introduction

Tokenization and part-of-speech (POS) tagging are considered core tasks in a standard Natural Language Processing (NLP) pipeline. NLP tasks, such as summarization, information extraction, event detection, machine translation, and many others, are typically based on machine learning algorithms which use the outcome of lower level NLP tasks, such as tokens or intermediate linguistic phenomena including parts-of-speech or grammatical relations, as features. Though tokenization and part-of-speech tagging are considered simple tasks, it is highly important to achieve high-quality results, as errors propagate to downstream applications, where they are hard to repair and may cause notable consequential errors. Thus, a major goal

is the minimization of the propagation of errors by using methods that perform as accurate as possible in lower level tasks on a diversity of texts and genres.

In this paper we present a simple, yet flexible and universally applicable system for tokenization and POS tagging German text. Our system participated in the EmpiriST shared task on "Automatic Linguistic Annotation of Computer-Mediated Communication / Social Media" (Beißwenger et al., 2016). For this task, we applied our solution to texts from two different genres: *a*) general, html-stripped *web data* and *b*) colloquial language from *social media texts*.

The paper is organized as follows: We first describe the shared task and related work Section 2. Our systems for tokenization and POS tagging are laid out in Section 3 and evaluated in Section 4, which includes a detailed error analysis. Section 5 concludes.

2 Task Description & Related Work

The main goal of the GSCL Shared Task "Automatic Linguistic Annotation of Computer-Mediated Communication / Social Media" was to encourage adaptation and development of language processing tools for German texts of computer-mediated communication genres. The shared task was divided into two subtasks, tokenization and POS tagging, which made use of an extended STTS-EmpiriST tag set. For both tasks, two data sets were provided for trial and training purposes.

- A computer-mediated communication data

Proceedings of the 10th Web as Corpus Workshop (WAC-X) and the EmpiriST Shared Task, pages 106–114,
Berlin, Germany, August 7-12, 2016. ©2016 Association for Computational Linguistics

set (CMC) that included chat texts, tweets, blogs and Wikipedia talk pages.

- A Web data set (WEB) with various web text genres.

The training data set includes 5,109 (WEB) and 6,034 (CMC) manually annotated and expert-checked tokens. System submissions for the tasks were evaluated by the organizers on 7,800 (WEB) and 6,142 (CMC) tokens of blind test data.

2.1 Tokenization

Tokenization is usually the first step in a NLP system. Even systems that do not follow the classical NLP pipeline architecture still mostly operate on the basis of tokens, including unified architectures starting from scratch (Collobert et al., 2011). This is common, since tokens – either directly or indirectly – are usually considered to bear the information in a text eventually. However, the importance of tokenization is often neglected, as simple methods like whitespace segmentation *can* yield acceptable accuracies for many languages at first sight (Webster and Kit, 1992). But errors in an early phase of an NLP pipeline can have severe effects to higher level tasks and influence their performance by a large margin.

Existing tokenizers can be organized into three categories: *a*) rule-based methods, *b*) supervised methods, *c*) unsupervised methods. Manning et al. (2014)[1], for example, internally use JFlex[2], which is a meta language for rules based on regular expressions and procedures to execute when a rule matches. In contrast, Jurish and Würzner (2013) present a supervised system for joint tokenization and sentence splitting, which employs a Hidden Markov Model on character features for boundary detection. Kiss and Strunk (2006) introduce *Punkt*, providing an unsupervised model for sentence splitting and tokenization. Kiss and Strunk (2006) use the fact that most ambiguous token or sentence boundaries happen around punctuation characters, such as periods/full stops. Punkt finds collocations of characters before and after punctuations, assuming that these collocations are typical abbreviations, initials, or ordinal numbers which can be maintained as a simple list of non-splittable tokens.

---

[1] As of the current version v3.6 of the Stanford Core Utils, the default PTBTokenizer uses JFlex.

[2] http://jflex.de/

Automatically learned models, both supervised and unsupervised, are typically hard to debug and the results might need post cleaning, e.g. post-merging or splitting of common mistakes, because modifying learned models is usually not trivial but need to be re-learned with different parameter settings or training data. However, it is important to offer the possibility to easily debug and change the outcome of the tokenization, hence, our goal is to implement a small and reasonable ruleset.

2.2 POS Tagging

Existing POS taggers for German primarily rely on the Stuttgart-Tübingen Tagset (STTS, Schiller et al. (1999)), which consists of 54 POS tags and distinguishes between eleven main parts of speech, which are further divided into various subcategories. The STTS tagset has become a de facto standard for German, as it is also used in major German treebanks, such as the Tiger treebank (Brants et al., 2004), called Tiger henceforth. Tiger consists of approx. 900,000 tokens of German newspaper text (taken from the Frankfurter Rundschau), and the POS annotations have been added semi-automatically. For this, the TnT tagger (Brants, 2000) was used, because it also outputs probabilities that can be used as confidence scores. Only POS tags with a low confidence score were checked for correctness by human annotators.

As the basis for the development of the STTS-tagset were newspaper corpora, STTS only contains six POS tags that describe categories other than the standard grammatical word categories (e.g., non-words or punctuation marks). In contrast, the extended version of STTS used in the EmpiriST shared task contains 18 additional tags for elements that are specific for computer-mediated communication, for example, tags for emoticons, hashtags and URLs, or tags for phenomena which are typical for spoken language.

State-of-the-art POS taggers use supervised machine learning to train a model from corpora annotated with POS tags. While there are several ways to model POS tagging as a machine learning problem, casting it as a sequence labeling problem is a frequent approach, used already for the early TnT tagger by Brants (2000). In sequence tagging, the learning algorithm – e.g. Hidden Markov Models or Conditional Random Fields (CRFs) – optimizes the most likely tags over the sequence, while taking interdependencies of tags into account – as opposed to a mere token-based classification.

Another annotation task that is a typical example of sequence labeling, is named entity recognition. For example, the GermaNER toolkit (Benikova et al., 2015) uses CRFs for learning to tag named entities. GermaNER has been built in a modular fashion and is highly configurable, which allows users to easily train it with new data and features sets, and hence we chose to build upon the GermaNER system for POS tagging in this shared task.

3 System Description

The systems we describe in the following subsections are available as open source components under the Apache v2 license.[3] For tokenization, we have not attempted to create different variants for the two text genres of the shared task, but rather provide a robust generic solution, since we would not want to adopt subsequent processing steps when applying them to a different genre.

3.1 Tokenization

We present a rule-based tokenizer where the rules describe merging routines of two or more conservatively segmented tokens. Rules are defined in terms of a list of common non-splittable terms and simple regular expressions. The tokenizer is configured with a set of configuration files, which we call a *ruleset*. A ruleset can be easily adapted or changed depending on a particular language. In the following we present the tokenizer's configuration options and show selected toy examples.

The main building blocks of the tokenizer are the following:

Conservative splits: A *base tokenizer* provides the initial tokens that are refined in the next steps. We chose a robust tokenizer that operates on general unicode character categories, i.e. a stream of characters is processed and for each character its general unicode category is retrieved. Based on the transition from the current character's unicode category to the next character's unicode category new token segments are created by some specified rules. More specifically, new token segments are created for empty space[4] to non-empty space

transitions, letter[5] to non-letter and number[6] to non-number transitions or vice versa.

Merge list: We maintain a list of common abbreviations, which contains words or expressions with non-letter characters such as dots or hyphens. Additionally, this list contains a collection of common text-based emojis. Some selected examples are listed in Listing 1. The file was manually compiled from various sources in the web, including Wikipedia.

Merge rules: Since merge lists contain only fixed tokens that must match entirely and hence do not allow for modifications within tokens, we additionally maintain a list of merge rules which are specified as regular expressions. This is particularly important for expressions involving digits, such as date expressions, usernames, etc. Rules are processed in the order of their definition. Unfortunately, as with potentially every rule-based system, too many handwritten rules start to interfere and introduce unwanted behavior. This is especially true if rules are too general, i.e. they match more examples than they should. We balance this trade-off between rule complexity and rule interaction by introducing *global* and *local reject rules*, i.e. merge rules are rejected iff a reject rule also matches. The scope of these reject rules can be defined globally, matching tokens that should never be considered for merging, or locally, matching tokens that should not be considered for merging only if a particular merge rule matched. Multiple consecutive reject rules are possible. Listing 2 shows a snippet of the respective configuration file.

The tokenizer is implemented in Java using the Java default regular expression engine. It was developed as part of the *lt-segmenter*[7] and is provided as a branch[8].

3.2 POS Tagging

For POS tagging, we have adapted the GermaNER system, an open-source named entity recognition

---

[3]https://github.com/AIPHES
[4]general unicode categories Zl, Zs, Zp
[5]general unicode categories Lu, Ll, Lt, Lm, Lo
[6]general unicode categories Nd, Nl, No
[7]https://tudarmstadt-lt.github.io/seg/
[8]https://github.com/AIPHES/tokenizer

```
## lookahead-list.txt
C-Jugend
Ü-Ei
altgriech.
24/7
2B~not2B
a-z
a.k.a.
>_<
:-}
X8-{}
...
```

Listing 1: Examples of fixed entries, i.e. non-splitable tokens in the tokenizer's look-ahead list. Comments begin with a # character.

```
## lookahead-rules.txt
# reject ) followed by ; globally
- \);

# email a@b.com
+ [\.+\w\-]+@([\w\-]+\.)+[\w]{2,6}

# reverse emoticons (-:
+ (\[\]\)\(DP*)\1{0,}-?'?[:;8B=]
# reject ):
- \) ?:

...
```

Listing 2: Examples for merge rules defined as regular expressions. Merge rules are defined with an initial '+' in the beginning of the line, whereas reject rules are defined with an initial '-'. Global reject rules are defined before any positive rule and comments begin with a # character. A description of the rules can be found as comment before the actual rule.

tool written in Java. *GermaPOS*[9] is a fork of the software, adapting the framework for this purpose. As a machine learning algorithm, a CRF sequence tagger (Lafferty et al., 2001) is used. Specifically the implementation provided by CRF-suite (Okazaki, 2007), as is in the clearTK framework is employed.

The architecture of *GermaPOS* is a highly extensible UIMA[10] pipeline (Ferrucci and Lally, 2004), providing a simple interface to both training a new tagger based on user-provided training data, as well as running a pretrained model on simple text files. The pipeline first reads a tab-separated input file. In a subsequent step, feature extraction is performed per token, using additional information from external sources, e.g. word lists. Feature extraction can further take into account any surrounding context of the current token, e.g. time-shifted features of relative position -2, -1, 0, $+1$, $+2$. In training mode, a CRF model is then built on the basis of feature annotations; at run-time the model provides POS tags as UIMA annotations. An optional output step in the pipeline produces a POS-annotated file. Alternatively, the pipeline can be used within UIMA projects out of the box. We perform a post-hoc assignment of POS tags based on a subset of our mapping rules that cover EmpiriST-specific conventions. For example a token *emojiQsmilingFace* will be assigned the tag *EMOIMG*, regardless of the output of the sequence tagger.

Features We adapt nearly the full feature set of *GermaNER*, with the exception of POS features. In the following list, we give a brief overview – a more detailed description can be found in (Benikova et al., 2015).

1. **Character n-grams** First and last character n-grams for $n \in \{1, 2, 3\}$ of the current token, as well as time-shifted versions of this feature with offset from -2 to 2 are extracted.

2. **Gazetteers and word lists** We adapt most gazetteers from GermaNER, containing mostly named entities (NE). As we gained no performance increase from a higher coverage of NEs in our datasets through Freebase (Bollacker et al., 2008), we omit this resource in favor of a more lightweight system. In addition, we incorporate word lists. We employ a small list of English words[11], as well as hand-crafted lists[12] of onomatopoeia, discourse markers, Internet abbreviations, intensity markers, as well as various types of particles.

3. **Similar words** JoBimText (Biemann and Riedl, 2013) to obtain a distributional thesaurus (DT) from which the four most similar words for the current token are used. The underlying motivation is to be able to correctly

---

[9]*GermaPOS* is available at https://github.com/AIPHES/GermaPOS

[10]Unified Information Management Architecture, https://uima.apache.org/

[11]We use a list of English words as these cover most occurrences of foreign language tags

[12]Partially compiled from Wikipedia and enriched by data from various internet sites e.g. internetslang.com.

tag infrequent or unseen targets, by expanding them with a frequent similar term, most likely sharing the same part of speech.

4. **Topic clusters** LDA topic modeling was applied on the DT defined above, resulting in a fixed number of topic clusters. For each token, and time-shifted context tokens, its topic index is extracted as a feature. We again build on existing work of GermaNER and use a precomputed set of 200 clusters.

5. **Syntax** We use simple syntactic features, such as the word position and casing of tokens. We generalize the original GermaPOS setup to use arbitrary regular expressions as binary features. We then use all regular expressions designed for tokenization as features. This way, we also cover most casing information.

Furthermore, we extract the character range of each token as a feature, in case all characters fall into the same class. Hence, if all characters are from the same Unicode code block, this block is extracted as a feature. This feature allows, for example, to capture Unicode emoticons, not specifically preprocessed as in the EmpiriST data.

Training In the context of the EmpiriST shared task, we train a separate model for both the CMC and WEB datasets. As the training data is comparatively small for the purpose of POS tagging, we add the Tiger dataset to the respective training sets. The Tiger corpus is annotated using the standard STTS tagset, whereas the task at hand provided an extended tagset. In order to make learning from Tiger feasible, we have manually converted the Tiger data to the extended tagset using a set of simple rules, which aim at covering most of the easy cases.

As with GermaNER, the selection of resources and software components was done in favor of choosing a permissive license rather than focusing on system performance. Although it is plausible to improve POS tagging performance by integrating high-quality resources, we have opted to release GermaPOS with only free components, i.e. those already employed in GermaNER as well as manual additions not encumbered with restrictive usage rights. Where applicable, the system can be customized to utilize additional resources. A possible extension is the integration of another third-party POS tagger to be utilized as a feature.

Usage *GermaPOS* is provided as a runnable jar file with a pre-bundled model trained on the data described above. The training format is – equivalent to the EmpiriST training data – a tab-separated file of one token-tag pair per line and sentences being separated by an empty line.

4 Evaluation

Following the EmpiriST task setup, we evaluate our tokenizer by measuring precision P, recall R, and the F_1 score as in Jurish and Würzner (2013). Precision denotes the proportion of correctly identified token boundaries over the total number of token boundaries proposed by our tokenizer and recall denotes the proportion of correctly identified token boundaries over the total number of token boundaries in the gold standard. The F_1 score is the harmonic mean of precision and recall.

For our POS tagger, we report the tagging accuracy. That is, we measure the fraction of correct tag guesses over the total number of tokens to tag. To enable a comparison of our tagger's results with previous work on German, we additionally use the STTS mapping provided by the shared task organizers and measure the tagging accuracy using the mapped tags.

Below, we first discuss our results according to these standardized metrics and then conduct a careful analysis of the most prominent errors of our tools.

4.1 Results

We present results according to the tasks evaluation. Table 1 shows the results for the tokenization task for the two datasets CMC and WEB. Without adapting the rules for the particular sub-tasks, we achieved good performance on both sets such that we positioned on rank two in both categories.

The results for the POS tagging task are shown in Table 2. We achieve clearly better results on the WEB dataset (second best results) than on the CMS dataset. One possible reason for that is the distribution of the new POS tag labels in the test set. As can be seen in Table 3, the CMC data make more use of the new labels. Another reason might be the adaption of our system to the text style, which is dominated by the much larger Tiger training set.

Genre	Rec	$Prec$	F_1	$Rank$
CMC	99.30	98.62	98.96	2
WEB	99.63	99.89	99.76	2

Table 1: Tokenization results. We achieved rank two of six submissions in both categories. Two submissions were non-competitive but do not change our rank.

Genre	Acc	$Rank$
CMC	84.22	5
CMC (STTS Map)	87.10	2
Web	93.27	2
Web (STTS Map)	94.30	2

Table 2: POS tagging results. Among 17 submissions from eight teams, of which two were out of competition, we ranked second on the web data and fifth on the CMC data.

Tag	CMC	Web
ONO	2	
DM	6	
PTKIFG	72	61
PTKMA	74	11
PTKMWL	10	14
VVPPER	6	
VAPPER	4	
KOUSPPER	1	1
PPERPPER	1	1
ADVART	3	
EMOASC	71	
EMOIMG	63	
AKW	60	
HST	42	
ADR	48	
URL	16	
EML		1

Table 3: Distribution of new POS tag labels in the test sets.

4.2 Common Errors

We identified three main sources of **tokenization errors**. Examples in the following show gold tokenization on the left and system tokens on the right, errors are marked with an asterisk.

1. **Rules are underspecified**, which means that certain rules were not specified or the look-ahead list did not contain the particular abbreviation. Also, note that we deviated from the annotation guidelines and did not perform token splitting at camel case boundaries.

   Examples:

```
*  Eingetr.           |  *  Eingetr
   Lebenspartnersch.  |  *  .

*  die                |  *  dieFeststellung
*  Feststellung       |     ,

   der                |     war
*  1.                 |  *  der1
   Teil               |  *  .
   meiner             |     Teil
```

2. **Rules are overspecified**, which means that rules are specified in our ruleset although they were not specified in the annotation guidelines.

   Example:

```
   Backlinks       |     Backlinks
   :               |     :
*  [[              |  *  [[sec:verschl]]
*  sec             |     Navigation
   :               |     Passwort-
   verschl         |     generator
```

3. **Current scheme cannot capture certain phenomena**, which happens on phenomena that are syntactically hard to distinguish. For instance, section listings that get identified as a date, e.g.

```
*  1.3.    |  *  1.
   Kekse   |  *  3.
```

POS tagging error analysis We have performed a post-hoc error analysis on the EmpiriST data. Table 4 shows a confusion matrix regarding classes of POS tags by their prefix (first character). Note that this matrix only lists tagging *errors*, so that the diagonal of the matrix denotes incorrect tagging within the same prefix class. It can be seen that the majority of errors happen within these classes, such as *N**. The most common tagging error is in fact mistagging *NE* and *NN*, which

111

	$*	AD*	AKW*	AP*	AR*	EML*	EMO*	N*	P*	PPER*	PT*	V*
$*	68	0	0	1	1	0	0	0	1	0	1	0	1
AD*	2	49	1	9	0	1	0	81	21	3	159	21	34
AKW*	0	1	0	0	0	0	0	1	0	0	0	0	3
AP*	2	0	0	4	0	0	0	0	1	0	6	2	10
AR*	0	1	0	0	0	0	0	0	22	0	2	0	0
EML*	0	0	0	0	0	0	0	0	0	0	0	0	0
EMO*	1	0	0	0	0	0	0	0	0	0	0	0	0
N*	1	25	2	3	3	0	2	163	3	2	6	16	43
P*	0	3	0	1	10	0	0	4	37	4	1	1	10
PPER*	0	0	0	0	0	0	0	0	7	0	0	0	0
PT*	0	34	0	5	0	0	0	1	7	0	16	0	0
V*	0	16	3	4	1	0	0	30	1	0	0	137| 7
other	11	10	5	9	1	0	1	28	9	1	5	1	25

Table 4: Confusion matrix for POS tag prefixes (errors only)

Error class	count	(%)
1. missed extended tagset	28	17.6
2. incorrectly assigned new tag	4	2.5
3. confusion of function word tags	22	13.6
4. mistagged *NN* due to lower case	23	14.4
5. mistagged *NE* as *NN* & vice-versa	20	12.5
6. mistagged *NE* as other	12	10.0
7. unknown emoticon	1	0.6
8. unknown foreign language word	2	1.3
9. error due to abbreviation	2	1.3
10. incorrect punctuation tag	20	12.5
11. other	26	16.3

Table 5: POS tagging error classes

is sometimes also difficult to discriminate for human annotators.

We define a number of error classes to better quantify the types of errors introduced by our tagger. For this, we construct an ordered list from which we select the first item that applies as the error class:

1. missed extended tagset

A tag from the extended set was required, but a standard STTS tag was assigned. Example:

```
wohl  PTKMA    |  wohl  ADV
```

2. incorrectly assigned new tag

A tag from the extended set was assigned incorrectly. Example:

```
mal ADV          |  mal PTKMA
gucken  VVINF    |  gucken  VVINF
```

3. confusion of function word tags

Incorrect tag within the class of function words. Example:

```
den ART          |  den ART
Irrsinn NN       |  Irrsinn NN
nicht PTKNEG     |  nicht PTKNEG
endlich ADJD     |  endlich ADV
beenden VVINF    |  beenden VVINF
```

4. mistagged *NN* due to lower case

A lower-case noun was not captured. Example:

```
ihre   PPOSAT         |  ihre   PPOSAT
entscheidung          |  entscheidung VVFIN
NN
```

5. mistagged *NE* as *NN* and vice versa

Incorrect tagging of named entities and nouns. Example:

```
HErr    NN       |  HErr    NE
Ozdemir NE       |  Ozdemir NE
```

6. mistagged *NE* as other

A named entity was not recognized and tagged with a tag other than *NN*. Example:

```
Frage NN              |  Frage NN
von APPR              |  von APPR
@DieMaJa22   NE       |  @DieMaJa22   ADR
```

7. unknown emoticon

An emoticon was not identified as such (due to not being covered by regular expressions). Example:

```
*<:-) EMOASC     |  *<:-) NE
```

8. **unknown foreign language word**

   A foreign word was not tagged as *FM*. Example:

```
meinst  VVFIN      meinst  VVFIN
du  PPER           du  PPER
bazdmeg FM         bazdmeg VVFIN
```

9. **error due to abbreviation**

   Word abbreviations leading to incorrect tagging. Example:

```
Anerkennung NN       Anerkennung NN
der ART              der ART
Eingetr. ADJA        Eingetr. NN
Partnerschaft NN     Partnerschaft NN
```

10. **incorrect punctuation tag**

    Errors within the class of punctuation tags. Example:

```
Thema NN             Thema NN
: $(                 : $.
Drogenpolitik NN     Drogenpolitik NN
... $.               ... $(
```

11. **other**

    if none of the other criteria apply

We then annotate the first 160 errors from the CMC test set with their respective error classes. The results are shown in Table 5. It can be observed that most errors are related to nouns or named entities. The tagger commonly confuses these two. For CMC data, a very common error which throws off the tagger are nouns written in lower case, which generally get assigned a completely different POS. As we have trained our tagger on a standard STTS-annotated corpus (with minimal postprocessing), some errors also stem from not capturing the new rules introduced by the extended EmpiriST tagset. There are also a few errors resulting from unknown foreign language words or emoticons not captured by our regular expressions, but regarding their quantity this is much less of a problem and they only account for a tiny percentage of errors.

5   Conclusion

We have presented our submission to the EmpiriST shared task on "Automatic Linguistic Annotation of Computer Mediated Communication / Social Media", comprising a rule-based tokenizer and a machine-learning-based POS tagger. Overall, we achieved a very good, but not the best performance amongst the participating systems, ranking second throughout except for CMC POS tagging with the extended tagset. Our submission was aimed at robustness; we have not tuned our tokenizer per genre, and show good POS tagging performance throughout. Both systems are freely available as open source under a permissive license.

Acknowledgments

This work has been supported by the German Research Foundation as part of the Research Training Group "Adaptive Preparation of Information from Heterogeneous Sources" (AIPHES) under grant No. GRK 1994/1 and by the German Institute for Educational Research (DIPF) under the KDSL program.

References

Michael Beißwenger, Sabine Bartsch, Stefan Evert, and Kay-Michael Würzner. 2016. Empirist 2015: A shared task on the automatic linguistic annotation of computer-mediated communication, social media and web corpora. In *Proceedings of the 10th Web as Corpus Workshop (WAC-X)*, Berlin, Germany.

Darina Benikova, Seid Muhie Yimam, and Chris Biemann. 2015. GermaNER: Free open German named entity recognition tool. In *International Conference of the German Society for Computational Linguistics and Language Technology (GSCL-2015)*, Essen, Germany.

Chris Biemann and Martin Riedl. 2013. Text: Now in 2D! a framework for lexical expansion with contextual similarity. *Journal of Language Modelling*, 1(1):55–95.

Kurt Bollacker, Colin Evans, Praveen Paritosh, Tim Sturge, and Jamie Taylor. 2008. Freebase: A collaboratively created graph database for structuring human knowledge. In *Proceedings of the 2008 ACM SIGMOD International Conference on Management of Data*, SIGMOD '08, pages 1247–1250, New York, NY, USA. ACM.

Sabine Brants, Stefanie Dipper, Peter Eisenberg, Silvia Hansen, Esther König, Wolfgang Lezius, Christian Rohrer, George Smith, and Hans Uszkoreit. 2004. TIGER: linguistic interpretation of a German corpus. *Research on Language and Computation*, 2(4):597–620.

Thorsten Brants. 2000. TnT: A Statistical Part-of-speech Tagger. In *Proceedings of the Sixth Conference on Applied Natural Language Processing*, pages 224–231, Seattle, Washington.

Ronan Collobert, Jason Weston, Léon Bottou, Michael Karlen, Koray Kavukcuoglu, and Pavel Kuksa. 2011. Natural language processing (almost) from scratch. *Journal of Machine Learning Research*, 12:2493–2537.

David Ferrucci and Adam Lally. 2004. UIMA: An architectural approach to unstructured information processing in the corporate research environment. *Natural Language Engineering*, 10(3-4):327–348.

Bryan Jurish and Kay-Michael Würzner. 2013. Word and sentence tokenization with Hidden Markov Models. *Journal for Language Technology and Computational Linguistics (JLCL)*, 28(2):61–83.

T. Kiss and J. Strunk. 2006. Unsupervised multilingual sentence boundary detection. *Computational Linguistics*, 32(4):485–525.

John D. Lafferty, Andrew McCallum, and Fernando C. N. Pereira. 2001. Conditional random fields: Probabilistic models for segmenting and labeling sequence data. In *Proceedings of the Eighteenth International Conference on Machine Learning*, ICML '01, pages 282–289, San Francisco, CA, USA. Morgan Kaufmann Publishers Inc.

Christopher Manning, Mihai Surdeanu, John Bauer, Jenny Finkel, Steven Bethard, and David McClosky. 2014. The Stanford CoreNLP natural language processing toolkit. In *Proceedings of 52nd Annual Meeting of the Association for Computational Linguistics: System Demonstrations*, pages 55–60, Baltimore, MD.

Naoaki Okazaki. 2007. CRFsuite: a fast implementation of conditional random fields (CRFs). *http://www.chokkan.org/software/crfsuite/*.

Anne Schiller, Simone Teufel, Christine Stöckert, and Christine Thielen. 1999. Guidelines für das Tagging deutscher Textcorpora mit STTS (Kleines und großes Tagset). Technical Report, Universität Stuttgart, Institut für Maschinelle Sprachverarbeitung.

Jonathan J. Webster and Chunyu Kit. 1992. Tokenization as the initial phase in NLP. In *The 15th International Conference on Computational Linguistics (COLING)*, pages 1106–1110, Nantes, France.

bot.zen @ EmpiriST 2015 - A minimally-deep learning PoS-tagger
(trained for German CMC and Web data)

Egon W. Stemle
EURAC research
Bozen-Bolzano, Italy
`egon.stemle@eurac.edu`

Abstract

This article describes the system that participated in the Part-of-speech tagging subtask of the *EmpiriST 2015 shared task on automatic linguistic annotation of computer-mediated communication / social media*.

The system combines a small assertion of trending techniques, which implement matured methods, from NLP and ML to achieve competitive results on PoS tagging of German CMC and Web corpus data; in particular, the system uses word embeddings and character-level representations of word beginnings and endings in a LSTM RNN architecture. Labelled data (Tiger v2.2 and EmpiriST) and unlabelled data (German Wikipedia) were used for training.

The system is available under the APLv2 open-source license.

1 Introduction

Part-of-speech (PoS) tagging is an essential processing stage for virtually all NLP applications. Subsequent tasks, like parsing, named-entity recognition, event detection, and machine translation, often utilise PoS tags, and benefit (directly or indirectly) from accurate tag sequences. However, frequent phenomena in computer-mediated communication (CMC) and Web corpora such as emoticons, acronyms, interaction words, iteration of letters, graphostylistics, shortenings, addressing terms, spelling variations, and boilerplate (Androutsopoulos, 2007; Bernardini et al., 2008; Beißwenger, 2013) deteriorate the performance of PoS-taggers (Giesbrecht and Evert, 2009; Baldwin et al., 2013).

To this end, the EmpiriST shared task (ST) invited developers of NLP applications to adapt their tokenisation and PoS tagging tools and resources for the processing of written German CMC and Web data (Beißwenger et al., 2016). The ST was divided into two subtasks, tokenisation and PoS tagging, and for each subtask two data sets were provided (see Subsection 4.1.3). The systems were evaluated by the organisers on raw data for the tokenisation subtask, and on unlabelled but pre-tokenised data for the PoS tagging subtask (both on the same approx. 14,000 tokens).

We participated in the PoS tagging subtask of the ST with our new minimally-deep learning PoS-tagger: We combine `word2vec` (`w2v`) word embeddings (WEs) with a single-layer Long Short Term Memory (LSTM) recurrent neural network (RNN) architecture; strictly speaking, `w2v` is *shallow*. Therefore we call the combination with a single hidden layer *minimally-deep*. The sequence of unlabelled `w2v` representations of words is accompanied by the sequence of n-grams of the word beginnings and endings, and is fed into the RNN which in turn predicts PoS labels.

The paper is organised as follows: We present our system design in Section 2, the implementation in Section 3, and its evaluation in Section 4. Section 5 concludes with an outlook on possible implementation improvements.

2 Design

Overall, our design takes inspiration from as far back as Benello et al. (1989) who used four preceding words and one following word in a feedforward neural network with backpropagation for PoS tagging, builds upon the strong foundation laid down by Collobert et al. (2011) for a NN architecture and learning algorithm that can be applied to various natural language processing tasks,

Proceedings of the 10th Web as Corpus Workshop (WAC-X) and the EmpiriST Shared Task, pages 115–119,
Berlin, Germany, August 7-12, 2016. ©2016 Association for Computational Linguistics

and ultimately is a variation of Nogueira dos Santos and Zadrozny (2014) who trained a NN for PoS tagging, with character-level and WE representations of words.

2.1 Word Embeddings

Recently, state-of-the-art results on various linguistic tasks were accomplished by architectures using neural-network based WEs. Baroni et al. (2014) conducted a set of experiments comparing the popular w2v (Mikolov et al., 2013a; Mikolov et al., 2013b) implementation for creating WEs to other distributional methods with state-of-the-art results across various (semantic) tasks. These results suggest that the word embeddings substantially outperform the other architectures on semantic similarity and analogy detection tasks. Subsequently, Levy et al. (2015) conducted a comprehensive set of experiments and comparisons that suggest that much of the improved results are due to the system design and parameter optimizations, rather than the selected method. They conclude that "there does not seem to be a consistent significant advantage to one approach over the other".

Word embeddings provide high-quality low dimensional vector representations of words from large corpora of unlabelled data, and the representations, typically computed using NNs, encode many linguistic regularities and patterns (Mikolov et al., 2013b).

2.2 Character-Level Sub-Word Information

The morphology of a word is opaque to WEs, and the relatedness of the meaning of a lemma's different word forms, i.e. its different string representations, is *not* systematically encoded. This means that in morphologically rich languages with long-tailed frequency distributions, even some WE representations for word forms of common lemmata may become very poor (Kim et al., 2015).

We agree with Nogueira dos Santos and Zadrozny (2014) and Kim et al. (2015) that subword information is very important for PoS tagging, and therefore we augment the WE representations with character-level representations of the word beginnings and endings; thereby, we also stay language agnostic—at least, as much as possible—by avoiding the need for, often language specific, morphological pre-processing.

2.3 Recurrent Neural Network Layer

Language Models are a central part of NLP. They are used to place distributions over word sequences that encode systematic structural properties of the sample of linguistic content they are built from, and can then be used on novel content, e.g. to rank it or predict some feature on it. For a detailed overview on language modelling research see Mikolov (2012).

A straight-forward approach to incorporate WEs into feature-based language models is to use the embeddings' vector representations as features. Having said that, WEs are also used in neural network architectures, where they constitute (part of) the input to the network.

Neural networks (NNs) consist of a large number of simple, highly interconnected processing nodes in an architecture loosely inspired by the structure of the cerebral cortex of the brain (O'Reilly and Munakata, 2000). The nodes receive weighted inputs through these connections and *fire* according to their individual thresholds of their shared activation function. A firing node passes on an activation to all successive connected nodes. During learning the input is propagated through the network and the output is compared to the desired output. Then, the weights of the connections (and the thresholds) are adjusted stepwise so as to more closely resemble a configuration that would produce the desired output. After all input cases have been presented, the process typically starts over again, and the output values will usually be closer to the correct values.

RNNs are NNs where the connections between the elements are directed cycles, i.e. the networks have loops, and this enables them to model sequential dependencies of the input. However, regular RNNs have fundamental difficulties learning long-term dependencies, and special kinds of RNNs need to be used (Hochreiter, 1991); a very popular kind is the so called long short-term memory (LSTM) network proposed by Hochreiter and Schmidhuber (1997).

3 Implementation

We maintain the implementation in a source code repository at `https://github.com/bot-zen/`. The version tagged as `0.9` comprises the version that was used to generate the results submitted to the ST. The version tagged as `1.0` is identical at its core but comes with explicit documentation on how to download and install external software, and how to download and pre-process required corpora.

Our system feeds WEs and character-level sub-word information into a single-layer RNN with a LSTM architecture.

3.1 Word Embeddings

We incorporates `w2v`'s original C implementation for learning WEs[1] in an independent pre-processing step, i.e. we pro-compute the WEs. Then, we use gensim[2], a Python tool for unsupervised semantic modelling from plain text, to load the data, and to extract the vector representations of the embedded words as input to our NN.

3.2 Character-Level Sub-Word Information

Our implementation uses a *one-hot encoding* with a few additional features for representing sub-word information. The one-hot encoding transforms a categorical feature into a vector where the categories are represented by equally many dimensions with binary values. We convert a letter to lower-case and use the sets of ASCII characters, digits, and punctuation marks as categories for the encoding. Then, we add dimensions to represent more binary features like *'uppercase'* (was uppercase prior to conversion), *'digit'* (is digit), *'punctuation'* (is punctuation mark), *whitespace* (is white space, except the new line character; note that this category is usually empty, because we expect our tokens to *not* include white space characters), and *unknown* (other characters, e.g. diacritics). This results in vectors with more than a single *one-hot* dimension.

3.3 Recurrent Neural Network Layer

Our implementation uses Keras, a minimalist, highly modular NNs library, written in Python and capable of running on top of either TensorFlow or Theano (Chollet, 2015). In our case it runs on top of Theano, a Python library that allows to define, optimize, and evaluate mathematical expressions involving multi-dimensional arrays efficiently (The Theano Development Team et al., 2016).

The input to our network are sequences of the same length as the sentences we process. During training we group sentences of the same length into batches. Each single word in the sequence is represented by its sub-word information and two WEs that come from two sources (see Section 4). Unknown words, i.e. words without a WE, are mapped to a randomly generated vector representation once, and this representation is reused later. In Total, each word is represented by $1,800$ features: two times 500 (WEs), and ten times 80 for two 5-grams (word beginning and ending). (If words are shorter than 5 characters their 5-grams are zero-padded.)

This sequential input is fed into a LSTM layer that, in turn, projects to a fully connected output layer with softmax activation function. We use categorical cross-entropy as loss function and backpropagation in conjunction with the RMSprop optimization for learning. At the time of writing, this was the Keras default—or the explicitly documented option to be used—for our type of architecture.

4 Case Study

We used our implementation to participate in the EmpiriST 2015 shared task. First, we describe the corpora used for training, and then the specific system configuration(s) for the ST.

4.1 Training Data for `w2v` and PoS Tagging

4.1.1 Tiger v2.2 (PoS)

Tiger v2.2[3] is version 2.2 of the TIGERCorpus (Brants et al., 2004) containing German newspaper texts. The corpus was semi-automatically PoS tagged, and is one of the standard corpora used for German PoS tagging. It contains 888,238 tokens in 50,472 sentences. For research and evaluation purposes, the TIGERCorpus can be downloaded for free.

4.1.2 German Wikipedia (`w2v`)

de.wiki'15[4] are user talk pages (messages from users to users, often questions and advice), article talk pages (questions, concerns or comments related to improving a Wikipedia article), and article pages of the German wikipedia from 2015, made available by the *Institut für Deutsche Sprache*[5]. The corpus contains 2 billion tokens (talk:379m,

---

[1] `https://code.google.com/archive/p/word2vec/`

[2] `https://radimrehurek.com/gensim/`

[3] `http://www.ims.uni-stuttgart.de/forschung/ressourcen/korpora/tiger.html`

[4] `http://www1.ids-mannheim.de/kl/projekte/korpora/verfuegbarkeit.html#Download`

[5] `http://www.ids-mannheim.de`

article talk:447m, article:1,1bn) in 79 million sentences (talk:15m, article talk:17m, article:47m), is well-sized for $w2v$, and also (partly) resembles or target data. It is available under the CC BY-SA 3.0[6] license.

4.1.3 EmpiriST 2015 Data (PoS and w2v)

empirist[7] is the CMC and Web data made available by the organizers of the ST. It contains data samples from different CMC genres and samples from text genres on the Web. The training corpus contains 10,053 tokens and was PoS tagged by two annotators (unclear cases were decided by a third person). The trial corpus contains around 3,600 tokens (2,100 CMC[8], 1,500 Web) and was PoS tagged by one annotator (without systematic error checks). See Beißwenger et al. (2016) for more details.

4.2 EmpiriST 2015 shared task

For the ST we used one overall configuration for the system, but we used three different corpus configurations for training. Consequently, we participated in the ST with three runs: we used PoS tags from *empirist* (run 1), from *Tiger v2.2* (run 2), and from both (run 3). For $w2v$ we trained a 500-dimensional skip-gram model on *empirist* that ignored all words with less than 3 occurrences within a window size of 10; it was trained with negative sampling (value 5) and erroneously[9] also with hierarchical softmax. We also trained a 500-dimensional continuous bag-of-words model on *de.wiki'15* that ignored all words with less than 25 occurrences within a window size of 10; it was trained with negative sampling (value 3) and erroneously also with hierarchical softmax.

---

[6]Creative Commons Attribution-ShareAlike 3.0 Unported, i.e. the data can be copied and redistributed, and adapted for any purpose, even commercially. See `http://creativecommons.org/licenses/by-sa/3.0/` for more details.

[7]`https://sites.google.com/site/empirist2015/home/shared-task-data`

[8]For evaluation during the development phase we used *empirist*-trial. Unfortunately, we found out only later that the CMC part of the trial data is also part of the training data, i.e. for the CMC data our evaluation data was identical with the training data.

[9]According to $w2v$'s author, technically negative sampling and hierarchical softmax can be combined but one should avoid combining them (see `https://groups.google.com/forum/#!topic/word2vec-toolkit/WUWad9fL0jU`).
We had forgotten to deactivate an option in a data processing script.

The rational behind training the two models differently was that according to $w2v$ author's experience[10] a skip-gram model "works well with small amount[s] of the training data, [and] represents well even rare words or phrases", and a cbow model is "several times faster to train than the skip-gram, [and has] slightly better accuracy for the frequent words". The other $w2v$ parameters were left at their default settings[11].

To optimize the system's output we ran a simple grid search for three parameters: the hidden LSTM layer's size, the dropout value for the projections from the LSTM to the output layer during training, and the number of epochs during training. The found values were size:1024, dropout:0.1, epochs:20.

	CMC	Web
(1) *empirist*	81.03	86.97
(2) *Tiger v2.2*	73.56	89.73
(3) *empirist+Tiger v2.2*	85.42	90.63
Winning Team	87.33	93.55

Table 1: Official results of our PoS tagger for the three runs on the EmpiriST 2015 shared task data.

5 Conclusion & Outlook

We presented our submission to the EmpiriST 2015 shared task, where we participated in the PoS tagging sub-task with fair results on the CMC data and adequate results on the Web data. Still, our implementation, albeit following state-of-the art designs and methods, is quite unpolished, and can certainly gain performance with more detailed tuning. For example, adding special sequence start and sequence stop symbols to the input is typically done as a pre-processing step, which might improve the results at the beginning and the end of sentences; or we might gain some performance by adding additional hidden layers to enable the network to learn more intermediate abstractions. A more profound design change could also help, e.g. Recurrent Memory Network are a novel recurrent architecture that have been shown to outperform LSTMs on some language modelling tasks. Finally, for learning the word embeddings we

---

[10]`https://groups.google.com/d/msg/word2vec-toolkit/NLvYXU99cAM/E5ld8LcDxlAJ`

[11]`-sample 1e-3 -iter 5 -alpha 0.025` for skip-gram and `-alpha 0.05` for continuous bag-of-words

could use different corpora, or selectively extract parts from large web-corpora resembling—as much as possible—the type of data that is to be tagged.

References

Jannis K. Androutsopoulos. 2007. Neue Medien – neue Schriftlichkeit? *Mitteilungen des Deutschen Germanistenverbandes*, 1:72–97.

Timothy Baldwin, Paul Cook, Marco Lui, Andrew MacKinlay, and Li Wang. 2013. How noisy social media text, how diffrnt social media sources? In *Proceedings of the Sixth International Joint Conference on Natural Language Processing*, pages 356–364, Nagoya, Japan, October. Asian Federation of Natural Language Processing.

Marco Baroni, Georgiana Dinu, and German Kruszewski. 2014. Don't count, predict! A systematic comparison of context-counting vs. context-predicting semantic vectors. In *Proceedings of the 52nd Annual Meeting of the Association for Computational Linguistics (Volume 1: Long Papers)*, pages 238–247. Association for Computational Linguistics.

Michael Beißwenger, Sabine Bartsch, Stefan Evert, and Kay-Michael Würzner. 2016. EmpiriST 2015: A Shared Task on the Automatic Linguistic Annotation of Computer-Mediated Communication, Social Media and Web Corpora. In *Proceedings of the 10th Web as Corpus Workshop (WAC-X)*, Berlin, Germany.

Michael Beißwenger. 2013. Das Dortmunder Chat-Korpus: ein annotiertes Korpus zur Sprachverwendung und sprachlichen Variation in der deutschsprachigen Chat-Kommunikation. *LINSE - Linguistik Server Essen*, pages 1–13.

Julian Benello, Andrew W. Mackie, and James A. Anderson. 1989. Syntactic category disambiguation with neural networks. *Computer Speech & Language*, 3(3):203–217, July.

Silvia Bernardini, Marco Baroni, and Stefan Evert. 2008. A WaCky Introduction. In *Wacky! Working papers on the Web as Corpus*, pages 9–40. GEDIT, Bologna, Italy.

Sabine Brants, Stefanie Dipper, Peter Eisenberg, Silvia Hansen-Schirra, Esther König, Wolfgang Lezius, Christian Rohrer, George Smith, and Hans Uszkoreit. 2004. TIGER: Linguistic Interpretation of a German Corpus. *Research on Language and Computation*, 2(4):597–620.

Franois Chollet. 2015. Keras: Deep Learning library for Theano and TensorFlow. https://github.com/fchollet/keras.

Ronan Collobert, Jason Weston, Léon Bottou, Michael Karlen, Koray Kavukcuoglu, and Pavel Kuksa. 2011. Natural Language Processing (almost) from Scratch. *Journal of Machine Learning Research*, 12:2493–2537.

Eugenie Giesbrecht and Stefan Evert. 2009. Is Part-of-Speech Tagging a Solved Task? An Evaluation of POS Taggers for the German Web as Corpus. *Web as Corpus Workshop (WAC5)*.

Sepp Hochreiter and Jürgen Schmidhuber. 1997. Long short-term memory. *Neural Computation*, 9(8):1735–1780, November.

Sepp Hochreiter. 1991. *Untersuchungen zu dynamischen neuronalen Netzen*. diploma thesis, TU München.

Yoon Kim, Yacine Jernite, David Sontag, and Alexander M. Rush. 2015. Character-Aware Neural Language Models. *CoRR*, abs/1508.0.

Omer Levy, Yoav Goldberg, and Ido Dagan. 2015. Improving distributional similarity with lessons learned from word embeddings. *Transactions of the Association for Computational Linguistics*, 3:211–225.

Tomas Mikolov, Kai Chen, Greg Corrado, and Jeffrey Dean. 2013a. Efficient Estimation of Word Representations in Vector Space. *CoRR*, abs/1301.3781.

Tomas Mikolov, Ilya Sutskever, Kai Chen, Greg Corrado, and Jeffrey Dean. 2013b. Distributed Representations of Words and Phrases and their Compositionality. *CoRR*, abs/1310.4546, October.

Tomáš Mikolov. 2012. *Statistical Language Models Based on Neural Networks*. Ph.D. thesis, Brno University of Technology.

Cícero Nogueira dos Santos and Bianca Zadrozny. 2014. Learning Character-level Representations for Part-of-Speech Tagging. In *Proceedings of the 31st International Conference on Machine Learning (ICML-14)*, pages 1818–1826.

Randall C. O'Reilly and Yuko Munakata. 2000. *Computational Explorations in Cognitive Neuroscience Understanding the Mind by Simulating the Brain*. MIT Press.

The Theano Development Team, Rami Al-Rfou, Guillaume Alain, Amjad Almahairi, and et al. 2016. Theano: A Python framework for fast computation of mathematical expressions. *CoRR*, abs/1605.02688.

LTL-UDE @ EmpiriST 2015:
Tokenization and PoS Tagging of Social Media Text

Tobias Horsmann   **Torsten Zesch**

Language Technology Lab

Department of Computer Science and Applied Cognitive Science

University of Duisburg-Essen, Germany

`{tobias.horsmann,torsten.zesch}@uni-due.de`

Abstract

We present a detailed description of our submission to the EmpiriST shared task 2015 for tokenization and part-of-speech tagging of German social media text. As relatively little training data is provided, neither tokenization nor PoS tagging can be learned from the data alone. For tokenization, our system uses regular expressions for general cases and word lists for exceptions. For PoS tagging, adding unsupervised knowledge beyond the available training data is the most important factor for reaching acceptable tagging accuracy. A learning curve experiment shows furthermore that more in-domain training data is very likely to further increase accuracy.

1   Introduction

Tokenization and part-of-speech (PoS) tagging are two fundamental NLP tasks. Tokenization aims at detecting word and sentence boundaries in text while PoS tagging uses the recognized words and assigns each word its syntactical category. Both tasks are especially challenging when applied on noisy social media texts (Eisenstein, 2013).

The main challenge when tokenizing social media text is the ambiguity of punctuation characters which occurs more frequently than in other domains. A major source of ambiguity are emoticons that show a surprising degree of complexity ranging from two-character emoticons such as *:)* to n-character emoticons such as *\(*.*#)*. Additionally challenges are introduced by missing whitespace characters and the use of non-standard abbreviations such as in *[...] aus meiner (Doz.)Sicht:) [...]*.

For PoS tagging, the main source of error are the frequently occurring unknown word forms that

are spelling variations of words found in the dictionary. Those spelling variations are usually not contained in the (newswire) training data of the model which leads to a strong decline in accuracy on social media data (Ritter et al., 2011; Eisenstein, 2013).

There has been little work for German social media processing, the EmpiriST (Beißwenger et al., 2016) provides for both tasks two data sets composing of dialogical and monological text of the social media domain to help the development of robust tools for German. The results of our approaches for tokenization and PoS tagging are reported under the name *LTL-UDE* in the EmpiriST rankings.

2   Tokenization

While tokenization usually comprises of two sub-tasks (sentence boundary detection and token boundary detection), in the EmpiriST shared task, the sentence boundaries are already given and only the token boundaries should be detected.

2.1   Task Analysis

A main challenge in this task lies in dealing with missing whitespace characters, Table 1 shows a few examples with their correct tokenization. In case (1), it is difficult to determine that in the character sequence '?"<-' the arrow symbol form a semantic unit that should not be split. This problem occurs in various forms such as in (2) where a dot indicates an abbreviation and a following word appear as single token, case (3) shows how numbers and following punctuation marks form a token and cannot just be separated.

While (1) is a case which might be solved by regular expressions, (2) requires to know that the first word is an abbreviation to which the dot belongs. An additional challenge comes from the

Proceedings of the 10th Web as Corpus Workshop (WAC-X) and the EmpiriST Shared Task, pages 120–126,
Berlin, Germany, August 7-12, 2016. ©2016 Association for Computational Linguistics

	(1)	(2)	(3)
Raw	*pdf?"<-Wenn*	*schriftl.Äquivalent*	*v.14.4*
Tokenized	pdf␣?␣"␣<-␣Wenn	schriftl.␣Äquivalent	v.␣14.␣4

Table 1: Examples of missing whitespace characters and their correctly tokenized form

tokenization rules defined in the EmpiriST guidelines. For example the version number *v.14.4* in (3) should be tokenized as *v.␣14.␣4* even if it is actually one entity.

2.2 Implementation

Our tokenizer performs three steps: In the first step, we split the input text into units at every whitespace character. In the second step, we use regular expressions to refine the splitting by separating alpha-numerical text segments from punctuation characters. This will also erroneously split up smilies and other character sequences. Thus, in the third step, we re-assemble sequences of punctuation characters which have been separated in the previous step. This mainly serves to restore smilies but also other symbols such as arrows and alike. We examined the training data to find the most common combinations of those character sequences and merge them to a single token when we encounter them. Furthermore, we use word lists to merge abbreviations with their following dot character. The list of abbreviations are obtained from the Tüba-DZ corpus (Telljohann et al., 2004), the German Web1T uni-gram corpus (Brants and Franz, 2006), and lists we manually obtained from Wikipedia.

Baseline Systems We compare our approach to three reference systems: a plain whitespace tokenization (i.e. the first step of our approach), tokenization with the Break-Iterator-Segmenter (BreakIter) as implemented in the NLP DKPro Core framework (Eckart de Castilho and Gurevych, 2014), and a specialized social media tokenizer from the ArkTools suite (Gimpel et al., 2011). Whitespace tokenization and BreakIter are expected to perform poorly as neither tool is designed for processing social media text. The ArkTools tokenizer is tailored to English Twitter messages which are quite similar to the EmpiriST dataset, but will obviously not capture phenomena that are specific for German.

2.3 Results & Discussion

In Table 2, we show the results of applying our methods and baseline systems to the provided training and test data. The CMC data set is harder to tokenize than the Web data. Our approach performed well on the training data set but fails to generalize to unseen data. Of our baselines systems, ArkTools is the only competitive one, which is not surprising as it aims at tokenizing tweets which are a subdomain of the provided data.

Challenging cases for our approach are situations when more than two tokens have to be separated because several whitespace characters are missing or punctuation marks belonging to abbreviations are involved. Table 3 shows examples for a few selected error cases. Example (1) shows a case of a dot terminated abbreviation which is not contained in our word lists. Example (2) shows an issue when more than one whitespace character is missing. We experimented with splitting camel case expressions but found on the training data that it does more harm than good and decided not to implement such a rule. In example (3) an abbreviation is involved which is based on two words shortened to a single letter each followed by a dot character. This abbreviation had to be split up into two tokens consisting of a letter and a dot in order to conform to the tokenization guidelines.

3 Part-of-Speech Tagging

Tagging social media text with off-the-shelve PoS taggers leads to a huge drop in accuracy compared to tagging newswire text (Ritter et al., 2011; Horsmann et al., 2015). The main cause for this drop is the high rate of out-of-vocabulary words, which are mainly caused by orthographical variations of known words (Eisenstein, 2013).

3.1 Shared Task Data

The EmpiriST training dataset contains about 10k tokens of PoS annotated German social media text (the test data contains about 13k tokens). The dataset is annotated with an extended version of the STTS tagset which adds 18 new PoS tags to account for German social media phenomena

	Method	CMC			Web			∅
		P	R	F_1	P	R	F_1	F_1
Train data	Whitespace	81.7	99.9	89.8	84.4	100	91.5	90.7
	BreakIter	99.4	90.2	94.5	99.7	98.3	99.0	96.8
	ArkTools	98.7	98.7	98.7	98.2	99.2	98.7	98.7
	LTL-UDE	99.7	99.7	99.7	99.9	99.9	99.9	**99.8**
Test data	Whitespace	80.7	99.8	89.2	87.0	99.9	93.0	91.1
	BreakIter	97.9	90.3	93.9	99.7	98.3	98.9	96.4
	ArkTools	97.5	98.4	97.9	99.3	99.0	99.1	98.5
	LTL-UDE	98.2	99.0	98.6	99.5	98.9	99.2	**98.9**

Table 2: Tokenization results

	(1)	(2)	(3)
Expected	Doz.	im␣Real␣Life	a.␣d.␣gestrigen
Actual	Doz␣.	imRealLife	a.d.gestrigen

Table 3: Tokenization errors

Empiri STTS PoS tags	Freq.	Standard STTS-PoS tags	Freq.
EMOASC	115	PTKANT	42
PTKMA	103	PWAV	39
PTKIFG	99	KOKOM	28
AKW	49	XY	28
HST	46	PDAT	28
ADR	35	VAINF	26
PTKMWL	28	PWS	23
EMOIMG	22	VVIMP	18
URL	18	TRUNC	12
VVPPER	7	KOUI	10
VAPPER	4	PWAT	8
DM	3	VVIZU	7
VMPPER	1	PIDAT	7
ADVART	1	PTKA	5
KOUSPPER	1	APZR	5
ONO	1	VMINF	3
PPERPPER	1	VAPP	3
EML	0	VMPP	1

Table 4: All 18 newly added PoS tags with their frequency of occurrence in the training data compared to the frequency of the 18 least frequent standard STTS PoS tags

(Beißwenger et al., 2015). Table 4 shows all newly added PoS tags with their frequency compared to the least frequent PoS tags that are annotated with a standard STTS PoS tag. As can be seen, 18 PoS tags from the new and standard STTS tagset occur ten times or less. The provided training data thus contains many rare phenomena that cannot be learned from the annotated data alone.

3.2 Implementation

We train a CRF classifier (Lafferty et al., 2001) using the FlexTag tagger (Zesch and Horsmann, 2016) which is based on the DKProTC (Daxenberger et al., 2014) machine learning framework. Our feature set uses a context window of ± 2 tokens, the five-hundred most-frequent character ngrams over all bi, tri and four-grams and boolean features if a token is capitalized, a number, etc.

General Domain Adaptation As the provided training data will not be sufficient to train a competitive model, we decided to apply a domain adaption strategy that has been proposed as an effective method for improving tagging accuracy on social media texts (Ritter et al., 2011; Rehbein, 2013). We closely follow the process outlined in our previous research, where we examined which domain adaption strategies are most likely to improve results (Horsmann and Zesch, 2015). We train a single model on the training data (*CMC* and *Web* subsets) and add additional 100k tokens of newswire text from the Tiger corpus (Brants et al., 2004). To inform the classifier about spelling variations of social media and German morphology we add the following resources:

- *Brown cluster* We create Brown clusters (Brown et al., 1992) from 70 million tokens of German Twitter messages. Spelling variations of the same word form tend to be placed into the same cluster (Ritter et al., 2011), e.g. the unknown word *i-wann* occurs in the same cluster as the correctly spelled and known word form *irgendwann*. This enables the classifier to learn that *i-wann* and *irgendwann* are distributional similar which provides a bias to assign *i-wann* the same PoS tag as *irgendwann*. We use 1000 clusters and consider words which occur at least 40 times as suggested by Ritter et al. (2011) we provide the resulting bit string in various length as feature to the classifier i.e. 2, 4, 6, ..., 16 (Owoputi et al., 2013) to inform the classifier about (partial) similarity between words.

- *Morphology lexicon* We extract the word class, number and comparative of a word from a German morphology lexicon[1] to inform the classifier about German morphology.

- *PoS dictionary* We create a PoS dictionary which stores the three most frequent PoS tags of a word. We build the dictionary using the Hamburg Dependency Treebank (Foth et al., 2014) which contains STTS annotated text from the technical German website `www.heise.de`. We choose this corpus for its size of almost five million tokens and its technical nature which let it seem more suited for the social media domain than a business newswire corpus.

EmpiriST-specific Adaptation As we have seen in Table 4, some PoS tags are rather rare in the training data and cannot be learned from the data. In order to tackle at least some of those cases, we utilize a post-processing step based on heuristics. For example, all instances of the token *sehr* in the training data are annotated with the same PoS tag. All occurrences of words that start with an @ character are set to *ADR* and those with # are set to *HST*. We also match Urls and Email addresses with regular expressions and assign *URL* or *EML* to them. The word form *sehr* is always assigned *PTKIFG*. Additionally, all words ending in a hyphen are set to *TRUNC*.

We use word lists from Wikipedia and Wiktionary to improve named entity recognition with name lists for person names, cities, countries etc. In those lists, we remove words which occur in the Tiger corpus with a word class other than named entity to filter for words that can occur with other

PoS tags, too. Due to unreliable upper- and lower-case usage in social media, we use case-insensitive matching.

A main drawback of adding data from a foreign text domain such as the Tiger corpus is a different annotation scheme and its dominating size that decreases the weight of the EmpiriST training data. This causes a bias for choosing the tags from the bigger Tiger corpus. We attempt to adjust for this bias by adding boolean features if a word can occur with a PoS tag for one of the sparse new word classes to assign a higher weight for choosing a new PoS tag. We added features for instance for focus particles such as *nur, schon, etwas* or words that are verbs merged with personal pronouns such as *schreibste, willste, machste*.

Baseline Systems We use the German model of TreeTagger (Schmid, 1995) as reference point for the performance of our PoS tagger. We report results of applying TreeTagger alone and additionally with our shared-task fitted post-processing to ensure a fair comparison.

3.3 Results & Discussion

Table 5 shows our results on the released gold test data. Each row shows a setting that is applied on the two subsets CMC and Web. For each data set we provide two accuracy values by applying the current setting in its *generic* form and with our shared task-specific (*ST-specific*) post-processing.

The first row in Table 5 shows the performance of the TreeTagger baseline which performs a lot better on the Web data than on CMC data which indicates that Web is much closer to standard German text on which the TreeTagger is known to perform well (Horsmann et al., 2015). The second row shows the performance of tagging the data with a model trained only on the provided EmpiriST training data which performs poorly due to data sparsity. In the third row, we add the foreign domain Tiger corpus which improves accuracy substantially and let our model even beat the baseline on CMC. The subsequent rows show the improvement of adding each of the three resources if added to the EmpiriST and Tiger training data. The morphological lexicon shows the smallest improvements on both data sets. Adding the Brown cluster increases accuracy by 4.6 percent points on the CMC data set but only by 2.5 points on the Web data. We assume that the higher similarity of the Web data to standard German also reduces

---

[1] `http://www.danielnaber.de/morphologie/`

	CMC		Web		∅	
	Generic	ST-specific	Generic	ST-specific	Generic	ST-specific
TreeTagger	73.8	77.3	91.6	91.8	84.2	84.6
EmpiriST	72.2	73.4	75.5	76.3	73.9	74.9
+Tiger	79.6	80.6	88.8	88.9	84.2	84.8
+Tiger+Brown	84.4	85.2	90.8	90.6	87.6	87.9
+Tiger+MorphLex	81.1	81.5	90.6	90.8	85.9	86.2
+Tiger+PosDict	82.4	83.8	91.0	91.4	86.7	87.6
All resources	85.6	86.1	92.0	92.1	88.8	89.1

Table 5: Results of applying our trained PoS tagger against the released gold test data, we present additional to the overall result the accuracy gain of adding 100k token Tiger and the gains of adding each individual resource compared to training on Empiri+Tiger. We compare our performance against the German TreeTagger model.

PoS tag	Occr.	Acc (%)
PTKMA	85	32.9
FM	49	26.5
VAPPER	4	25.0
VVIMP	32	15.6
PTKIFG	133	15.0
PTKMWL	24	8.3
XY	17	5.9
ADVART	3	0
APPO	1	0
DM	6	0
KOUSPPER	2	0
ONO	2	0
PIDAT	4	0
PPERPPER	1	0

Table 6: Accuracy per word class with an accuracy of less than 50%. PoS tags newly added in the extended STTS tagset are highlighted in grey.

the number of spelling variations in the text which explains the smaller effect of the Brown cluster on the Web data set. The PoS dictionary is with an improvement of 2.5 percent points most effective on the Web data set . If we combine all resources, we improve accuracy on CMC by 8.8 percent points compared to our baseline. On the Web data, the baseline is already quite high, but we still slightly improve by 0.3 points.

To better understand the challenge arising from data sparsity, we show the PoS tags of the test data set which have an accuracy below 50% and are thus especially difficult to tag in Table 6. Noteworthy is that seven word classes have an accuracy of zero. Five of those classes are newly added tags which confirms our assumption that they are too infrequent to be reliably learned.

Figure 1 shows the learning curve of our classifier using both, the provided training data and gold test data. We computed the learning curve as an averaged value with 10fold cross validation. The blue learning curve (triangle) shows the accuracy gain without using any resources. The red curve (square) shows the accuracy gain by additionally adding all of our resources including our shared-task post-processing. The curve without any resources confirms the data sparsity issue. The curve with our resources shows how well our resources compensate data sparsity, but still indicates that more actual training data of the target domain will bring further improvements. Thus, we consider annotating more training data as a promising method to achieve further accuracy improvements.

4 Summary

We presented our approach in the EmpiriST shared task 2015 for the tokenization and PoS tagging of German social media text. We tackled the tokenization task with regular expressions and word lists.

An analysis of the provided training and test data for PoS tagging showes that many of the fine word class distinctions do not occur frequently enough to be learned effectively. We thus utilize foreign domain data, PoS and morphological dictionaries, and clusters of distributional word similarity to overcome sparsity of training data. The added resources show a much higher effectiveness on the CMC data set than on the Web data set,

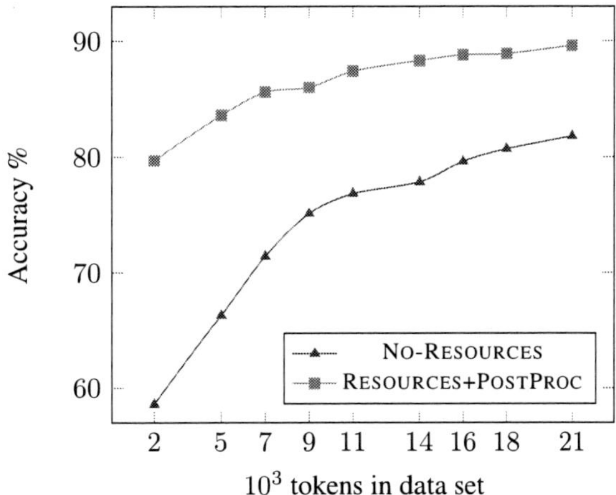

Figure 1: Learning Curve on Empiri-Train and Empiri-Test data averaged in 10fold cross validation, learning curve is shown for using no resources and for using all resources including our post processing.

probably as the Web data set is much closer to standard German text than the CMC data. Furthermore, we presented a learning curve experiment that shows that using more annotated data is likely to yield further improvements.

We make the source code of our experiments publicly available.[2]

References

Michael Beißwenger, Thomas Bartz, Angelika Storrer, and Swantje Westpfahl. 2015. Tagset und Richtlinie für das Part-of-Speech-Tagging von Sprachdaten aus Genres internetbasierter Kommunikation.

Michael Beißwenger, Sabine Bartsch, Stefan Evert, and Kay-Michael Würzner. 2016. EmpiriST 2015: A Shared Task on the Automatic Linguistic Annotation of Computer-Mediated Communication, Social Media and Web Corpora. In *Proceedings of the 10th Web as Corpus Workshop (WAC-X)*, Berlin, Germany.

Thorsten Brants and Alex Franz. 2006. Web 1T 5-gram corpus version 1.1. *Linguistic Data Consortium*.

Sabine Brants, Stefanie Dipper, Peter Eisenberg, Silvia Hansen-Schirra, Esther König, Wolfgang Lezius, Christian Rohrer, George Smith, and Hans Uszkoreit. 2004. TIGER: Linguistic Interpretation of a German Corpus. *Research on Language and Computation*, 2(4):597–620.

Peter F Brown, Peter V DeSouza, Robert L Mercer, Vincent J Della Pietra, and Jenifer C Lai. 1992. Class-Based n-gram Models of Natural Language. *Computational Linguistics*, 18:467–479.

Johannes Daxenberger, Oliver Ferschke, Iryna Gurevych, and Torsten Zesch. 2014. DKPro TC: A java-based framework for supervised learning experiments on textual data. In *Proceedings of 52nd Annual Meeting of the Association for Computational Linguistics: System Demonstrations*, pages 61–66, Baltimore, Maryland.

Richard Eckart de Castilho and Iryna Gurevych. 2014. A broad-coverage collection of portable NLP components for building shareable analysis pipelines. In *Proceedings of the Workshop on Open Infrastructures and Analysis Frameworks for HLT (OIAF4HLT) at COLING 2014*, pages 1–11, Dublin, Ireland, August. Association for Computational Linguistics and Dublin City University.

Jacob Eisenstein. 2013. What to do about bad language on the internet. In *Proceedings of the 2013 Conference of the North American Chapter of the Association for Computational Linguistics: Human Language Technologies*, pages 359–369, Atlanta, Georgia.

Kilian A. Foth, Arne Köhn, Niels Beuck, and Wolfgang Menzel. 2014. Because Size Does Matter: The Hamburg Dependency Treebank. In *Proceedings of the Ninth International Conference on Language Resources and Evaluation (LREC'14)*, Reykjavik, Iceland, may. European Language Resources Association (ELRA).

Kevin Gimpel, Nathan Schneider, Brendan O'Connor, Dipanjan Das, Daniel Mills, Jacob Eisenstein, Michael Heilman, Dani Yogatama, Jeffrey Flanigan, and Noah A. Smith. 2011. Part-of-speech Tagging for Twitter: Annotation, Features, and Experiments. In *Proceedings of the 49th Annual Meeting of the Association for Computational Linguistics: Human

---

[2]https://github.com/Horsmann/EmpiriSharedTask2015.git

Language Technologies: Short Papers - Volume 2, HLT '11, pages 42–47, Stroudsburg, PA, USA. Association for Computational Linguistics.

Tobias Horsmann and Torsten Zesch. 2015. Effectiveness of Domain Adaptation Approaches for Social Media PoS Tagging. In *Proceeding of the Second Italian Conference on Computational Linguistics*, pages 166–170, Trento, Italy. Accademia University Press.

Tobias Horsmann, Nicolai Erbs, and Torsten Zesch. 2015. Fast or Accurate ? – A Comparative Evaluation of PoS Tagging Models. In *Proceedings of the International Conference of the German Society for Computational Linguistics and Language Technology (GSCL-2015)*, Essen, Germany.

John D Lafferty, Andrew McCallum, and Fernando C N Pereira. 2001. Conditional Random Fields: Probabilistic Models for Segmenting and Labeling Sequence Data. In *Proceedings of the Eighteenth International Conference on Machine Learning*, ICML '01, pages 282–289, San Francisco, CA, USA.

Olutobi Owoputi, Chris Dyer, Kevin Gimpel, Nathan Schneider, and Noah A Smith. 2013. Improved part-of-speech tagging for online conversational text with word clusters. In *Proceedings of the 2013 Conference of the North American Chapter of the Association for Computational Linguistics: Human Language Technologies*.

Ines Rehbein. 2013. Fine-Grained POS Tagging of German Tweets. In Iryna Gurevych, Chris Biemann, and Torsten Zesch, editors, *Language Processing and Knowledge in the Web*, volume 8105 of *Lecture Notes in Computer Science*, pages 162–175.

Alan Ritter, Sam Clark, Mausam, and Oren Etzioni. 2011. Named Entity Recognition in Tweets: An Experimental Study. In *Proceedings of the Conference on Empirical Methods in Natural Language Processing*, EMNLP '11, pages 1524–1534, Stroudsburg, PA, USA.

Helmut Schmid. 1995. Improvements In Part-of-Speech Tagging With an Application To German. In *Proceedings of the ACL SIGDAT-Workshop*, pages 47–50.

Heike Telljohann, Erhard Hinrichs, and Sandra Kübler. 2004. The Tüba-D/Z Treebank: Annotating German with a Context-Free Backbone. In *Proceedings of the Fourth International Conference on Language Resources and Evaluation (LREC-2004)*, Lisbon, Portugal, May. European Language Resources Association (ELRA). ACL Anthology Identifier: L04-1096.

Torsten Zesch and Tobias Horsmann. 2016. Flextag: A highly flexible pos tagging framework. In *Proceedings of the Tenth International Conference on Language Resources and Evaluation (LREC 2016)*, pages 4259–4263, Portorož, Slovenia. European Language Resources Association (ELRA).

Author Index

Association for Computational Linguistics
209 N. Eighth Street
Stroudsburg, Pennsylvania 18360

ISBN 978-1-5108-2769-1